VLADIMIR
THE RUSSIAN VIKING

VLADIMIR THE RUSSIAN VIKING

Vladimir Volkoff

The Overlook Press
Woodstock, New York

First published in 1985 by
The Overlook Press
Lewis Hollow Road
Woodstock, New York

Library of Congress Cataloging in Publication Data

Volkoff, Vladimir.
    Vladimir the Russian Viking.

    Bibliography: p.
    Includes index.
    1. Vladimir, Grand-Duke of Kiev, ca. 956-1015.
2. Soviet Union—Kings and rulers—biography.
3. Soviet Union—History—Vladimir, 972-1015.
DK75.V65   1985   947'.02'0924 [B]s   84-22741
ISBN 0-87951-993-2 (cloth)
ISBN 0-87951-234-2 (paper)

Third printing 1998

*A country crystallizes its saints
as a mountain its diamonds.*

Archbishop John of San Francisco

Contents

Contents

List of Illustrations

List of Maps

Foreword

To forestall an observant reader's curiosity, it may as well be stated at the outset that there is no coincidence in the same name appearing twice on the title page of this work: once for the hero and once for the author. The author's life was entrusted at birth to the hero's care, and it is only fair that some of the author's care should now be spent on the hero's life. So much for that. On the other hand, not to disappoint lovers of coincidences, significant or otherwise, how about this one, which the author confesses to find rather piquant: Russia begins with Vladimir the baptist and ends with Vladimir the apostate?

Before that span of nearly one thousand years which extends from Vladimir's violent accession to the throne (978) to Lenin's October Revolution (1917) and during which the country grew into a vast empire known as Holy Russia, she was a loose conglomerate of towns and tribes; after that period, she was broken up into fifteen federated republics, less a nation and a state than, at least officially, 'the material and technical base for the expansion of world communism'.

Vladimir the First and Vladimir the Last were both of partly non-native origin; both forcefully severed their ties with heritage and tradition; both grafted on to the body of Russia an imported faith; by so doing, both ended up changing the face of the world. Both were rewarded by canonization in their respective folds: while for Orthodox, Catholic and Anglican Christians alike Vladimir of Kiev is a saint – the Russians in particular revere him as 'Equal to the Apostles' in spiritual rank – Vladimir Lenin has undergone among Communists a sort of materialistic apotheosis; his features are reproduced on books, canvases, newspapers, vases, coins, stamps, medals, posters, flags; his works, translated into nearly all modern languages, constitute his followers' Bible; his patronymic, Ilich, is uttered in Russia with sacred awe. The earthly bodies of the two Vladimirs have known, after their demises, not dissimilar fates: one of the two – or what remains of it under the wax and make-up – lies enshrined in the porphyry mausoleum on Red Square; the other one was conveniently divided into pieces to be venerated as relics: one hand went to St Sophia Cathedral in Kiev, the head minus the jaw to the Pechersk Monastery, the jaw itself was sent by Metropolitan Peter Mogila to Tsar Michael. Finally both Vladimirs must have been firmly attached to their common name, since the Prince kept it even after having been christened Basil, and the revolutionary went back to it after using for some time the pseudonym Nicholas, although he never bothered to resume his real family name, Ulianov.

There the coincidental resemblance stops. For, whereas Lenin's success in creating a beneficial political structure and in fostering a viable creed remains, at least for non-communist historians, debatable, even communist ones, in spite of their militant atheism, recognize the excellence of Vladimir's reign and commend the baptism of Russia, which they consider progressive for its time. Later we shall examine in some detail the consequences of the momentous event of 989, but here it will be appropriate to point out the two most prominent ones: from a spiritual and cultural standpoint, how much poorer mankind would be without Russia's saints, mystics and philosophers, her religious music, her incomparable icons, her Tolstoys and her Dostoievskys! From an historical standpoint, what would have happened to the civilization of medieval Europe – and consequently of America – if the Russian millions had sided with the Tartars or the Turks instead of the Greeks?

The Orthodox Church likes to compare Vladimir to Paul and to Constantine. Like Paul's, his conversion was directly instrumental in bringing about numberless other conversions; like Constantine, he was, for better or for worse, the founder of a Christian state destined to reconcile the interests of Caesar with those of God. Among the Russian people, his memory has been preserved through the centuries in the most colourful images: his personal lustiness, his entourage of gallant or wise *bogatyri* (knights-errant), his munificence toward the poor, his standing among other monarchs – and maybe more than all the rest, the Gargantuan banquets he loved to offer at the slightest provocation – have made him Russia's most popular sovereign, a recurrent inspiration for her poets, from the anonymous minstrels of the early Middle Ages to an Aleksey Tolstoy in the nineteenth century, her historical Charlemagne, her legendary King Arthur. The very nickname of Krasnoe Solnyshko – literally 'The Red Sun', more faithfully 'Darling Beautiful Sun' – which spontaneously arose for him from the people, radiates warmth and light. To sum up, we have in Vladimir, the saintly Prince, one of the most charismatic personalities to have left their mark on the world.

Nevertheless not one whole historical work has, to our knowledge, been dedicated to the man, either in

Icon 'of all the Russian saints' in the Holy Trinity Monastery, Jordanville, New York. The left-hand panel shows Vladimir directing the baptism of the Russians in the Dniepr. In the middle panel, the figure of the Great Prince, and all the canonized saints. In the right-hand panel, all those who, according to the painter and to popular belief, may be canonized one day. It is worth noting that history has already begun to justify this belief: Hermann of Alaska has been recognized as a saint by the Russian Orthodox Church.

Russia or outside it. Hagiography has its limitations; Semen Sklyarenko's fictional biography can hardly be taken seriously; as to the numerous books and numberless articles which have been published in the field, they concern either more generally Kievan Russia or more specifically individual episodes in Vladimir's life. The result is that the public's imagination is allowed to run wild (in Russia) or not allowed to run at all (outside). Such a lacuna can be primarily attributed to an unhealthy source situation, the crux of the matter being that seventy-five per cent of what we know about Vladimir comes from one main source, and no more than twenty-five per cent from a number of minor ones.

Let us have a look at the minor sources first. They can be split into five categories:

– Arabic historians, reliable as to mores, and, being good at astronomy, precious for the verification of a few dates, but scantily informed about facts★

– Western chroniclers, put out by Vladimir because he accepted his faith from the Eastern Church†

– Icelandic bards, somewhat excessively gifted with imagination and mainly concerned with their own heroes‡

– Greek chroniclers and historians, trying their best to sound uninterested in Vladimir, probably because Russia became Christian on his, not the Basileus', terms§

– most Russian chroniclers, hagiographers and orators, or rather those few whose works survived three hundred years of Tartar rampages (thirteenth to

---

★ Ibn Rusteh, Ibn Fadlan, Marvazi, Yahya, El-Macin, Abu-Shyjac, Ibn-al-Athyr.
† Thietmar's Chronicles.
‡ The cycle of sagas concerning Olaf Tryggvison.
§ Leo the Deacon, Cedrenus, Zonaras, Psellus, Bandouri.

fifteenth century).* With the exception of Metropolitan Hilarion and Jacob the Monk, whose value resides in the fact that they were practically contemporaries of Vladimir, but who have so little to tell us that no extensive biography could be based upon them, these sources elaborate *ad infinitum* on the same few elements, and while it is curious to watch anecdotes grow into episodes and lines into pages with the centuries, the historical benefit derived from such evolutions is at best nil. As to documents, treaties, decrees and the like, all originals have disappeared and copies must naturally be viewed with extreme wariness.[1]

On the other hand, we do possess one main source, entitled *The Chronicle of Bygone Years* (and hereafter simply called *The Chronicle*), which, since it starts at the biblical flood and ends in AD 1111, covers quite satisfactorily Vladimir's reign (978–1015), into which it even delves at some length. Unfortunately, although the basic redaction may date from 1111, the earliest available manuscript (the Laurentian) was transcribed in 1377, and we do not know what changes may have occurred in the interval. The next available manuscript (the Hypatian), transcribed in 1450 and somewhat different from the first one, throws little light upon the matter. Since even the first redaction (which we do not possess) was obviously a compilation of facts, fantasies, interpretations, materials of different origins, interpolated discourses, imitations of other sources and fortuitous or nonfortuitous omissions, modern historians have had a jolly time tearing down the flimsy edifice. No wonder if it

---

* Chronicles of Arkhangelsk, Novgorod, Tver; chronicle by Nikon; chronicle by Joachim in Tatishchev; continuation of Laurentian manuscript; Pliginsky manuscript; Public Library manuscript; *Life of St Vladimir*; *Prologue Life of St Vladimir*; *Life of Boris and Gleb*; *Passion and Encomium of Boris and Gleb*; Jacob the Monk; Metropolitan Hilarion.

collapsed satisfactorily over their own heads. For, having discarded all the evidence, and having nowhere else to look for more, they began replacing it with wishful figments of imagination, each expert brilliantly succeeding in proving exactly what he had set out to prove.

Historians' feuds would make dramatic history by themselves. Westerners consider 'Russian scholars notorious for misrepresenting the history of Eastern Europe';[2] Russians complain that Western histories of Russia 'are based on an almost total rejection of the Russian sources; . . . their authors reveal an inadequate knowledge of Russian church practice and of Russian literature'.[3] Christians recognize only religious motives; agnostics reject them altogether. Those who identify with the Vikings – the so-called Normanist school – give them the lion's part in every commendable event; those who do not approve of them pretend they scarcely existed. Belated occidentalists and resurrected Slavophiles dig out their hatchets. Baumgarten manages to leave in our minds the idea that Vladimir may have been baptized by an Anglo-Saxon priest, which is about as probable as that Napoleon married Marie-Antoinette; Tatishchev works on a manuscript which has since disappeared, and whose main pages were already missing in his time. A startling example of what can be done along these lines is afforded by Taube who proposes to demonstrate that Askold, one of Vladimir's predecessors on the Kievan throne, was a Roman Catholic: true, it is not even known whether he was a Christian at all, but a chapel dedicated to St Nicholas was erected on the site of his tomb (as, by the way, was often done in specifically pagan locations); now one of the contemporary Popes was called Nicholas; it follows, as the night the day, that

Askold was a Roman Catholic christened Nicholas in honour of the Pope. Q.E.D.

In the face of such fancifulness on the one hand and utter scepticism on the other, a moderate attitude could be in order. This may be deplorable, but *The Chronicle* is our main constructive source, and so, whenever it is not contradicted by other relevant and reliable information or simply by common sense, it seems reasonable to listen to what it has to say, not without caution, but certainly without going out of one's way to prove that it might be wrong. For our part, while supplementing its evidence with background information and at the same time keeping our own imagination under control,[4] we intend to challenge *The Chronicle* only when there is serious reason to do so, and, so as not to bore the reader with professional bickering, to consign the nicer points under dispute to the endnotes, bringing only the most important ones into the limelight. Such a course of action is not without risk: by choosing to believe *The Chronicle* whenever there is no known cause to disbelieve it, we may inadvertently acquire some of its bias. Although this is undoubtedly so, we tend to think that little harm will be done, for *The Chronicle*'s bias, pro-Christian, pro-Orthodox, pro-Vladimirian, somewhat pro-Greek, contaminated by neither Slav nor Viking extremism, is upheld, in the long run, by the subsequent development of Russian history. After all, no one contests that Russia became a Christian country of the Orthodox variety, that Vladimir was a great ruler, and that, whatever problems may have arisen at some time or other, Russian culture as such is a happy blend of Slav, Norse and Greek ingredients. The danger therefore, in following *The Chronicle* too closely, is not of straying from the truth, but rather of anticipating it, stylizing it, so to speak, instead of presenting it in its original variegation. So be it. The source situation being what it is, we shall probably be better off with oversimplification than with cynicism or fantasy.

Legend is the live part of history. The past as such is dead; but if it becomes myth, it lives on in us, nourishing and nurturing both our conscious and our unconscious selves. Where history is concerned, Pygmalion's story should read backwards: it is the masterpiece that makes the master come alive.

Such is the perspective in which we place ourselves. What is attempted here is not religious edification; neither is it in any way fiction; nor the bare result of scholarly research. Whilst trying to conform to the strictest standards of modern history, the author feels no iconoclastic compulsion to reduce his hero to the dimensions of ordinary men. Born half a prince and a pagan, Vladimir became an illustrious sovereign and an eminent saint: not exactly a common destiny. His memory has inspired the author to cope with more than one ordeal in his personal life; he would like to offer this modest work in the spirit of an ex-voto.

V.V.

Acknowledgements

The author wishes to thank Archimandrite Kiprian of the Holy Trinity Monastery in Jordanville, New York, the Reverend Father John Townsend of St Mary of Egypt in Atlanta, Georgia, the Reverend Father Alexis Kniazev of St Sergius in Paris, Mrs Zalessky, President of the Icon Association in Paris, Dr I. G. Spassky of the Hermitage Museum, Professor Jamie Cockfield of Mercer University in Macon, Georgia, and especially

Acknowledgements

Miss Lilian Newman of Atlanta, Georgia, for help generously provided.

The author and the publishers wish to thank Julliard/ L'Age d'Homme for permission to reproduce the illustrations and maps.

Note on transcription of proper names

Proper names have been transcribed according to tradition, which is sometimes incoherent, rather than according to modern scientific usage, which would have seemed unfamiliar to many readers.

Family Tree of the Early Rurikids

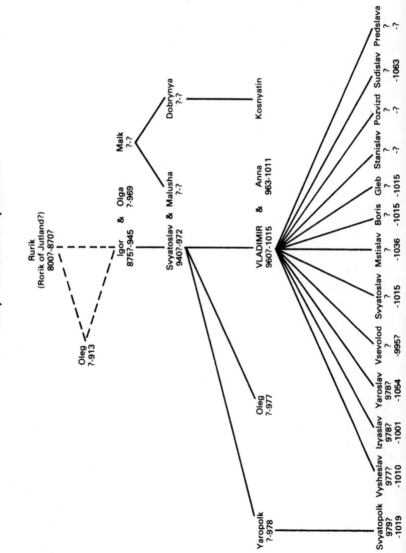

CHAPTER ONE

Boy

1 A narrow escape

> Peaceful is Ukraine's night.
> The sky translucent. The stars gleam.
> To drowsiness succumbs the air.
> The silver poplars' leaves are barely
> Shivering. The placid moon shines from on high.
> And all is quiet, quiet everywhere.[5]

Such is Pushkin's serene description of a nocturnal Kievan landscape, but on that particular night when, in AD 968, Vladimir first enters history, it could not have been less accurate. The valleys surrounding the wooden city sprawling on its three hills, as well as the plain beyond, were aglow with reddish campfires whose pungent smoke rising in the air hid moon and stars from view. Poplars and pines were being hewn down to keep the fires going, and crashed heavily to the ground. Foreign shouts, foreign whines, foreign laughter mingled with the neighing of horses, with the clatter of hooves, with snatches of voluptuous oriental songs issuing from the coarse leather tents,[6] and with the clanking of exotic curved sabres being sharpened for tomorrow's action. Innumerable herds milled around in the dark. A powerful, foreign stench – a mixture of roasting meat, sweat, manure, sour curd and rancid butter – floated all the way from the besiegers to the besieged, and filled the nostrils of the young, handsome boy, who stood by a second-floor window in his grandmother's stone palace, gazing down with fascination at the city laid out at his feet and at the foreign hordes that were going to storm it the next morning or the one after.

The invaders were Pechenegs,[7] a Turko-Tartar nomadic nation, who, about one hundred years before, had sprung out of the boundless Eastern steppes beyond the Volga. The Khazars had wisely conceded them free passage (870–880), the Magyars[8] had been pushed off into the West, and here they were, half cattle-breeders half-marauders, roaming in the plains between Danube and Don. The whole nation counted eight tribes, and one of them had elected the region south of Kiev as its territory. Part of the time they were content with capturing travellers on roads and rivers and selling cattle to the Russians, but one day's trip would take them to the earthen ramparts of Kiev, and this time it looked as if they had made up their minds to take the Russian capital, loot it, and raze it to the ground.

When the sun rose, the fate of the city appeared settled. The Pechenegs were all around in countless numbers, and kept arriving. They looked like ants, like swarming termites. A nameless bard must have remembered such an invasion when he described an oriental potentate gathering

> his forces from forty lands,
> From forty lands and from forty kings,
> Each one bringing forty thousand,
> And himself, the dog, more than one could count.[9]

When the potentate orders every soldier to pick up a pebble, all the pebbles thrown in a heap make up a huge mountain, and 'from the steam of all those horses, the red sun grows dim'.

If only Father were here! thought the boy. Prince Svyatoslav would ride at a gallop into the midst of the enemy, with his horse he would trample them, with his spear he would skewer them, with his flail he would mow them down like green grass: one wave and a road would open, one waft and an alley would unfurl.[10] But Father was somewhere on the Danube, around Pereyaslavets, seven hundred kilometres away, teaching the Christians a lesson or two. Grandmother, 'the wisest of all women', had been left in command. If she had been younger, she would have been quite capable of galvanizing her people into victorious resistance even without an army, but in her old age she seemed to be losing her grip on reality. Had she not elected to join that shameful new religion, made for cowards and slaves, a ridiculous denomination of which Father always made such great fun? And as for the boy's older brothers, that milksop Yaropolk and that blunderer Oleg, they lacked the inspiration to rally the common people around them and to shake and shape them into a fighting force. Of course, just across the Dniepr, on the left bank, there was still General Pretich's detachment, operational and intact. But it was not strong enough to take on the whole Pecheneg horde; besides, Pretich did not know how desperate the city's position was, and there was no way to call him to the rescue: the capital was sealed . . . One thing was clear: if the Pechenegs did not succeed in storming the walls, hunger and thirst, which had already taken their toll, would overcome whatever defence the Kievans were willing to provide. And so, on that day, the people met in the market square, and, by general consent, decided to surrender on the morrow.

The boy watched the proceedings, and who knows what feelings went through his heart? Anger, shame, fear? Surrendering to the Pechenegs could mean death, but for him it would probably be worse: slavery. The child would be sold in one of the Crimean ports to a Greek master who would then own him body and soul. Oh! if Vladimir had been older, he would have known how to bring these men to their senses, how to lead them into battle and either win a great victory or die an honourable death! But he could not have been more than ten, and, even in those days of early maturity, men would not follow a ten-year-old leader.[11]

It was a boy, however, scarcely older than Vladimir himself, who stepped forward and announced that he knew a way, if not to save the city, at least to attempt it. 'I can swim,' he said, 'and I know the Pecheneg tongue. Give me an old bridle, and I'll see what I can do.'

That bridle! How close it brings to us those events which happened more than one thousand years ago! Vladimir's heart must have gone out to the brave youth, and in his child's mind he must have admired the simple cunning of the plan. From his window, he watched the unpretentious hero slipping out of the city,[12] mingling with the besiegers, taken for one of them, showing his bridle and asking everyone the same question: 'Where is my horse? Have you seen my horse?'

All those Pecheneg horses, small, tough, with long hair and bushy manes, were alike. Finding one among all the others was an impossible job. And so, accompanied by jibes and banter and maybe even some show of concern, the young Russian progressed toward the Dniepr, which watered the foot of the hill. Suddenly he threw off his clothes, dived into the stream and swam out. 'Stop him! Stop him!' shouted the Pechenegs. One could hear the hue and cry from the palace. There were few good swimmers among the nomads, but many excellent archers, who ran to their bows. Rocks were already falling like hail on the water; soon hundreds of arrows

4

were aimed at the fugitive, who plunged and dodged as best he could. The marksmen were out of luck that day, and the Russian escaped beyond their range. It was now a question of whether he would be able to swim as far as the other shore.

The Dniepr at that point is pretty wide, but Pretich's men caught sight of the swimmer and rowed out in a boat to meet him. They took him, dripping, to headquarters. 'What message bring you?' asked the general. 'If the city is not relieved by tomorrow, it will surrender,' answered the youth, standing in the middle of a small puddle.

His work was done, and here he exits from history. We shall not hear of him any more. But had it not been for that old bridle and a bit of teenage pluck and inventiveness, Russia might well have turned Pecheneg and later Moslem – at least, if Tolstoy is wrong and if men do change the course of events.[13]

Pretich was a perceptive man who knew his Svyatoslav. 'We have to rescue his mother and three young sons, or else we are all dead men when the Prince returns,' he observed, and his men gloomily agreed. When strength is lacking, use ruse. Pretich waited for night to fall. The Pechenegs, seeing that no one was bothering them, forgot all about the youth and his bridle. It was a little before dawn and they had not yet armed themselves for the final assault, when trumpets resounded over the water and boats loomed out of the mist, approaching at full speed, oars splashing, sails swelling in the morning breeze. A great shout rose from the city. The confused Pechenegs thought that the Prince himself was back, and such was Svyatoslav's reputation that, in utter panic, they took to their heels. When, having put some distance between the city and themselves, they stopped to consider what should be done next, Pretich had already established a beachhead on the right bank of the Dniepr, and the princely family had been whisked off to safety on the left bank. Not exactly a dignified retreat, but what would an old woman and three boys have done against a horde of savages? One of them at least would live to prove that he could do better than flee in the face of danger.

Wondering at the events of the night, the Pecheneg chieftain, having more or less recovered his wits, asked for permission to parley with the newcomers. Permission was granted. 'What is all this pandemonium about?' inquired the Pecheneg. 'Just some reinforcements from the opposite bank,' replied Pretich lightly. Reinforcements could only come from Svyatoslav. 'In that case . . . could you be the Prince?' asked the chieftain in awed tones. Pretich looked shocked. He drew himself together. 'I am proud to be his vassal,' he answered, 'and the leader of his vanguard. The Prince follows with forces untold. He has but now finished obliterating the Bulgars . . .' The chieftain twirled his drooping moustache, and took the hint. 'If that is so,' he offered with a sly leer, 'why don't you and I become friends?'

Given the circumstances, this sounded like a good idea, and Pretich extended his hand, which the Pecheneg solemnly shook. A symbolic exchange of weapons followed. The chieftain acquired a breastplate, a shield and a two-edged sword, which may have come from a Frankish smithy, while Pretich wondered what he would do with a few arrows and a short sabre, ancestor of the scimitar, not to mention a spear somewhat similar to his own. Having become the friend of a Kievan general, the Pecheneg chieftain could do no less than raise the siege, the sooner the better. It still took a number of days, so that the inhabitants dared not come out to water their horses in the Lybed, an affluent of the Dniepr which they had previously considered convenient for that use: anything, they thought, was better than meeting face to face those new allies of theirs.

As soon as the landscape surrounding Kiev was left in confusion – at least in deserted confusion, the embers in the campfires dying out and the cowdung steaming slightly in the chilly dawn – the Russians put their heads together and chose the most able penman among them to inscribe on birchbark the following epistle to their master. 'Prince,' they wrote, 'you often visit foreign lands. [Nothing could be more correct. Out of the ten odd years that Svyatoslav reigned without his mother's supervision, he hardly spent two at home.] But while you neglect your own country [typical firm Slavo-Viking way of addressing one's sovereign] the Pechenegs have all but taken us captives [and now a personal dig:], including your mother and children. Unless you return to protect us, they will attack again [Friendship was all right as far as it went; you could not, however, trust a nomad too far. The last words are truly poignant: even Svyatoslav could not help being moved:], that is, if you have no pity on your native land, on your mother in her old age, and on your children . . .'

Abandoning his newly made conquests, Svyatoslav rushed back to rescue the city where he had been born but which he had never loved. One fine day, Vladimir would recognize his Father, whom he could scarcely remember, riding at the head of his men into the exulting crowds who would gratefully hail him as their protector and lord.

2 Father

It was a great festive occasion when, in 968, Svyatoslav returned from Pereyaslavets. Dressed in dazzling white from head to foot, he jumped down from his horse and ran up the steps into the light-brown marble hall, his boots thumping on the fine brick slabs. He embraced his mother, kissed his sons, and lifted the youngest in his powerful arms. He expressed regret at the dangers they had run without him, and showered them with gifts. What may they have been? Silks and gold for the Princess, weapons mounted in silver and fiery steeds for the boys. When the cries of admiration had subsided, 'I have something even better for you, Yaropolk,' he said to his eldest, a shifty, pimply youth. 'It is high time you began behaving like a man. Trust my taste: she is a jewel.'[14] He turned toward a veiled feminine figure who had remained bashfully standing at the door, and at whom Princess Olga had looked askance more than once. 'Come here, my dear. This is your new abbot. He will teach you prayers of another kind. Just think! If I had not ransacked that Greek convent of yours, all your beauty would have gone to waste.' He tore the veil off, revealing a girl, slender and dark in her silk tunic. She stood there silently and with eyes downcast, the features of an icon, the body of a goddess. 'A nun,' he explained. 'She was a nun. Aren't those Christians fools? Or aren't they men? One good thing, however: all their nonsense means she is a guaranteed virgin. Take her, Yaropolk.'

Yaropolk led his prize away, but there is reason to believe that some time went by before he appreciated his father's gift to its full extent. Two pairs of eyes followed the receding couple: the old Princess's, appalled at the blasphemy if not at the injustice – would there never be an end to that monstrous Viking carnality which held nothing sacred? – and Vladimir's, who had never seen such beauty in his life, and in whose heart a new and deadly fire stirred for the first time. Ten years later he would show that he had not forgotten the childhood scene.

For the time being, Vladimir may well have been the happiest member of the family at the conqueror's homecoming. Such a son could only be passionately proud of such a father. Of medium but strong build, with broad shoulders, a bull's neck and a lordly bearing, Svyatoslav looked 'gloomy and savage'[15] to his enemies, but his boy must have thought him the embodiment of all virile virtues. Under his bushy eyebrows, his blue eyes were those of his Viking forebears, but his snub-nose suggested that someone along the line, maybe old Rurik himself, the founder of the dynasty as far as Russia was concerned, had taken a native wife. Although Svyatoslav shaved his head and chin, he wore a long, thick moustache, plus one lock of hair over one temple to indicate his princely rank. Vladimir could remember that when Father bent over his cradle – it already seemed so long ago – he would let him play with the beautiful golden ear-ring (a ruby between two pearls) which adorned one of his ears.

As an administrator, Svyatoslav was non-existent, but what poetry is there in administration? As a warrior, on the contrary, he had the stature of a small Alexander. He was to die at approximately the same age (thirty-two or even thirty), after leading five titanic campaigns of which only the last was not entirely victorious, against the Khazars, the Vyatichans, the Yassians (Ossetians), the Kassagians (Cherkesses), the Volga Bulgars, the Western Bulgars, the Pechenegs, again the Western

Bulgars, and the Greeks. The first, the most brilliant, which he undertook when he could not have been more than twenty-five years old, took him more than five thousand kilometres into enemy territory. He started it with a modest enough incursion into the Crimea to protect its Greek and Gothic inhabitants – in particular those of the city of Cherson (about which more will follow later on) – at their own request, against Khazar raids. Successful there, he decided to push further and, living off the land, never stopped until he had taken the Khazar cities of Bela Vezha (Sarkel), Semender, and Itil, the metropolis: forty thousand vineyards had been planted there, and he is said to have left 'not a leaf, not a raisin'. In between, he had scaled the northern slopes of the Caucasus and defeated the natives there. On the way home, he thought he would make a small detour, something like a thousand kilometres as the crow flies, to destroy Bulgar, the capital of the Volga Bulgars, which he did. Such expeditions were launched sometimes for sheer loot, sometimes for a consideration (Calocyras of Cherson paid Svyatoslav an advance of fifteen hundred pounds of gold on inviting him to the Crimea, and Nicephorus Phocas 108 thousand gold solidi on suggesting that he invade Bulgaria), sometimes to exact tributes from the vanquished foe (as was the case with the Vyatichans, from whom he obtained a silver-piece per ploughshare), sometimes to gain control of trade routes (at the end of his reign, he was master of all land and water itineraries connecting the West to the Orient and the North of Europe to the Mediterranean in his part of the world) – and always, of course, because war was in his blood.

Wielding the oar like his men, dressed like them although he changed shirts more often, a modern drill

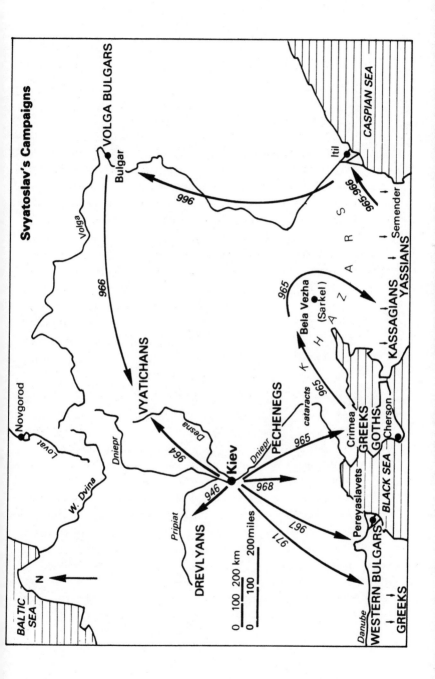

Svyatoslav's Campaigns

sergeant would have seemed a sissy to him. His retinue led, under orders, a hard but exhilarating life; no impedimenta would slow down his progress because he would not allow any, not even kettles to boil meat; he travelled thousands of miles without a baggage-train; the men would eat beef, horseflesh or game, roasted on campfires, and the Prince would set them an example, cutting his own strips of meat and cooking it over the coals. Tents? None. Pillows? None. Blankets? Yes, he would tolerate a horse-blanket under him, and with his head propped on his saddle, he would lie on the ground, looking up at the stars and dreaming of future victories. He could be cruel at times: according to the Greeks (who hated him), twenty thousand Bulgars were impaled at his command. But there was also a chivalrous streak in him: he never attacked anyone by surprise, but would always send a fair, though laconic, warning: 'I am setting forth against you.' This anecdote from his early boyhood paints him in bright colours.

His father, Prince Igor,[16] had been slain by a neighbouring Slavic tribe, the Drevlyans, for demanding from them the same tribute for the third time. The Drevlyans were a dark, backward people; they lived north of Kiev, in deep forests, where they extracted iron from the ground; they would eat anything, kill one another, marry by kidnapping their future wives, and even, as an indignant chronicler assures us, use obscene language before their daughters-in-law! What could be more foul? Igor died at their hands in gruesome circumstances: it appears he was tied to two bent saplings, which were then released and tore him apart. The murder may have been justifiable, but naturally revenge had to be exacted. The two armies took up their positions opposite each other. The Kievans were led by two

Viking generals, Sveinald and Asmund; the orphan Prince Svyatoslav, however, was present. Taking his part seriously, the child – he must have been four at the time – hurled his spear at the enemy. The point barely cleared his own horse's head and the heavy shaft struck the animal's leg. But the boy's gallantry was inspiring. 'The Prince has begun battle!' laughed Asmund, who was his tutor. 'Press on, men! After the Prince!' shouted Sveinald, prancing and strutting on his costly steed. And the Drevlyans were crushed under the assault.

Vladimir had heard the story hundreds of times from proud men-at-arms and ecstatic chambermaids. Whenever he looked at his father, he felt ashamed that he had already attained the ripe age of eight without having found the slightest opportunity to prove his mettle in the field. Even now, although Svyatoslav, as soon as he had arrived, gathered his forces and easily threw back Pretich's new 'friends' into their steppes, Vladimir was probably not allowed to accompany him into battle. Svyatoslav may have been annoyed at his elder son's lack of military gusto, but he treated his youngest with somewhat less interest than the boy's talents deserved. There were reasons for this.

3 Grandmother

Another member of the household to be passionately admired – though not without reservations – was Grandmother. Stories were told about her youth that would make your hair stand on end, and even now there was something forbidding about her tall, austere figure. As a young widow, she had taken an active and imaginative part in avenging her husband Igor's death. The gist of a popular ballad went like this:

Russia's two great evangelists, grandmother and grandson: Saint Olga and Saint Vladimir. Icon in Arkhangelsk Cathedral.
(*Photo J. da Cunha-Plon. Courtesy of Mme Zalessky.*)

After the murder, the Prince of the Drevlyans had made her offers of marriage which she feigned to accept. Her only request was that his ambassadors should behave with extreme arrogance and indeed demand to be carried into her presence in their boat. So they did, to comply with her wishes, not reflecting that boats, in those times, were also used for coffins. Sniggering up their sleeves, the Kievans whimpered aloud: 'Our Prince is dead, our Princess marries our enemy, we shall be nothing but slaves', and they hoisted the heavy boat on to their backs. The ambassadors, lording it on their cross-benches, puffed up in their great, provincial-looking robes, were beginning to like their parts in the comedy. They did not enjoy themselves for long, for the boat was soon dropped into a trench which Princess Olga had arranged to be dug out in her courtyard in front of her windows. 'Do you find so much honour to your taste?' she sneered, as the shovels went into action and buried the ambassadors alive. End of first gentle stanza.

Thereupon Olga informed the Drevlyan Prince Mal that her own people would not let her come to him, unless he sent his noblest lords to accompany her. Mal was only too glad, since his intention was to marry the widow, to 'work his will' upon the orphaned Svyato-slav, and then to take possession of the throne of Kiev. The lords came. According to the Russian tradition, they were offered a steam bath. As soon as they had been ushered in, the bathhouse was locked and burned down. End of second stanza.

In the third one, Olga announces her arrival: 'So prepare much mead in the city where you killed my hus-band, that I may weep over his grave and hold a funeral feast for him.' The mead is prepared in suitable quan-tities and while the Drevlyans fall to, Olga's retainers humbly wait on them, hiding their poniards in their sleeves. When the guests are drunk, out come the poniards. As to Olga, she 'went around egging on her retinue to the massacre.' Five thousand are supposed to have died on that day. This, of course, was just another hors-d'oeuvre: Iskorosten, the capital of the Drevlyans, had to be taken.

And taken it was, as the fourth and final stanza described. After a year of siege, seeing that she had achieved nothing, Olga sent into the town a conciliatory message: 'All your other cities have surrendered to me and pay tribute; their inhabitants till their fields and their lands in peace. Why would you want to starve to death?' The Drevlyans replied that they would be happy to pay up, but were afraid of Olga's revenge. She declared that enough was enough, even for her, and that she would be content with a token tribute: not silver, not furs, not honey, only three pigeons and three sparrows per house. 'I will not impose a heavy burden on you, like my husband, for you are impoverished by the siege,' added the petticoated Machiavelli with a touch of sadism. All the boys began catching birds and soon hundreds of them, their legs tied together, amongst much twittering and fluttering, were brought to Olga by overjoyed Iskorosten citizens. 'Be sure to return to your city tonight; tomorrow I am leaving for Kiev,' graciously advised the Princess. That evening, while the Drevlyans sang and danced, the Kievans took pieces of sulphur wrapped in cloth and tied them with thread to each pigeon and sparrow. Then they set the sulphur on fire and released the birds, who flew in a panic to their nests, 'the pigeons to the cotes, the sparrows under the eaves'. Coops, porches, haystacks, everything blazed at the same time. The people fled the city, only to fall into Olga's ambushes.

Some she killed, some she gave as slaves to her own men, some she left alive and free to work in order to collect a heavy tribute from them.

Such was the ballad, not a particularly original one, since the motif of the incendiary bird is a common one in Viking lore, but on one point at least it told the truth: there was only one happy ending for Olga, and that was when somebody paid a new tax into her exchequer. Grandmother had the mind of a financier, which she proved by organizing, around 947, the first Russian internal revenue service.

Born in the North, some specify in the town of Izborsk, colonized according to tradition around 860 by Viking Prince Truvor, who may even have been Rurik's youngest brother if he really existed (which is doubtful), Olga belonged to a very rich family[17] and possessed in her own right several villages – Vyshgorod, Olzhichi, Budutino – and also hunting grounds and game preserves. To these vast properties she applied, as was usual, one third of the state revenues, the two other thirds being deposited in the Kiev exchequer. Before her regency, the Prince – Askold, Oleg, Igor himself – would have been merely based in his capital city. In November of each year, as soon as the snow transformed all Russia into one gigantic road, he would set out to visit all the lands that were supposed to pay taxes to him. This collection round, called the *poludie*, lasted all winter, with incidents along the way: robbers attacking, tribes refusing to pay, or being taken over by other, sometimes more powerful, exploiters. In April, the Prince would return to Kiev with his sleighs full of furs, silver dirhems or other coins, and even honey. In the meantime, up the Dniepr and its affluents, riverside villagers had been building boats (Russians were famous for the quality of their boats), and as soon as the ice gave, they floated them down to Kiev, where they would sell them to the Prince. The retinue would then load the booty, to which, as arranged with the Greeks, slaves and grain would be added. The huge convoy would float down the Dniepr to Vitichev, where it would await other convoys from Novgorod, Smolensk, Lubech, Chernigov, Vyshgorod. Then on to Constantinople, without the Prince, who would generally take advantage of the nice weather to go and beat up some of his neighbours, whom he found too greedy for his taste.

Olga changed all that. She abolished the impractical *poludie*, creating instead local tax units. Each one was called a *pogost* and operated under a tax-collector employed and salaried by the state. In addition to that important reform, she installed boundary-posts, which allowed a more rational collecting of taxes, and, in the Viking tradition, trading-posts, which added fluidity to the circulation of goods. The system was centralized in Kiev, but extended even further north than Novgorod, where Rurik, the founder of the dynasty, had had his seat, and which Olga was careful to visit, so as to keep it, so to speak, in the Kiev gravitational ensemble. As a result, an area of approximately five hundred thousand square kilometres – not unlike the state of Washington or two Great Britains – was being slowly transformed, through financial organization, into a unified country governed by the house of Rurik. How much of all this Vladimir understood as a child, we do not know, but, when the time came for him to gather the reins of power in his hands, he did not miss the opportunity, and went one step further, giving the status of nation to what, two generations earlier, had been hardly more than a hunting preserve.

Olga had not been Igor's only wife, but it is said that he always respected her more than the others 'on account of her wisdom'. Anyway she does not seem to have encountered any political opposition from any other member of his harem. She ruled strongly and peacefully for about ten years, and then, either because of her wisdom or, as Svyatoslav would have said, in spite of it, a staggering change came over her: she abandoned the proud faith of her forefathers and began to worship a crucified God. A chaplain called Gregory accompanied her everywhere like her shadow, and she even took it into her head to go to Constantinople, the Eastern capital of the Christians. She is said to have been baptized there; whatever may be the case, she chose as her new name Helena, in honour of St Helena, Constantine I's mother, and as a gesture of courtesy toward Helena, Constantine VII's wife. From then on, no more atrocities are ascribed to her credit; her lifestyle changed drastically; 'a woman in body, but as wise as a man', she destroyed some places of pagan worship, perhaps built in Kiev a wooden church dedicated to St Sophia, devoted part of her income to charity, her time to prayer, her efforts to the conversion of her people. Of course Vladimir took all that for granted: he had never known his grandmother as a pagan, and her stern and somewhat formidable personality must have stamped itself on his mind as that of an eminently successful head of state, with one regrettable oddity: her religion.

As a matter of fact, religion was the only point on which success betrayed her. Not only did her subjects remain for the most part pagan, but even with her sponsor in Christianity, the Emperor of Constantinople, she ran into trouble. Both the Russian chronicler and the Basileus himself have preserved for us an account of

21

Olga's trip to Constantinople, and although they are by no means consonant, one thing appears clearly: Olga, mighty Princess of the North, bringing a golden plate as an offering, expected to be treated as the Queen of Sheba at the court of Solomon, whereas the Basileus felt he was honouring her more than she deserved when he graciously allowed her to have dinner with the Empress's ladies-in-waiting. Wittingly or unwittingly, he obviously snubbed her in many ways. She had become a Christian, but she never forgot that, in the person of her own self, a Russian princess had been slighted. When, after her return to Kiev, Constantine sent envoys to her to solicit presents of slaves, wax and furs as well as soldiers, she replied that she would gladly grant his request if he came to formulate it in person; of course he would have to wait at her door as long as she had waited at his. Another aspect of the question, which will have its importance hereafter, may have weighed more than a few disagreements about etiquette. The Greeks tended to consider that any foreign prince who accepted their faith became *ipso facto* a vassal of their emperor. Such definitely was not Olga's intention. Refined and sophisticated as the Greeks might be, and as much as she believed in their God, she was a regent in her own right, and felt she had been on the verge of compromising her independence by making that trip to Constantinople. Like the great stateswoman she was, she decided to restore a proper balance by applying for missionaries to the Western Church instead of to the Eastern one. That would teach the arrogant Constantine with whom he had to deal.

In 959 Russian envoys reached the court of Otto I, King of Germania, future first sovereign of the Holy Empire. They wanted a bishop and some priests for their

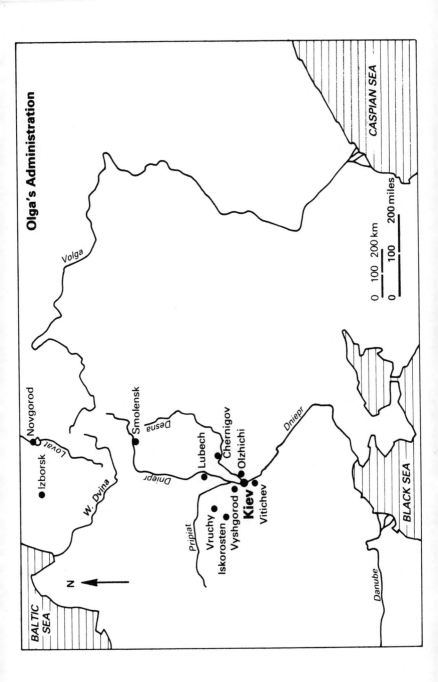

Olga's Administration

people. The Germans took their time to fulfil the request. In 960 a bishop was appointed, but he died the next year, before he had even left Frankfurt. His place was finally given to Adalbert of Trier, of the monastery of St Maximin, who set out after having been provided by the King with everything he might need for the execution of his holy mission in remote, barbaric lands. The lack of enthusiasm shown by the Western Church or the German government had serious consequences. In 962 Svyatoslav was already a grown man, ready to confront his mother on an issue on which he happened to have strong feelings. While he was Prince of Kiev, his people were not to be taught meekness, patience, forbearance, humility, and all that nonsense; they would not be persuaded to turn the other cheek or to sheathe the sword. Vladimir was very young in 962 but one of his first memories may have been seeing in that year a foreign character, who had looked very important on his arrival, hastily tucking his robes into his boots before beating a speedy retreat. Adalbert was fortunate to escape with his life: several of his companions were killed on the way back, and if he had stayed, he might have provided the necessary object for a good old Viking human sacrifice.

Olga had been thwarted, but she refused to acknowledge defeat. For years she tried to share her happiness as a Christian with her beloved son. 'I have learned to know God. It is such a joy!' she exclaimed. 'If you know him too, you also will rejoice.' Svyatoslav smiled and shook his head: frankly, Christianity seemed very stupid to him. Besides, he had pragmatic reasons for sticking to the beliefs of his people: 'Mother, my retinue will laugh at me if I become a do-gooder. Yours is not a faith for soldiers and princes.' Grandmother was never at a loss for a good argument. 'If you were to be converted, your subjects would follow your example, my son, and we should become a Christian nation, like the Greeks.' 'May Perun avert such a disgrace!' Father would retort, good-naturedly enough. Like most pagans, he was fundamentally tolerant. If some of his men turned Christian, he would scoff at them: 'Here comes another of Mother's converts! Have you exchanged the sword for the cross, man? Will you give your breeches to the Greeks if they ask for your shirt?' But he instituted no persecutions. So long as a soldier fought like a pagan, what did it matter what god he worshipped? True, rumours did circulate to the effect that in the rare cases he was defeated, he would lay the blame on the Christians among his soldiers, and execute a few as an example.[18] Grandmother had no recourse except in the exhortations of her chaplain and in prayer. 'Night and day,' says the chronicler, 'she prayed for her dear son and for her people: "If God wishes to have pity on my family and the land of Russia, let him lead my son's heart as he led mine."'

There were also, between the old Princess and the young Prince, misunderstandings of a more personal nature. One of them, Vladimir knew, had been caused by his own appearance in the world. Polygamy was a fact of life among Vikings, but Olga, it seems, had acquired Christian prejudices on that point, and, like many a mother, she was bent on preserving her son's virtue. She felt responsible for it even after he was married and had fathered two sons. Young Svyatoslav, however, had no such inhibitions, and – apparently while his righteous mother was excursioning in Constantinople – he distinguished her own housekeeper, the sister of one of his best captains, Dobrynya. It is a matter of surmise whether Dobrynya deliberately pushed his sister into the Prince's arms; whatever the truth of the matter may be, he later had good reason to be pleased with the result of his brotherly broadmindedness and maybe forethought. As to poor Malusha, she did not enjoy her master's favours for long. The mistress came back, not in the best of dispositions. As soon as she learned about what to her was an illicit relationship, she forced the pregnant housekeeper to surrender her keys, and sent her away to the village of Budutino, where Vladimir was probably born.[19] A Victorian plot if ever there was one. Also in the Victorian tradition, the stern benefactress relented after a time, not toward sin but toward its child: Vladimir was carried back to the palace and raised there with his two half-brothers. What became of Malusha will be discussed later.

Svyatoslav's last return to Kiev, happy as it was, brought about some more confrontations between him and his aged mother. He stayed at home for a whole year, with the exception of one short campaign against the Pechenegs, and nearly died of boredom. Building a keep outside the city, to protect it to some extent from further invasions – could such a tame occupation absorb his ebullient energies? Besides, what was Russia to him? He had never even been to Novgorod,[20] and all his attention was focused on the South. 'Pereyaslavets,' he used to say, 'is the real centre of my realm.' This only shows how little sense of geography he had – which, strangely enough, is often the case with Alexanders and Napoleons of all descriptions. Svyatoslav was fascinated by the circulation of goods that was taking place at the mouth of the Danube: gold, wines, fruit, silks and brocades came from Greece, silver and horses from Hungary and Bohemia, furs, wax, honey, slaves from Russia. What more could a man want? Oh! much more.

Svyatoslav talked about Pereyaslavets, but he must have quietly entertained a much greater ambition: after all, he was to reach Adrianopolis, which is a bare two hundred kilometres from Constantinople herself. And looting what they called Miklagard had always been the Vikings' dream. Obviously, to attack Constantinople, Pereyaslavets was a better base than Kiev. So Svyatoslav announced several times that he wished to set off again for the blessed South. Olga could not help being disappointed at the idea that her life's work – she had made Kiev the organic centre of Russia – would go to waste; she also did not want to let go her beloved son when her health made it obvious that she was seeing him for the last time. She begged him to wait for her death: then he could do as he pleased. Being a dutiful and grateful son, he complied, although his hand must have itched for the hilt of his sword. She did not make him wait too long: on July 11, 969, she died, bequeathing[21] the whole village of Budutino to the Church.

Naturally Svyatoslav wanted to bury his mother according to pagan customs: a feast, some carousing and a few warlike games would fittingly express the survivors' grief. Then the body would be laid in a boat which would be set afire; and in no time at all the soul of the Princess would be reunited with her ancestors. But Olga had expressly forbidden such satanic practices, and, much to Vladimir's dismay, his pagan father organized a Christian funeral. In the midst of great mourning – the whole population of Kiev sincerely bewailed the disappearance of a great ruler, even the indomitable Svyatoslav crying like a child – a priest, perhaps Gregory the chaplain, performed the last rites over the body of the great convert whom, one day, the Church would recognize as one of her saints. Her flesh, it seems, did not decay, and this, for the Christians, was a sure sign that God had glorified her who had glorified Him. Little Vladimir did not care. He heard the chanting, he smelled the incense, but all this was quite foreign to him. He knew only one thing, that he would never again see his stern, kind, awe-inspiring grandmother. And he wept. The chronicler has explicitly preserved for us the memory of these tears.

4 The setting

The importance of Kiev, a key city from an economic standpoint, has to do with its hydrography. A look at the map will show that the West extends toward Russia by means of a triple fork whose prongs are called the West Dvina, the Niemen and the Vistula. A fourth prong can be identified as the Gulf of Finland, to the north of Novgorod. To meet this four-pronged thrust, Russia, on its side, extends two willing arms: the Volga system and the Dniepr system. In between 'quietly flows the Don', less important because it takes its source further east. As soon as the *Drang nach Osten* began from the North-west, the Volga, with its infinite net of tributaries, could not but catch a considerable amount of traffic, because it was eminently navigable and opened directly into the Caspian Sea, which in turn led conveniently to Baghdad, one of the main stops on the Westerner's route to India. But the Dniepr system, which looks, if a poetic metaphor may be pardoned for clarity's sake, like a three-petalled flower rising high on its stem, collected all travellers and merchants whose business took them to Constantinople, whether they came from Germany, Poland, Lithuania, Scandinavia, even England, or from the flourishing Viking-Russian market of Novgorod. Kiev found itself at the very heart of this flower of rivers, allowing easy communication not only with 'the Western fork' but also with the North, through the Lovat and the lakes, with the North-east through the Oka which led into the Volga, with the East through the Don, and with the South-east through the Donets. Moreover, thanks to the moisture preserved by forests which were much more numerous then than they are now, many of the lesser tributaries, not even marked on the map, would be quite navigable, especially for Viking ships with a small draft. Therefore the famous route 'from the Vikings to the Greeks' (Gulf of Finland, Neva, Lake Ladoga, Volkhov, Lake Ilmen, West Dvina, Dniepr, Black Sea, Bosphorus) necessitated only a few short portages, and of course Kiev profited by the added convenience.

Interesting markets could also be found much closer to Kiev than Constantinople, since, dating back to 600 BC, the Greeks had sprinkled the Black Sea coast with colonies many of which prospered. Besides Cherson, already mentioned, there were Olbia, Theodosia, Phanagoria, and others.

Land roads, not as safe as water ones, but still used whenever the weather would permit, formed a knot in Kiev. The main one, the route of the caravans, stretched as far as Western Europe, and through Mainz, Prague, Cracov, Kiev, wound its way to the shores of the Caspian: Araby, India, China, lay beyond; east of Kiev it was known as the Zalozny road. Another one went to the Crimea: it was the salt route, the Solony. Another came from Warsaw and North-eastern Europe. Another went to Kursk. Yet another one linked Kiev with Bulgaria and Constantinople, the capital of what was still known as the Roman Empire. Not only foreigners

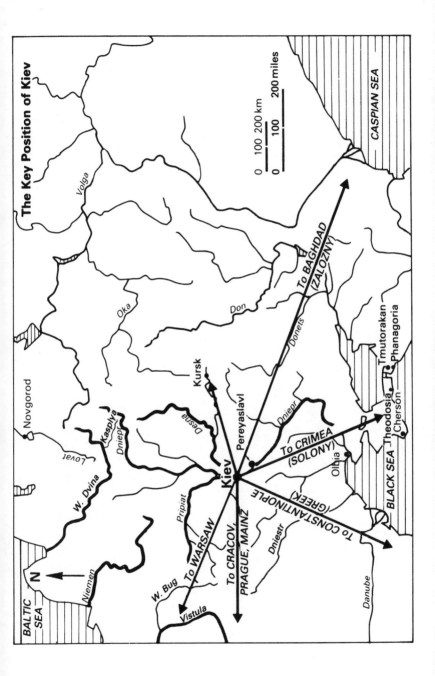

The Key Position of Kiev

travelled these roads: the Russians themselves were renowned merchants at the time; they were seen as far as
Baghdad if not further.

The very position of Kiev at the extreme limit of the
northern forests and the southern steppes, which
allowed the city to make the best of two complementary
economies (hunting, forestry, wild honey on the one
hand, agriculture and cattle-raising on the other), also
exercised some influence in its being singled out for the
major part it was to play in the history of Russia, the
more so as the Slavs had a traditional tendency to group
around cities, the best situated being of course the preferred ones. It would be quite beyond the scope of this
study to go back to pre-Slavic times or even to tackle the
controversial question of the origin of Slavs, but it is
important to realize that, for Eastern Slavs, attraction to
towns was always more decisive than tribal derivation.
A tribe that did not manage to build a town was absorbed into the neighbouring tribe; a tribe that built two
towns split into two communities. Between the Ladoga
lake (north of Novgorod) and Kiev, lived eight tribes:
four of them, the Dregovichans, Radimichans, Vyatichans and Drevlyans disappeared by absorption,
whereas the four other ones, the Lake Ilmen Slavs,
Krivichans, Severyans and Polyans, formed six
provinces around six cities, respectively Novgorod,
Polotsk, Smolensk, Chernigov, Pereyaslavl, and Kiev.
It is not for nothing that the Vikings called Russia Gardariki: the country of towns. True, Kiev was not at the
geographic centre of that complex, but it controlled
communications, and that was enough. In a very short
time, scarcely more than a century, it became, from just
another town, the principal one, and very soon after
that, it held all the others under its thumb. Oleg called

Kiev 'the mother of Russian cities', and he was right: her 'daughters' were entirely dependent upon her, since all the outlets of Russian commerce (except the northern ones, which are much less practical since most Russian rivers flow in a north-south direction) were gathered in her hand: she could let the stream of goods pour out, or allow it to seep through, or choke it to death. Some towns, like Smolensk, bowed gracefully, paid dues and prospered; some tribes, like the Drevlyans, tried to resist and were crushed. A powerful centralization was the result. Not, of course, that a favourable economic combination is sufficient to determine the fate of any city: it takes men, and the men were there, as well as one brilliant woman. This is where Vladimir's family comes in.

These men were Vikings.[22] In our peace-loving times Vikings do not enjoy a very good press; they are seen by most as mere professional bandits who ravaged the coasts of Europe for a good two hundred years. This is not untrue as far as it goes, but it is a one-sided view of a many-sided question. The military feats of that extraordinary people began in the eighth century and lasted in fact as late as the seventeenth with Gustav-Adolphus, to end in the eighteenth with Karl XII, at the hand of Peter the Great. Their value on the battlefield was only one aspect of an absolutely unique vitality, which exploded in the 700s and knew no bounds until first Christianity and then sheer exhaustion forced it to subside. In the meantime they had led the crusades, discovered Iceland, Greenland, and, with Leif Ericsson, in Vladimir's lifetime, America, colonized Scotland and Ireland, plundered France, Italy and Greece, taken over Normandy in the time of Vladimir's grandfather, conquered and organized England in the time of his sons, opened roads to the Orient when Spain had fallen to the Moor, created

34

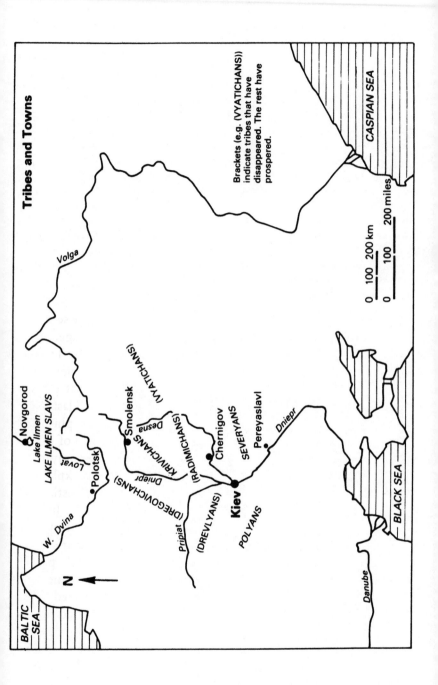

Tribes and Towns

Brackets (e.g. (VYATICHANS)) indicate tribes that have disappeared. The rest have prospered.

0   100   200 km
0   100   200 miles

CASPIAN SEA

BALTIC SEA

Volga

Novgorod
Lake Ilmen
LAKE ILMEN SLAVS

W. Dvina

Polotsk
(DREGOVICHANS)

Smolensk
Dniepr
(KRIVICHANS)
Desna
(VYATICHANS)
(RADIMICHANS)

Lovat

Pripiat
(DREVLYANS)

Chernigov
SEVERYANS
Pereyaslavl

Kiev
POLYANS

Dniepr

BLACK SEA

Danube

N

Russia out of a practically virgin desert, founded the prosperous and tolerant state of Sicily, served as the bodyguard of the Emperors of Constantinople, and given Europe a large part of her hereditary nobility, which kept them in ruling positions for a few hundred years more. One cannot help wondering at such a gigantic bubbling over of the Scandinavian kettle, and one of the explanations that come to mind is naturally polygamy. How well it served Islam, by causing a demographic tidewave in the wake of a few thousand Arab warriors! It may have rendered the same service to the Scandinavian farmers who sent their cohorts of bastards to fecundate the world. Why be stingy? In case of mishap nothing was easier than to replace them.

Although greatly feared, the Vikings of the period in which our main interest lies did receive some deserved admiration from contemporary observers. Admittedly, they had a reputation for cruelty – they would use prisoners of war for target practice with the bow or drive nails through their heads just for the fun of it, and one Arab writer disapproves of their filthy habits: they all wash every day, he says, in the same large bowl carried around the hall. This may not have been extremely hygienic, but at least they washed, and other Arabs take a definitely less dim view of their customs. For one thing, they were found to be handsome, elegant, richly attired. Then they treated their slaves well, never submitting them to the ignominy of public auctions. They did not oppress the native Slavs; on the contrary, they intermarried with them. Not interested in villages, estates, fields, they had only towns, which they used as trading-posts. They were both trustful and trustworthy, leaving their furs in specially marked clearings, where Arab merchants would examine them at leisure and leave in exchange the amount of silver indicated on the label, or somewhat less if they did not agree with the price; or the Arabs would display their silver artifacts, and the Vikings would come to have a look at them, and complete the deal only if they liked it. Sometimes such bartering would go on for quite some time, the Arab or the Viking adding to his silver or to his skins, and no one would pick up the other's goods before both were satisfied. Isn't such honesty something to dream about? 'They are generous with their possessions,' writes the Arab, Ibn Rusteh about the Vikings, 'they treat their guests honourably and act handsomely toward strangers who take refuge with them and all those who accept their hospitality, not allowing any of their own people to do them the slightest harm.'

It is hazardous to try and date the arrival of the Vikings in the land which we now call Russia. In the eleventh century, Arabs observed that they had become so intermingled with the Slavs as to have adopted their tongue. This should not surprise us, as the Vikings were never deeply attached to their own culture, unless they found no native one where they landed, as in Iceland. For instance, William Longsword, the son of Rollo, founder of Normandy, had to send his own son from his capital Rouen to Bayeux so that he might learn Danish: he already spoke only French. Western sources mention a Russian Viking attack on Constantinople as early as 860, although it is still doubtful whether Kiev or Tmutorakan[23] served as its base. In 839 some of them appeared to have at least travelled through Russia, and some historians think that Viking settlements already existed on Russian soil in the eighth century. Whatever the truth of the matter, the general pattern of colonization seems to have been as follows:

– step one, Viking clan A executes raids against given objective

– step two, after a number of raids, native population hires Viking clan B to protect it against A, for a fee

– step three, B moves in and builds forts with permanent garrisons, set on hilltops

– step four, progressively voluntary fee becomes forced tribute, servants turn into masters

– step five, Vikings trade with local population. Their passion for trade is well known. After taking the city of Angiers in France, they reserved the right to stay around for some time after peace was signed, in order to open a market where they sold back what they had just acquired by loot

– step six, traders from different regions are attracted to fortified centres, craftsmen settle down at foot of hills

– step seven, Viking warriors marry native women, bravest of young natives volunteer to join Viking army – or, technically, the retinue of the Viking prince – and, in a matter of generations, the two peoples become one.

So it must have happened when, around 860 according to *The Chronicle*, envoys from the Slavs sailed overseas to deliver to the Vikings the famous sentence: 'Our land is vast and rich, but there is no order in it. Come and rule over us.' What a *Contrat social*![24] The Vikings were only too happy to accommodate, and the foremost among them was Rurik,[25] who settled down first in Staraya Ladoga, north of Novgorod, then in Novgorod itself.

Rurik may have been, as some historians think, the same man as the notorious Rorik of Jutland. This, on the whole, seems probable, but even if Rurik was not Rorik, he must have been very much like him, and tales of similar youthful adventures must have played an important part in the building up of Vladimir's imagination.

Rorik's father, of the clan of Skioldung, had lost his Jutland fief in Denmark and entered the service of Charlemagne, which did not prevent him from trying to get back what was his. That he never succeeded in doing, but in compensation, his eldest son Harald received from Emperor Louis the Pious, Charlemagne's son, the district of Rustringen in Friesland. Rorik, who is supposed to have been born around 800, inherited the region from Harald but lost it after Louis' death and Lothaire's accession to the throne. He had already spent his youth fighting against the King of Denmark, and earning his living by the sword was nothing new to him. A medieval Dubrovsky,[26] he gathered 'a few good men' and, at their head, raided now the continent, now the British Isles. In 845 he sailed up the Elbe; the same year he plundered northern France; in 850, with three hundred and fifty boats, he laid waste the coasts of England; then it was the turn of the mouth of the Rhine and of his own Friesland. Meanwhile he had acquired the picturesque nickname of *Fel Christianitatis*, the gall of Christendom. Finally Lothaire had to give in: 'Friesland will be returned to you, provided you defend the North Sea shores against other Vikings.' The old story: only Vikings could control Vikings. Rorik accepted the deal, but that was no reason to give up the kind of life he loved. Since the Baltic was open for hunting, he shifted his attention in that direction, especially when Lothaire, after some deliberation, asked him to accept, in exchange for Friesland, his own hereditary southern Jutland which, for a Viking, was a stone's throw from the coasts of Russia. No wonder that a very short time later (around 855), either invited (as legend will have it) or not, he showed up with his dragon-shaped ships on the shores of Lake Ladoga. And small wonder if, on June 18,

860, under one of Rurik's captains, Askold,[27] a nation so far 'obscure, insignificant, of no account, uncaptained, equipped in servile fashion, not even known to exist until then',[28] suddenly appeared in the port of Constantinople and, after much killing and looting, could be defeated only by a storm which arose in answer to the frantic prayers of Patriarch Photius carrying the Holy Virgin's robe in a procession and dipping it into the sea.

Constantinople! The city of purple! What spells the name alone cast upon the efficient barbarians of the North! From then on, the obscure, insignificant nation never ceased to be obsessed with it, mixing regular trading routine with intermittent forays, like the doubtful one of 907, under Oleg, when the Viking's shield is supposed to have been nailed, in defiance, to the gates of the city, or like the authentic one of 941, under Igor, Vladimir's grandfather. Whenever the boy looked at the dust rising over the 'Greek' road which led south, he could not help dreaming of the immense riches – gold, silks, brocades, jewels, mountains of pearls, beautiful shining statues of horses and men – that lay in that direction. Of course, if he ever went there, he would not take the impractical dirt road, but, as his ancestors had done before him, he would sail down the superb, convenient, majestic Dniepr, which rolled its full waters straight into the sea. You could throw into it a little stick with which you had just been playing, and one day it might scratch at the stone piers of the imperial city. Yes, one day Vladimir would show those Christians what blows a Russian prince could strike for honour (and profit).

The romantic family saga did not end with Rurik. Oleg, a kinsman, succeeded him. Two generals, Askold and Dir, having established themselves in Kiev, Oleg found the location ideal and decided to do something about it. He hid his soldiers, and, under false pretences, was admitted into the city: he was just a fellow Viking, he said, on a business trip to Constantinople. Then, when the people gathered to gape at the stranger, he suddenly showed them the little boy Igor (even younger than Vladimir was now) whom he carried in his arms: 'In his veins,' he cried, 'runs Rurik's blood. As to you,' he turned toward Askold and Dir, 'you are not even of princely stock!' The soldiers sprang out of their boats and slew the two lords, who understood a little late that they had been too forward for their station. The populace acclaimed the execution, and Oleg, not Igor, became Prince of Kiev. How the scene must have impressed Vladimir! First, the presence of a child, in a mute but essential part, and then the admirable economy of it all. A little guile, two murders and a silent boy: no more was needed to conquer a capital.

Making Kiev the centre of his realm, Oleg imposed tributes on all neighbouring tribes: some paid a silver piece, some a black marten skin per person, and Novgorod 300 grivnas a year.[29] Oleg was a good provider, a great general, and an excellent diplomat: his treaty with the Greeks is a detailed document full of sensible and just stipulations. But, although he was considered to be a bit of a magician, fate played a sinister trick on him. Soothsayers had foretold that his favourite horse would be the cause of his death; so he ordered that the animal be well taken care of, but never again mounted him. Five years later, he inquired about him and learned that he was dead. Ridiculing the prediction, he decided to go and have a look at what was left of the steed.

42

There the bones lie.
They are washed by the rains, they are covered with dust,
Feathergrass over them gently waves in the wind.

The prince sets his foot on the horse's head and makes an ironic speech about destiny.

Meanwhile, from the skull of the horse,
Hissing, a sepulchre snake has crept out,
And like a black garter it circles his leg.
The prince utters a cry: he is bitten to death.[30]

The story was not necessarily true – indeed it had been heard before about other characters – but still, when told in whispers by some toothless old nurse who strongly believed in the power of the *tchernobogi* (evil gods), it would easily make you shiver in the dusk.

Grandfather Igor had ruled in Kiev after Oleg; then, Father; some time it would be Yaropolk's day. As to Vladimir, he had good reason to believe that his father's keep, his grandmother's palace, these streets and alleys, these mansions and hovels that he knew so well, would never be his. If he wanted a princedom, he would have to carve one for himself from some wild and unknown country, where everything would have to start from the beginning. His ambition might be to rule some day a civilized nation, but, frankly, he had not a chance.

5   The end of a childhood

It was not that Vladimir was a half-breed.[31] As Pierre Gripari aptly puts it, you can either be a racist or a colonialist, but you cannot afford to be both if you want to be consistent, and the Vikings were the most consistent colonialists that ever lived. A Slavic mother was not a disadvantage, rather the opposite, among men who were systematically pushing their roots into Slavic soil.

It was not that Vladimir was probably illegitimate.[32] In a polygamous society, ideas about legitimacy are necessarily a little vague, and in a pagan one there can scarcely be any religious blemish attached to sex outside wedlock. To compare, William the Conqueror was the descendant of a long line of natural sons which included three reigning dukes (with his father, Robert II, the only legitimately born of the lot); his correspondence was officially signed 'William the Bastard', which may sound brazen, but was merely technically correct, as far as he was concerned. Christianity would, in its occasional narrow-mindedness, modify society's attitudes and impose cruel prejudices and discrimination against 'the children of love', but around the year 970, a man of good blood was still a man of good blood, no matter how he had happened to acquire it.

It was not so much that Vladimir was the youngest son, although primogeniture, not as an absolute right but as a practical way of doing things, was already prevalent in Viking families: among a number of sons, the oldest naturally succeded his father, if only because he had been the strongest for years and was still more experienced than his siblings. Still, there is a pattern here that deserves noticing. Many Russian fairy-tales present three brothers, the two older ones handsome, intelligent, and apparently destined for great success, the youngest a kind of idiot. But when put to the test, the older ones behave like fools or like knaves; the last one, on the contrary, demonstrates courage, honesty and common sense, not without a dose of opportunism, so that in the end he is the one to marry the Tsar's daughter. Agreed, the archetype is not entirely different from

Joseph's, Cordelia's or Cinderella's, and the underdog appeal, coupled with aesthetic necessities such as surprise and suspense, does make an outsider's story more satisfactory than a favourite's. There is, however, in such a reversal of values something particularly enjoyable for a Russian: if Vladimir's intense popularity did not originate in his apparently inferior position, at least it was substantially served by it.

For on one point his position was definitely inferior. Even if Yaropolk's and Oleg's mother was not, as some would like to believe, a Hungarian princess, we can deduce from later events that she was definitely of better stock than Malusha the housekeeper daughter of Malk, from Lubech. It is reasonable to surmise that the older boys made Vladimir feel the difference, teasing him because he was not born in the palace, ridiculing his uncle Dobrynya's aptitude at social climbing, remembering the menial tasks Malusha must have performed for everybody to see. This angle should not be over-emphasized: the Vikings were essentially a simple-minded people, concerned with achievement more than with lineage, ignorant of the refined delights of snobbery, and prone to measure a man's quality by the weight of his sword rather than by the designs on his shield. Yet Vladimir was but half a prince, and his hopes of inheriting even a portion of his father's appanage were small.

In the meantime, in spite of being, according to Thietmar, of a weak constitution, he led the same life as his half-brothers, receiving a princely education, or as much of it as was available. There is no proof that he could read and write, but since such accomplishments could already be obtained in Kiev, since his interest in learning became obvious in later years, and since his son Yaroslav was quite a scholar, it is to be assumed that he could, and we may imagine him engraving his name on the trees in the woods, or perhaps even sending short messages to his father's headquarters in Pereyaslavets.[33] He learned to ride a horse, to throw a javelin, to fence with a double-edged sword and to shoot with a bow. His instructor in such manly sports was Uncle Dobrynya, who devoted himself to the service of his princely nephew, knowing that he was not wasting his time. Most of Vladimir's days would be spent hunting, which is the best schooling for war, war being of course the *raison d'être* of princes. Game was superabundant in Russia; it was staple food for the people, and naturally the Prince's sons could enjoy any kind of hunting they liked. Vladimir would hunt on horseback or on foot, he would use baying hounds or silent, deadly falcons; he would aim arrows, hurl spears, set snares, pitch nets, or even lasso his quarry. Not to mention small game, he would capture wild horses, attack stags, bison, leopards, wild boars, fighting them hand to paw, his flesh torn by their claws, his bones exposed by their horns and tusks. Accidents happened: he would fall from his horse, or an elk would trample him under foot, or a buffalo throw him in the air, or a bear bite his thigh, or a wolf would jump upon his horse's neck with teeth bared.[34] But he knew all this was good. It was making a man of him, and in those times you had to be quite a man before you could qualify as a Viking, and a prince to boot. If he was at all like the great-grandson who transmitted to us those images of Russian hunts a thousand years ago, he spared neither his health nor his life. At an early age his body was already decorated with scars, he had cracked his skull once or twice, broken a limb or two, in short he was used to danger, suffering, and all the hardships of an adventurous life. As to killing, it had become a necessary habit. Strictly following Uncle Dobrynya's recommendations, whatever he would demand of his men he would first do himself, day or night, in the cold or in the heat, 'never giving himself one moment's rest'. So he roamed his native forests, with companions and guides, fortifying his muscles, steeling his heart, and getting acquainted at first hand with the resources of the land and of the people.

At night, when he finally lay down on the ground, he forgot all about wild beasts: other shadows lurked between the trees, other voices spoke to him in the dark. In a wood, it would be the local *leshy* intent on making the hunters lose their way as soon as they got up at daybreak; by a stream, it would be the *russalka* combing her wavy, green hair and crooning a song to lure men into the water; near a well, it would be the *vodyanik* popping in and out, in marshes, the *didko* peeping from a hollow tree. Even worse encounters were possible in the vicinity of watermills: all millers were wizards, that was certain. Compared with wizards, the spirits of the earth and waters were really not so bad: they could be propitiated by secret formulas known to professional sorcerers and by appropriate sacrifices. But the drowned rising from the dead and pressing their blue faces against your windows, the werewolves changing form at will when the moon was full, the vampires crawling out of their graves, these typical inhabitants of Slavic lands were greatly to be feared. Fortunately some supernatural protection could be obtained from the *rod*, the genie of the family, brandishing the hereditary trident of the Rurikids, from the *rozhanitsa*, a helpful female angel bending over every human soul, from the *domovoy*, the spirit of Grandmother's palace – only he was no good out of doors – and from the *choor*, the soul of Grand-father Igor, who had known how to pummel those odious, blasphemous Christians, while he lived, and would know how to protect his grandson, now that he himself had been reunited with the pure forces of the upper world. All his life Vladimir was deeply aware of the superficial and ephemeral aspects of man's condition on this earth; all his life, he hungered for communication with the beyond. We can easily imagine the wraiths of his native land hovering over him like fairies around a cradle; little did they know what gift they were secretly depositing at his feet.

While the boy was growing, Svyatoslav, having fulfilled his promise to his mother, made elaborate preparations for his long-delayed expedition into Bulgaria and, if the gods were with him, Greece. Collecting money, building boats, gathering and training an army: in such occupations he spent two years. His plans were grandiose: he wanted to transfer his capital from Kiev to Pereyaslavets, and that, even in those non-bureaucratic days, implied some organization. It may be a significant trait of the history of Russia that she never had for long an indisputable capital. Distances and communications being what they were, Svyatoslav felt the need to leave someone in authority behind him, and he naturally entrusted Kiev to Yaropolk his first-born, and the newly colonized lands of the Drevlyans to his second son Oleg. 'And me?' Vladimir could have asked. But no throne was vacant for the housekeeper's son, who anyway could not have been older than ten or twelve at the time.[35]

At that point some envoys arrived from Novgorod, twisting their fur hats in their hands. 'What brings you here?' asked Svyatoslav, foreseeing trouble. They replied, like the Hebrews of yore: 'Since everybody else gets a prince, we want one too.' The Novgorodians had always been a wilful, unruly people; they would no sooner hire a prince than they would kick him out, because he had displeased them one way or another. Svyatoslav had no patience with them, and it is significant that he had not even bothered to find a solution to the Novgorod problem. So they would not accept to be under Yaropolk? Certainly not. There was, and always would be, a strong antipathy between Northerners and Southerners, *katsaps* and *khokhols*. To accept the rule of an adult prince residing in Kiev was hard enough; the Novgorodians would have nothing to do with an immature substitute whom they did not even know. All the bitterness that must have been felt nearly one hundred years before, when Oleg moved 'down South', came now to the surface. 'We want a prince,' stubbornly repeated the Novgorodians. Could they not rule themselves as they had done so far, and be content with paying their tribute to Svyatoslav, who remained, after all, the overall master?[36] That was out of the question. If even that paltry Iskorosten rated a viceroy, certainly the old, mighty city of Novgorod, which traded with the whole world, needed one. 'We want a prince.' And being impudent Novgorodians, the envoys added: 'If you do not give us one, we shall find one elsewhere.' This was a serious threat. Svyatoslav was dreaming and he needed the prosperous Novgorodian merchants to pay for his dream. Anxious to please them, he summoned Yaropolk and offered him the northern city. Yaropolk shook his head: Kiev was a merry capital, admired by foreigners, with a relatively mild climate. Why would he exchange it for a gloomy, misty tradepost buried in snow half the year? Moreover, he

49

may have had Christian sympathies[37] or at least interests, and Kiev was the place to be in order to maintain contact with Greek traders and Bulgarian evangelists. His ex-nun of a wife did not relish the idea of being relegated to a still more remote place of exile. 'I will not go, Father,' said Yaropolk. Svyatoslav called in Oleg, whose forest dwellers and iron-miners could prove less than jolly subjects. But he did not like the idea of Novgorod either. Maybe, being passionately addicted to hunting, he distrusted the frozen lakes of the north. Maybe the challenge of change frightened him. Maybe he just wanted to remain close to Kiev, and two hundred kilometres is closer than one thousand. 'Father,' he said, 'I will not go.' The Novgorodians were getting fidgety; they wanted a prince and they could have any Viking pirate for the asking; Svyatoslav felt at a loss; it was precisely the kind of petty, annoying puzzle that he did not know how to tackle.

Dobrynya had been biding his time. Standing in the background as befitted his rank, he had not, so far, said one word. But now, 'Why not the child Vladimir?' he whispered in his sovereign's ear. Had Svyatoslav forgotten his third son? It is possible: he must have had a number of bastards, and although this one had been raised in the palace and, so to speak, recognized, fatherly attention does not seem to have been lavished on him. Did he think the child was too young? This again is possible, although Vsevolod III would not hesitate to send a four-year-old babe, his son Svyatoslav, to reign over the same Novgorod – but two centuries later, when, at least in theory, legitimacy would have taken precedence over valour. Anyway, prompted by Dobrynya, the Prince thought this was a good idea and immediately offered his bantling to the obdurate Novgorodians.

They agreed. The handsome boy was a descendant of Rurik and he would be all their own. They intimated that Svyatoslav should have thought of him before, and that they at least would treat him according to his rank. Was Vladimir consulted? At his age, perhaps not, since Svyatoslav must have been quite relieved at seeing his predicament so happily resolved. But if the housekeeper's son's opinion was asked, he probably could scarcely hide his excitement. Distances and adventures did not frighten him; getting closer to the land from which his forefathers came must have appealed to him; and the rich city of Novgorod was quite a morsel for anyone with princely tastes. 'Father, I will go,' he answered forthwith, with shining eyes.

Quite pleased with themselves, the taciturn Novgorodians carried him off to a fur-lined barge, and weighed anchor. The sails flapped, the oars bent against the current, and she turned her stem northward. That was the end of a childhood.

CHAPTER TWO

Teens

1 Going north

His brothers' taunts resounded a long time in the boy's ears. 'A Novgorodian? Congratulations!' mocked Yaropolk. 'Do you know that Novgorodians cannot ride a horse? They will soon have you trotting like a pregnant matron, brotherkin!' 'On the other hand, they are very excellent carpenters,' scoffed Oleg. 'Will you build a palace for me, Vladimir, when you have learned to wield a drill and an adze, or even one of those ridiculous modern saws?' 'One nice thing,' added Yaropolk, 'is that every time you go to the steam-bath, you will get a sound thrashing with birch twigs. It is the custom in Novgorod, and, in my opinion, it will do you a lot of good.' 'Besides it might help you scrub off the tannic acid you will always be anointed with. Ugh!' cried Oleg, holding his nose as if the stink of the *usnianny kvas* was already unbearable. 'Mock away, my lads,' thought Vladimir, as he lay in the barge and observed familiar landmarks recede into the distance. 'I am now a reigning prince, and your equal, whether you like it or not. You can have your dirty Iskorosten and even your Kiev. I do not envy you one little bit. I shall be perfectly happy in *my* Novgorod.' And he dreamed about the powerful merchant city which the Vikings called Holmgardr (Hill-town), and the Russians Novgorod (New-town), to differentiate it from the older Viking settlement at Ladoga.

From time to time, the *strugi* (river boats) would

53

touch shore; later it was sometimes necessary to disembark and ride portions of the road on horseback, while slaves would fit rollers under the hulls, tie and strain ropes, and push and pull the big, heavy things, which looked so graceful in the water and so clumsy on the road. These were good opportunities to study the changing landscape. Although, through his hunting experience, Vladimir knew what a forest was like, he was mainly used to boundless steppes where the *chernoziom* was so rich that you could plough it once, after letting it lie fallow for several years, and then harvest wheat a number of times without bothering any more about tilling. Not so in the North. Here woods were everywhere and you had to burn out patches before ploughing them by means of a wooden hack equipped with three teeth. Vladimir – he was to be famous for his interest in the common people – would rein in his horse as soon as he saw working men to whom he could talk. 'What are you doing? Explain.' The men would bare their heads to the princely boy, squint at the imposing figure of Dobrynya riding a fat charger in the background, and answer in their regional dialect, which Vladimir tried very hard to understand: 'Prince, we are working on a *podseka*. Once the fire has burned out, we shall have this *lyado* to cultivate.' 'And what do you call this funny plough? I have never seen the like.' 'This, master, is a *sokha*.' 'And what are you going to sow?' 'Oats, master. Or barley. Or rye.' Rye seemed to be the password of the North. Even the Prince had to adapt himself to local culture and eat rye bread. Vladimir did not mind. He was absorbing his new realm through all his pores.

The physical type of the population changed also. The Polyans were tall men, with a short skull and a broad forehead. The Northern Slavs were as tall, but their skulls were longer and narrower. They had a reputation for being slow-witted, and true enough, they were neither as merry nor as sly as the Southerners, but they seemed more dependable, more strongly attached to their values, good soldier material if you only knew how to use them, as Uncle Dobrynya pointed out.

As one approached Novgorod, there was more and more marshland, and agriculture became scarce, but fishing settlements were to be seen everywhere. Vladimir's descendant, the Fisherman Prince Alexander Nevsky, was to show particular interest in this way of making one's living, and it is fair to assume that young Vladimir also was curious at seeing small rivers barred with pales; in the paling, there would be holes, and behind them creels, into which the fish would be driven. The boy was full of admiration: 'In Kiev, we know seines, and dragnets, and of course angling, but this paling of rivers looks like a neat trick!' Uncle Dobrynya, perhaps, would be surprised at a prince showing interest in something which was neither war nor hunting. But, being a far-sighted man, he must have approved of this concern for economics: times were changing and princes were to become something they had never been: organizers. Besides, the paling trick might be adaptable to warfare, who knows?

One day, the travellers reached Lake Ilmen, and the *strugi*, hoisting up their sails – canvas for most ships, silk for the one which had the honour of carrying the Prince – caught the wind. Novgorod, surrounded by wooden palisades and earthen ramparts, appeared on its hill. Through the vaporous northern clouds, a huge wooden pillar seemed to tower over it. As you came closer, you saw it was not a pillar at all, but, erected in the middle of a circular area comprising eight lobes, the gigantic statue of a god, holding a club in his hand. Vladimir's heart must have beaten fast: this was his city, this would be his god. Besides he had a fondness for statues. 'Who is it?' he asked, descrying the enormous features coarsely hewn out of a tree trunk. 'The great Perun, the god of lightning,' answered the helmsman with reverence. Vladimir, religious as ever, bowed devoutly before the thing, while Dobrynya, if he was at all gifted with prognostication, must have peered at it with some misgivings. Dobrynya, one imagines, did not believe too much in either god or devil, but the day was not very far off when the god of lightning and the ambitious general would come to grips.[38]

2 Novgorod

Novgorod stood on the left (western) bank of the Volkhov, at the very point where that river was born from the overflow of Lake Ilmen. Quite a modern city, smaller but much cleaner than Kiev, it had an air of prosperity and well-being, not without a touch of complacency, it must be confessed. The harbour was a forest of masts belonging to the smaller *strugi*, to the larger *nasady*, which would cost you up to three grivnas[39] but could face the storms of the Baltic Sea, and to foreign ships of every description. Piers stretched out into the water; wooden landing stages belonging to individual merchants ran alongside the shore. How convenient for the loading and unloading of passengers and goods!

Two men were waiting on the embankment with a none too respectful crowd gathered behind them. They were the two main dignitaries of the city, the *posadnik*[40] (city mayor) and the *tysyatsky* (chief of the militia).

Although they were bringing the traditional bread and salt of hospitality on a silver platter, they awaited the new Prince with somewhat mixed feelings. They held their offices from the people, whence, in Novgorod, all power sprang. On the other hand this boy, who had just jumped over the side of the *strug*, and whose boots clattered so gaily on the wooden wharf, possessed something else, more and less important at the same time. In his veins ran the blood of Rurik. As such he was a symbol of a concept which was still extremely vague in Russia: sovereignty. This somehow gave him one chance to reign. If he bungled it, he would promptly be sent away, but the chance was his, and the field of power was felt to be still wide enough for his prerogatives not to conflict with those of the mayor and police commissioner. The people wanted a prince: let them at least have a Rurikid – if the Rurikid was any good. On the other hand, they had their doubts about that Dobrynya fellow, whose massive figure loomed in the background. As the Prince's tutor, and to make matters worse, his uncle, he would for a time exercise all the Prince's functions. Who was he? Would his ambition clash with theirs? Would this upstart know how to treat the chiefs of the old Novgorodian families, and the *veche*, the all-powerful assembly of the people? All this crossed their minds as they bowed with dignity before the newcomers, fairly low to the Prince, much less low to his factotum.

Seeing no reason to hide his curiosity about *his* city, Vladimir, while graciously accepting the gifts of hospitality, twisted and turned his head right and left to observe everything. A sturdy bridge, built by the most famous bridge-builders of Eastern Europe, linked the *Podol* (riverside quarter of the old city) to the newer settlements on the other bank of the Volkhov, 'the market side', as the dignitaries explained. They were justly proud of a wooden sewerage system consisting of pipes and barrels. The main street, they mentioned, was paved with timber, another luxury unheard of in Kiev. The superb work of the carpenters was evident everywhere. The wooden *kreml* (citadel) and its *detinets* (keep) dominated the old city, and on entering them Vladimir felt he was following very closely in the footsteps of his Viking ancestors, who had simultaneously colonized and protected this people, before blending with it. He too, he decided, would both serve it and reign over it as efficiently as he would know how.

The next days were spent in getting acquainted with the population. Novgorod comprised five autonomous communes, each one called a *konets*. They were the Slovensky, the Plotnitsky (carpenters' own), the Zagorodsky (suburban), the Goncharsky (potters' own) and the Nerevsky, in charge respectively of the Bezhetskaya, the Obonezhskaya, the Shelonskaya, the Derevskaya and the Vodskaya provinces. Every commune elected a *starosta* (elder) for internal administration. There were also two foreign settlements: a German one, and another, whose inhabitants came from the Scandinavian island of Gotland. This did not strike Vladimir as particularly exotic: in Kiev, in addition to the Germans, he was used to seeing Jews, Armenians and Greeks, who had chosen to live in the Russian capital. Far more intriguing for him was the Zavolozhye colony, which lay north of Vologda and extended no one knew how far. It was a mysterious land, frequented only by those fearless sailors who would go out into the White Sea and Arctic Ocean to hunt walruses, since 'fish teeth' were very much in demand. They would tell incredible stories of white nights, the midnight sun, and limitless deserts of eternal ice.

The city of Novgorod was strictly organized according to professions, with specialist streets and 'rows'; founders', nailers', shieldmakers' unions were well known; carpenters lustily handled their axes, their chisels, their drills; the builders' association was comparable to the famous Kiev one. 'And what is this crackpot doing? Boiling water in a frying pan?' 'Yes, Prince. It is sea water, and the man is a salt producer, which is an honourable profession.' A trade was to be taken seriously in Novgorod, whatever it was, and none more so than commerce itself. All businesses had their guilds, leagues, syndicates. It was especially prestigious to be an overseas merchant – the time would soon come when this select group would organize itself into an exclusive corporation called the St John Guild, with an exorbitant admission fee of 50 grivnas, to export furs, hides, wax, resin, alkali or building timber; yet, in the good old Viking tradition, local trade was not to be despised either. A tradesman was, in this curious civilization, a poetic figure, and the adventures of the famous Sadko were to inspire not only folk bards but also, in the nineteenth century, Aleksey Tolstoy and Rimsky-Korsakov.

Social organization was mainly based on financial considerations. At the top were the boyars, who, coming from affluent families, served the Prince in war and administration; the *zhitye lyudi*, businessmen on a large scale; next the *kuptsy*, merchants also but not so wealthy, and finally the *molodshie* (younger) or *chornye* (black) people, who were neither black nor particularly young, but had not yet acquired the capital necessary to join one of the higher classes. Slaves of course did not count. Justice was generally rendered according to Viking traditions: in most cases fines were applied rather than physical chastisement. The fines were calculated in proportion to the defendants' means: centuries later, for the same charge of contempt of court, a boyar for instance would pay five times as much as a commoner. Such social fair play was unknown in more 'civilized' countries, and Vladimir, with his sympathy for the destitute, doubtless admired it at its worth.

Politically, the customs were startling for a new-comer, but they pleased the people and worked efficiently enough. All important decisions were taken by the famous *veche*, which all citizens attended but in which only heads of families could vote. Every decision had to be reached *unanimously*. This, naturally, raised a few problems, but the Novgorodians had devised a solution. If two parties were of different opinions, they would repair to the famous Novgorod bridge, where they would fight with fists and more or less blunt weapons until party A had convinced party B that it was right. This extremely democratic, though muscular, legislature, operated quite satisfactorily for centuries and had its own bards who described not only the convocations:

> You would think it was the spring flood
> Overflowing in the meadows,
> But it is the crowd of Novgorod
> Swelling-surging in Rogatitsa.
> You would think it was geese and swans
> Rising on Ilmen lake,
> But it is all the men of Novgorod
> Gathering on the Volkhov bridge

but also the pitiful results of such manly debates:

All the heads are broken with the flail,
All the arms are bandaged with kerchiefs,
All the legs are tied with belts.[41]

A particularly droll incident takes place when one of the politicians seizes a carriage axle and fells his opponents in neat rows, like rye in a storm, until one of them hides under a brass bell weighing eighteen hundred kilograms. This does not prevent the astute fellow from reaching the Volkhov bridge, since he smartly uses the clapper as a crutch. But when the axle hits the bell, what music resounds through Novgorod!

Traditionally, the Novgorodians had been jealous of their privileges and hard to govern; they were to remain so, as Vladimir's son Yaroslav would learn a few years later. But Vladimir himself, wisely advised by Dobrynya, was quite a success with them. Not that, for the time being, his responsibilities were very heavy. His role as a prince was limited to the executive and the judicial; he was responsible for applying the laws and decisions that the *veche* had, literally, thrashed out; he entertained foreign guests, mainly merchants; he would have led the army if there had been a war; as it was, he commanded his own retinue, which played the triple role of bodyguard, peacetime army and police force; finally he collected taxes from peoples subject to Novgorod, and sent on to Kiev the tribute exacted by brother Yaropolk. At first, his duties were of course fulfilled by his uncle, but people matured fast in the Middle Ages, and as soon as he was in his teens he began assuming more and more of them. The future was to show that he not only performed them well, but also managed to make himself extremely popular in the process. These were, in literary terms, his *Lehrjahre*, and he put them to good use.

3 A messenger

According to the Norse sagas, Vladimir's mother lived in Novgorod. There is really nothing improbable in the idea that the young Prince might have sent to Budutino for her or even brought her out with him on his trip north. After all, no one else seemed to want her. If he did, this adds to his moral portrait the characteristics of an affectionate son, and we may find some gratification in thinking that the once abused housekeeper spent the end of her life honoured and pampered at her son's court. On the other hand, the sagas describe her as very old, which can hardly have been the case, since Vladimir himself was barely in his teens at the time. A severe illness could account for the fact that she did not leave her bed, and on great occasions was brought on it into the main hall to prophesy the fortunes of the realm. If such were indeed her gifts, did she foresee the tragic end of the man who had been her lover if not her husband?

On a hot day in the summer of 972, a messenger arrived from Kiev, was introduced into Vladimir's presence, and announced to the twelve-year-old boy: 'Prince, your father is dead.'

The invincible Svyatoslav had succumbed.

'How?'

The story was an inspiring blend of woe, heroism and naïveté. Father, Vladimir learned, had set out for Pereyaslavets, considering that it was 'the centre of his realm'. Such was not the opinion of its Bulgarian inhabitants, who received him as an enemy and closed the city gates. He attacked. The defence was obstinate and bloody. A Bulgarian sally made great carnage of the Russians. The campaign had scarcely begun, and already it seemed doomed. 'Brothers! Friends!' called Father to

his men. 'We may have to die, but we shall die like men.'
The Russians, galvanized by his leadership, scaled the
walls once again, and took the city. So far the Greeks had
encouraged Svyatoslav to invade Bulgaria in order to
wear out one barbarian nation against the other; this was
standard Byzantine policy. But now they were not too
pleased with the result and suggested that Svyatoslav go
back whence he had come. He replied that such were not
his plans: as a matter of fact, he intended to pitch camp in
Constantinople in the near future. War broke out
between Russians and Greeks. This time Fortune did not
smile on Svyatoslav as she had been wont to do.
Although at one point he reached Adrianopolis, he was
leading a losing campaign against an enemy ten times
superior in numbers, and inferior neither in courage nor
in craft. 'Flight would not save us,' said Svyatoslav to
his troops arrayed for battle. 'Whether we want to fight
or not, we have to. Let us not shame our country. What
if our bones lie here? There is no disgrace for the dead.
Stand firm. I shall march before you. When my head
falls, look to yourselves.' Father had a way with his men.
They struck their swords against their shields and replied: 'Where your head falls, there ours will remain.'
And Svyatoslav carried the day. Some negotiations
ensued, but to no avail.

The next year, the Greeks took Pereyaslavets, where
Svyatoslav had left a garrison of eight thousand men,
who burned to death in the besieged palace. Svyatoslav
rushed to confront the Greeks. After a whole day of
battle, during which victory seemed to change sides up
to *twelve* times, the Russians were beaten back and surrounded in the city of Dorostol, which they hastily
fortified. A *Götterdämmerung* atmosphere prevailed
among these men, who knew they were doomed. The

manly religion of their fathers appeared to them as their only hope against the Christians. By moonlight, they would swarm out of their entrenchments to burn their slain brothers lying in the field; they would sacrifice prisoners over the smoking pyres, and drown little children in the misty waters of the Danube; by day, they would sally forth to strike at the Greek camp, and the Russian women, whom they had brought with them, would also come out and fight side by side with their men. The retreats were orderly: the men would hang their shields on their backs and withdraw into the city with contemptuous slowness; if a soldier had no hope of escaping, he plunged his sword into his own heart in order to avoid serving his killer as a slave in a future life. The losses were tremendous. Once, Father managed to effect a sortie by boat and to bring back some wheat for his starving troops, but he could not expect to do it twice. He resolved to fight a final desperate battle, led his army into the field and had the city gates locked, so that flight would not even enter anyone's mind. Thousands died that day; the Russians could not break through the Greek ranks; the Greeks could not crush the Russians. Emperor Tzimisches offered to meet Svyato-slav in single combat, so as to spare 'many lives'. But Father knew that his army would be lost without him; he also suspected a trick, and he declined the honour. It was clever of him! The Greeks had been trying to murder him for days. The battle was renewed. Finally the south wind rose, blew into the Russians' faces and blinded them with dust. In the clouds of sand the Christians descried St Theodore Stratilate himself on his white horse, trampling the pagan hordes. It had taken super-natural forces to defeat Svyatoslav.

'Is St Theodore really stronger than Father?' 'We did

not actually see St Theodore, Prince. There was too much sand whirling in the wind, but the Christians say they were able to recognize him beyond a doubt.' This was something to think about. For the second time, the Christian God intervened on behalf of the Greeks, and always with complete success. First the Virgin and the storm at sea, now St Theodore and the sand storm . . . Could it mean something? No, Vladimir refused to dwell on such treacherous thoughts.

Peace was signed. Not very satisfactory, but honourable. By the great Perun and by Volos, god of cattle, Svyatoslav swore eternal friendship for and alliance with Tzimisches. He renounced all his claims on Greece, Bulgaria and the Crimea. The 'centre of his realm' did not even belong to him any more. If ever he betrayed his oath, he wished to become *yellow as gold* and be cut to pieces with his own weapons. In exchange, the Basileus allowed the remnants of the Russian army to leave Bulgaria unharmed, provided it with food and other necessities, and promised to send envoys to the Pechenegs, with whom he was on friendly terms, to ask them to let the Russians cross their lands in peace. After so much bloodshed, the Basileus in his gilt armour and the Prince in his white tunic met on amicable terms. How sincere they were is another question. With a bloodless and exhausted army, which was but the shadow of itself, Svyatoslav set sail, and safely reached the mouth of the Dniepr. But the Pechenegs were not as congenial as they should have been, and it was necessary to spend the winter on the coast. It was not difficult for young Vladimir to imagine what this winter had been like for his father. Extreme starvation – a horse's head for a grivna – was not the worst. Svyatoslav must have spent his nights remembering his impassioned speech under the walls of Dorostol: 'Can life be sweet for those who have saved it by flight? Shall we not be despised by our neighbours, who are used to dreading the very name *Russian*?' True, he had not fled, but neither had he conquered or died. He had amazed the Greeks by the dauntless fortitude of his men and by his mastery over them, but he was returning beaten to a city for which he had no liking and which would have no respect for him. So many of his companions had died, and what had he to show for it? How would he face his sons, Yaropolk, Oleg, and even, in faraway Novgorod, that boy Vladimir? ('Oh! if only I had been there, in Dorostol!' thought Vladimir. 'If only I had known how badly Father needed me and my retinue! Could I not have made the difference? And too bad for St Theodore!')

At the first sign of spring, Svyatoslav struck camp. Old General Sveinald, the same who had guided the Prince in his first battle and seen him throw the famous spear which had hit his own horse, recommended, in view of the situation, that the boats be abandoned and that the army cross the steppes in battle order. Svyatoslav was too heartbroken to listen to him. With an army consisting of worn-out invalids, it was so much easier and faster to sail up the Dniepr. It was easy and fast until the cataracts were reached. There, they could not avoid disembarking and resorting to portage.

Could it be that Tzimisches' envoys had brought to the Pechenegs a secret message different from the official one? Or had the Bulgars wanted to make sure that Pereyaslavets would never be a Russian capital? Anyway the nomads were warned of the Russians' approach and they lay in wait. Fresh and lusty, they pounced upon the battered outfit. After a whole winter of hunger, the men could scarcely lift their arms to fight back.

'And then?' 'And then, Prince, Kurya, the Pecheneg chieftain, cut off your father's head and made a cup of the skull and overlayed it with gold and is drinking mead from it.'

4 Many gods

In the Viking tradition, one of the Prince's most important duties was to maintain contact with the gods on behalf of his people. In a religion without priests, the Prince was the priest.

As Vladimir grew, his religious dispositions had also grown. Now he was less concerned with the lower divinities of field and wood, although he still felt they had their place in nature; he was less afraid of the minor 'black' gods, Div and his owl, Mara and her epidemics; and even Moargana, the goddess of death, was but one more spook out of childhood. On the other hand, his soul opened to the higher aspects of Slavic paganism. Most peoples begin by worshipping natural forces and then personify them in a more or less anthropomorphic style. The Slavic style was less anthropomorphic than, say, the Ancient Greek one, and at the same time less inclined toward symbolism. Vladimir believed first of all in a god of gods magnificently called Svarog (the Heaven-walker), sometimes identified with a trinitarian divinity named Troyar or Triglav (the Three-headed one). All other major gods were *svarozhichi*, not so much Svarog's sons as manifestations of his might: Dazhbog, god of the sun; Stribog, god of the winds; Khors, god without portfolio. There was also Volos, god of poetry and oracles, money and cattle and trade, a kind of Slavic Mercury; Perun, god of lightning, the Slavic version of the Viking Thor and a great favourite with Vladimir;

and the lusty Yarilo, also known as Yarovit, Rugevit, Yason or Tur, god of fertility, war and sensual delights, who was yearly buried among great festivities in the shape of an unmistakably male wooden doll. They all testified to the fact that the universe we see around us is not the only one, but rather the visible expression of another, more real world, with which Vladimir felt the need to communicate constantly through prayer and sacrifice.

Although the Slavs knew no priests, they had wizards, soothsayers, magicians, witch doctors. Vladimir had not much use for them. What good could such charlatans be to him, when he, like any other man – and even more so since he was the Prince – could address directly the god of his choice? At the beginning of any undertaking, he would sacrifice bread, meat, onions, milk or mead, in front of a tall wooden post with a carved human face at the top. Then he would bow and kneel before it, asking for his prayers to be heard. In case of failure, he would turn to other, better disposed divinities; but if his requests were granted, he would slaughter several cattle, give part of the meat to the poor, and offer the rest to the god. Stakes would have been driven into the ground around the idol, and the victims' heads would be hung from them, composing a gory spectacle which was supposed to be agreeable to the heavenly powers. Vladimir, knife in hand, would stand in the middle of the bloody circle, and passionately invoke Perun, Dazhbog, Stribog or even Svarog, the Godhead itself. At harvest time, he would attend to less sanguinary ceremonies. He would put some grain in a scoop, lift it toward the sky, and pray aloud: 'O Lord, Thou who feeds us, this time also be generous with us.' The people around him would fall to the ground and adore the

Almighty, secure in the feeling that this young prince was their advocate before Him.[42]

Years went by, and some time around 976 – Vladimir was approximately sixteen – a suitable marriage was arranged for him by his good uncle.[43] Olava, it seems, knew a handsome boy when she saw one, and was probably flattered at being number one in the Prince's future harem. There was the usual symbolic fight between the bridegroom's party and the family of the bride: swords clashed against shields, spears against breastplates, with much laughter and many songs. The men sang warlike songs, and maybe some ribald ones; the women, sad songs about departing girls and unplaited hair. The next morning, Vladimir presented his father-in-law with a gift, the traditional *veno* or ransom of the bride.

With marriage, a more than vigorous sensuality awoke in Vladimir, and he may, at that time, have sacrificed to Yarilo as much as to Perun. Whether he still remembered his beautiful Greek sister-in-law is doubtful, but Olava lost no time in presenting him with a son, who received the Slavic name Vysheslav, although Vladimir's own was adopted and adapted from the Norse Valdemar. Rurik's graft was doing well on the Russian stock.

5 A friend

A few years after Vladimir had seen the light in southern Russia, another Viking prince was born,[44] also in unusual circumstances, on an island in the middle of a Swedish lake. His father Tryggvi Olafsson, King of Norway (or, more modestly, of Oslofjord), had been killed by treachery even before the child was born, and the pregnant mother, Astrid, was in hiding with two women and her son's future tutor, old Thorolf, who also responded to the picturesque, if not very hygienic, nickname of Ljusaskägg (Lousebeard). She had fled from Norway to Sweden in the hope of reaching the lands of the Prince of Novgorod, where her brother Sigurd had a good position in Valdemar's (Vladimir's) retinue. It took her several years to find a means of getting to the Baltic and secretly hiring a boat. Finally the sail was hoisted, and the cold waves carried the fugitives away. A few more hours and the poor Queen and her child would have safely made the friendly Russian shores; they would have conveniently sailed up the Neva, through the Ladoga and up the Volkhov; Sigurd would have greeted his sister and nephew with open arms. The happy reunion was not to be. Esthonian pirates captured the ship. The Queen, the woman and the little boy, whose name was Olaf, were sold into slavery. As for Lousebeard, 'You are too old, grandfather. No one would buy you,' said the Esthonian Klerkon, and killed him on the spot. Olaf's master was kind to him; still the proud boy suffered from his position as a slave. Years went by, and General Sigurd appeared in Esthonia to collect the tribute for Novgorod. His nephew made himself known, and the overjoyed uncle ransomed him and brought him back to Russia.

Olaf was already a youth, when, sauntering around the market square on the right bank of the Volkhov and twirling a hatchet in his hands, whom should he recognize among the passers-by but Klerkon, the murderer of Thorolf, whom Olaf had loved as a foster-father. The impetuous Tryggvison did not hesitate: he sank the hatchet into the villain's head 'down to the brain'. This, on the whole, may have been a healthy reaction, but murdering peaceful foreigners was frowned upon by the

Novgorodians; death was the recognized penalty for such rashness. Olaf ran to his uncle, who had his entrées at the palace, and immediately took him to the Princess. She judged him at one look: 'It is not proper that such a comely youth be killed,' she said, and ordered her personal bodyguards to put on their armour. The crowd, in the meantime, had gathered outside, and were clamouring for justice. With a people as conscious of their rights as the Novgorodians, the situation might easily have become dangerous, but Vladimir – it is the first time we see him in action, and he was approximately seventeen – managed to pacify everybody. The old Viking tradition was to exact money for blood; a fine would serve as well as an execution; Olaf would be condemned to pay a sum of money which he did not possess, but since the Princess was so intent on saving him, she could acquit it from her own means. Olava was happy to do so, Klerkon's relatives received handsome compensation and ceased to cry for revenge, the crowds dispersed, the bodyguards took off their armour, and Vladimir acquired a personal friend, maybe the only one he ever had.

He loved him, the sagas say, as he would have loved his own son, and, to make up for the time Olaf had lost as a slave, he instructed him in all the arts that befitted a prince, except head-breaking, which Olaf obviously had already acquired by himself. They fenced, they rode, they hunted, they studied together. Olaf's romantic posthumous birth and his supposed ability to predict the future by watching birds, which had earned him the nickname Craccoben (Crowbone), added to his natural charm; the young Princess, who had saved his life, treated him with affection; as soon as she had set eyes upon his face, she had realized that he would bring only

71

good things to his protectors. On one point, however, Olaf annoyed the princely couple very much: they would have liked him even more than they did, if he had not been so foolish and obdurate on religious matters. At first, Vladimir had graciously invited him to participate in public sacrifices, but he refused. At least, he should attend. He refused again, and although at ordinary times Vladimir and he would be well-nigh inseparable, he would remain standing on the threshold of the sacred places where the sacrifices were offered, and patiently wait while his friend was pouring milk and cutting throats.

'Olaf,' Vladimir said with some irritation, 'you are going to make the gods very angry. They will cut you down in your youth.' But Olaf, during his time as a slave, had been corrupted by Christian fantasies, and although he was not yet baptized, he was ready to throw in his lot with those blasphemous scoundrels. He replied, smiling: 'Prince, I have no fear of your gods. Can they speak? Can they see? Can they hear? Can they rejoice? Can they understand? If not, why should I be afraid of your wooden poles?' This made Vladimir lose his temper. 'Your attitude, my dear fellow, is extremely improper. Believe me, it is much wiser to be always on the right side of the gods. You must bow before them and try to propitiate them in every possible way. For your own safety, I beg you to do so.' At that Olaf shook his head. Never would he bend the dignity of man before a carpenter's artefact. Vladimir could not understand such foolhardiness, sensitive as he was to the power the gods had over him. 'Olaf, if you do not minister to them, fondly and faithfully, I shudder at the punishments they might heap upon your head. Why put yourself in such danger?' 'I am in no danger. But even if I feared your stupid idols, I would not worship them. It is my destiny to deny them, and if I do not overturn them and hack them to pieces right now, it is only out of respect and affection for you, who are better than they. Look at yourself, Prince. You, whose face is always so kind and serene, how dark and sinister it becomes when you perform your vile sacrifices!' exclaimed Olaf with some heat. 'By this I rightly judge the nature of your gods: if they reign over anything, it must be over night and gloom.'

How true to life this speech sounds, even if it was invented by an anonymous Icelandic bard! And how well we imagine darkness descending over Vladimir's tortured brow, as he lifts his knife at the feet of Perun, to sacrifice more and more flesh to the insatiable appetite of that famous gormandizer among gods.

The conflict between the two young men was resolved later, and in a way that the crows did not reveal to Olaf.

6 *The second messenger*

Vladimir reigned quietly in Novgorod for about seven years, throwing lavish parties for great and small, assuming more and more responsibilities, and managing not to displease his self-willed subjects in anything. Given the fact that these subjects still fancied themselves to be employers of a sort, this must have taken quite some flair, but on flair Vladimir was never short. Dutifully, he sent his yearly tribute to his older brother in Kiev, but otherwise ruled independently of the Great Prince, as the sovereign of Kiev was beginning to be called. It was in 977 that a new messenger brought another sad tale. Although it did not concern him directly, Vladimir was quick to perceive that it boded no good for him.

Many of Svyatoslav's men had perished at the cataracts, but the old Viking general Sveinald had fought his way through the Pechenegs and had brought back a handful of warriors. He was a loyal and extremely successful soldier, but, as it appears, something of a troublemaker. Thirty-two years before, it was the spectacle of his arrogantly displayed wealth that had led Igor's retinue to demand more loot, which finally resulted in Igor's death at the hands of the Drevlyans. Now, Sveinald was again to bring trials upon those Rurikids whom he served so faithfully and with so much profit (to them and to himself). His son Lyut was an addicted hunter, and had little consideration for private preserves, even princely ones. The rich Sveinald certainly had enough land of his own, but Lyut decided to try his hand at killing some of Oleg's game. The two young men met in a forest belonging to the prince of the Drevlyans. Did they quarrel? Did Lyut intimate that as Sveinald's son he hunted where he pleased? Did brother Oleg, clumsy as ever, over-react? Anyway he found it necessary to kill the trespasser then and there.

Only revenge could appease the old general's sorrow, and he began working day and night to set Oleg and Yaropolk by the ears. Sveinald had been the brother-at-arms of Yaropolk's father and grandfather; he would have saved Svyatoslav if only the Prince had taken his advice; Yaropolk could do no less than listen to him. Besides, there were really good reasons for doing away with that impractical realm of Dereva, with its small towns and savage tribes. What did it weigh against Kiev? How sensible it would be if all the country surrounding the capital belonged directly to the Great Prince! How much easier to administrate justice and collect tributes! People did not talk about 'the direction of history' yet, but was it not obvious that some communities are viable and some are not, and that Dereva fell into the second category? Yaropolk let himself be persuaded. He took the offensive, without enthusiasm, but still he took it. Like the fool he was, Oleg rushed out to meet him. Sveinald's experience and decision made it very easy for brother Yaropolk. At the first clash, Oleg turned back and fled toward Vruchy (or Ovruch), a fortified town on the Noryna, a tributary of the Uzh, which in turn empties itself into the Pripiat. Nothing remarkable about Vruchy, except that its craftsmen made excellent cross-pieces for spindles. It must have been a pretty frantic rout, with Sveinald in pursuit, thirsting for revenge, the panic-stricken infantry running for their lives, the cavalry crushing them with their horses in their own haste to reach the gates.

The town was surrounded by a moat, and there was a bridge over it. That bridge meant life for a thousand men, who wanted to cross it at once. No one obeyed orders, no one even gave them any more, it was every man for himself. Horses rearing and neighing, weapons clanging, soldiers falling into the water and drowning under the weight of armour – it was an ugly scene, and the confusion was such that no one paid attention to Prince Oleg himself, who, like any other terrified soul, had been caught in the pitiless stampede. Pushed over the parapet by the press, he fell into the moat which was filling with corpses. Other bodies – of men and horses – fell on top of him. Was he drowned, or choked, or squashed? We shall never know, but whatever the case it was a pathetic death for a son of Svyatoslav.

The town did not defend itself, and, having brilliantly defeated an army of spindle-makers, Yaropolk marched straight to his brother's palace. He wanted Oleg's dispossession, not his death, and he sent soldiers to look for him everywhere, maybe with the intention of protecting him against Sveinald. 'Still the fumbler, aren't you, Oleg, old fellow?' he would say, and pat the prisoner on the back, before allocating to him a handsome allowance in exchange for his lands. But there was no prisoner. Oleg could not be found. 'Search every nook for him!' It was the next morning before one of the defeated Drevlyans came forward with the shocking information that the Prince had been pushed off the bridge by his own men. Unbelievable and frankly insulting as the news sounded, Yaropolk decided to investigate. Prisoners began dragging the bodies out of the moat, and by the hour of noon, Oleg's corpse was discovered, in what state can only be imagined. At that time, Yaropolk was holding court in the captured palace, with the beaming Sveinald at his side. The body was brought to the Great Prince and laid out at his feet, upon a rug, says the chronicler. Yaropolk knelt down over his dead brother, and was not able to restrain his sobs. It seemed only yesterday that Oleg and he had played together and fought over their toys, and now . . . Poor old clumsy Oleg, who never could do anything right! Yaropolk turned toward Sveinald, and, looking up at him through his tears, exclaimed with more feeling than it is generally advisable for conquerors to experience: 'Is that what you wanted?' Undoubtedly, it was.

Vladimir listened to the story without betraying any emotion, at least as far as we know. Uncle Dobrynya was consulted, of course. Deplorable as they were, the events down south would have to be taken into consideration. Oleg had got himself into a scrape, as usual, and paid for it; there was nothing to be done about it. There seems to have been no love lost between Svyatoslav's sons, and the idea of avenging his brother never entered Vladimir's head. Yaropolk had wept over Oleg's body, that was very touching – but the lands of the Drevlyans were now absorbed in the Kiev complex, and that was disquieting. What if Yaropolk's appetite had been whetted by a too easy victory? What if he decided to swallow up Novgorod after Iskorosten?

Novgorod, it is true, was a wealthy city, in love with its independence, and Vladimir had made himself popular among the people. But would they fight for him? And if they fought, were they capable of winning? They were traders and carpenters, not warriors; as cavalry, they were no good; they had no army, just a civilian militia. To indulge in political fisticuffs was one thing; to meet Sveinald in the field, quite another. If the city's security was at stake, then yes, they could put up a tremendous resistance and show those lazy-bones from the South what sober, grim Northerners could do at a pinch. But if it was just a question of princes, let princes decide their princely business between themselves – that might be Novgorod's attitude.

It was doubtless Dobrynya who explained all these considerations to Vladimir, who was then in his teens, and it is remarkable and significant that the young Prince saw that his uncle was right and that the time had not yet come for him to show what he was worth. Surely his first impulse must have been to go and meet his brother in open battle, and maybe his second to stay where he was and defend himself if attacked. But he was already capable of learning through other people's mistakes: he would not commit any of Oleg's, neither risking combat with an unprepared army nor putting himself at the mercy of as yet untried subjects. He could also have reasoned thus: 'I have not hurt Sveinald, I have not offended Yaropolk in any way; there is nothing to show that my brother is going to make a habit of fratricide, quite the contrary; maybe, if I do not react in any way and go on paying my tribute, he will leave me to reign in peace in Novgorod.' But here another thought must have come to him.

So far, Vladimir had been a dutiful younger brother, quite willing to respect in all things his dead father's wishes; it is probable that, if Yaropolk had not seized Dereva, Vladimir would never have attempted to become Prince of Kiev. But now the rules had been broken: would he alone be so foolish as to abide by them? For him, Yaropolk's greed might yet prove the best chance he had ever had. He had a right to defend himself, had he not? And was it not a recognized principle of warfare that offence is the best defence? The unexpected conclusion of that train of thought was that, since offence could not, at this time, be undertaken with any chance of success, the most intelligent move would be . . . to withdraw temporarily from the game. What must it have cost the fiery young Prince to be thought a fool or, worse, a coward! But, although he might have attacked, or defended himself, or simply done nothing, Vladimir did what he thought would serve him best.

Without any threat from Kiev, without any pressure from Yaropolk, anticipating a decision which he practically forced upon his brother, he explained to the *posadnik*, the *tysyatsky*, the boyars and all the people of Novgorod that it was not convenient for him to remain with them any longer, and bowed, packed, and was off. He did not flee in the face of danger, no, but he most decidedly left before the danger arose. An astonishing display of self-control, purposefulness and foresight in one so young.

Would Yaropolk have attacked if Vladimir had held his ground? It is doubtful. But Vladimir knew his Yaropolk well: the younger brother had scarcely left Novgorod when the older one sent his own men to take it over. The city submitted gracefully. The Great Prince was master of all Russia.

CHAPTER THREE

Man

1 Return

About Vladimir's *Wanderjahre* we know nothing. That period lasted approximately two years, probably a little less, and what he did during it will always, one imagines, remain a mystery. Some historians have him plundering the coasts of France and Italy with his friend Olaf, and that is quite possible, but he may also have spent his time travelling peacefully in Sweden, Denmark, or Norway, or even have gone to earth somewhere, preparing his return 'with Varangian [Viking] allies', to quote *The Chronicle*. Among these, we can count Olaf, since the sagas inform us that he eventually conquered several provinces for Vladimir, and it seems reasonable to presume that the two uncles, Dobrynya and Sigurd, accompanied the two nephews with a more or less numerous retinue. What happened from then on to Olava is not known; as to the infant Vysheslav, we shall meet him again, much later.

Problems must have arisen very soon, and first of all, financial ones. Olaf was still an outcast from his country and could not lend a *nogata* to his protector. Vladimir may have borrowed a few sable skins from the Novgorod exchequer, but not enough to levy troops. Fortunately, professional soldiers were willing to serve for credit if the prospects were good, and it seems that Vladimir managed to pay his followers with promises. Still they had to be fed: hence the hypothesis of plundering along European coasts. This occupation would also have provided Vladimir with some knowledge of combat: he later showed himself a very successful general, and he must have acquired experience somewhere. Another problem may have been the doubtful reception afforded by the Vikings to this Viking prince who could not speak Norse and who looked as if he was running away from his enemies. It would be unrealistic to assume that Vladimir found among them any rich cousins of his who welcomed him with open arms to the family fold. He probably had no family left in Scandinavia; if he had, they probably turned their backs upon him with disgust. One more possible source of trouble was that it must have taken the young prince quite some time to adapt himself to the ways of the Vikings, who were, and again were not, his people. (A Mississippian returning to Scotland after a hundred years of Spanish moss and Southern drawl . . .) Yes, he was a Rurikid, but also a Slav, and the gentler, lazier habits of Kiev, the softer winds of the Orient and Constantinople, had partly changed his nature and his outlook on life. He came from a nation which was gradually being organized and civilized, where monarchy and centralization were in progress, where trading had replaced looting and taxes were collected instead of war tributes. He may easily have shied at the almost pathological, almost metaphysical, Viking obsession with bloodshed as the only possible way of life (not that all Viking farmers were also warriors; but there is little doubt that war was in fact the main native industry). On the other hand, after a period of adjustment it may also be – as events seem to show – that Vladimir found himself at home among the worshippers of the warlike Thor, and that, having fighting in mind, he appreciated the society of men who knew no other profession, except perhaps trade, and no other relaxation, except most assuredly lechery.

Among other Viking singularities, and although Russia was still at the time a country where everyone could have his say, Vladimir must have noticed, with some surprise, the people's outspokenness toward their leaders. In an official meeting at Uppsala, farmer Torgny once said to king Olaf: 'If you will not follow what the farmers say, we shall rise against you and kill you, and not put up with any disturbances and law-breaking from you. Our forebears have done it before. They threw five kings, who were just as full of arrogance as you, down a well at Mula.' Such was the tone between subject and sovereign; the idea that the sovereigns were there to serve the subjects was still very much alive.

The Vikings' relationship to women was also something at which to wonder. Their lust was, it seems, prodigious, and it may not be irrelevant to note that, in modern times, Scandinavian countries were the first to do away with all sexual taboos. Adam of Bremen writes that the Vikings despised riches and gold (this may have been an unjustified generalization) and that it was only in *mulierum copula* that they knew no moderation (*modum nesciunt*). In conquered countries no woman would be spared: 'married women they defiled, virgins they raped,' specifies Dudo Viromandensis. In their own country, although each Viking had, according to his fortune, two or three or more wives – as to the rich men, theirs were 'without number' – very strict laws had to be promulgated against sexual assault: 'If anyone knew somebody's wife or ravished a maid,' mentions Thietmar, 'capital punishment must be his sentence.' And that in a culture where a fine was deemed to be adequate chastisement for murder! Contemporary Arabs, who of course had their own refined harems, were shocked at the Vikings' excesses and lack of decorum in such matters. According to them, women – and not only slaves – would be freely enjoyed in public; sometimes collective orgies would be organized, and everyone present would be invited to participate. In spite of this, Viking women were not considered as pleasure cattle – exactly the reverse. Widows became practically family heads; wives were showered with gifts – neck-rings of gold or silver according to their husbands' wealth, strings of green glass beads, tortoiseshell brooches. Slaying a woman was a crime punished by the exaction of both wergeld and bloodwite (compensation and fine); girls who wanted to were permitted to put on men's clothes and appear in the field, cheerfully swinging a battleaxe from their right shoulder. This, of course, was the supreme consecration: the two sexes may not have been equal in rights, but both had a full share of the only honour that counted, that which consists in proving one's courage to live a victor or die a hero.

Vladimir watched the mores of this people, and whatever small mishaps he may have encountered – the Vikings were supposed to be ill-tempered, quarrelsome, arrogant, addicted to brawls and duels – the day came pretty soon when he knew he had come to the right place in search of allies. This happened, one imagines, when for the first time a son was born to one of his followers. While the child cried in the happy mother's arms, the proud father took his sword from its scabbard and threw it on the floor where it clanged on the flagstones. 'My son, I shall leave you nothing; you will only have what you win by the sword,' he uttered in fierce tones. Such was the ritual phrase, and Vladimir wondered if Svyatoslav had pronounced it over his cradle. If he had, the prophecy was soon to be fulfilled. Whatever Vladimir once had, he had lost: the sword was his sole recourse.

Season followed season, and more and more temporarily unemployed Vikings decided to gamble on the young Rurikid who would lead them to Gardariki, the country of towns. They would liberate Holmgardr (Novgorod), storm Kiev, and then – who knows? – perhaps sail down the Dniepr to Miklagard (Constantinople). Any private who participated in the sacking of the richest of all cities would be an independent man for the rest of his life, and if this Prince Valdemar was the true Viking he looked, he would not settle for the certainty of Kiev once he had the hope of Miklagard. In the meantime, he would pay and pay well. A grivna per man may have been promised, and a grivna, wisely invested in business, would in the long run make a modest man's fortune. How many of the jobless joined Vladimir's retinue can only be guessed. A few thousand seems a probable figure. To transport the army to Novgorod and further, some old ships were used, but also some new ones must have been built. They were made of oak, about twenty metres long, with a draught of one to two metres. The planks were fixed with clinch nails to the ribs and carefully tarred. What a gay noise the hammers made in the crisp Scandinavian mornings! Vladimir would come down to the shipyard and listen to it, and smell the wood, the brine and the tar, and think that soon he would entrust his fate to these boards and masts. That in itself was good: for a Viking, a ship was always a friend. At one point, some two hundred of them were moored in a Scandinavian harbour – we do not know which one – ready to sail at the Prince's will. Julius Caesar when he crossed the Rubicon, Napoleon on the 17th of Brumaire, must have experienced feelings comparable to those of Vladimir contemplating his flotilla, and, with a single gesture, setting it in motion. But Napoleon was thirty and Caesar fifty-two at the time of their great decisions; Vladimir was at most twenty. How exhilarating it must have been to know that he would soon be leading into action the best soldiers in the world! The 'good' intention of re-conquering what had been his own was an added incentive: he was not violating a republic, he was only claiming his inheritance.

It did not take long to cross the Baltic, and one day the Novgorodians awoke with a whole fleet at their gates, gently swaying on the waves of Lake Ilmen, the high bows and sterns and the even higher staffs giving the ships that unmistakable Viking curve which, by now, meant terror in all civilized lands. The sails were down; the shields were displayed in rows along the boards, and the unfurled flags rustled in the breeze. Olaf, the sagas tell us, had two ships, a smaller and a larger one, which, not being overgifted with imagination, he had named Short Dragon and Long Dragon, because their prows were decorated with gilt dragon heads. Vladimir's ship may not have been such a fancy one, but it was probably painted red according to the Russian Vikings' custom, and the flag which waved over it bore the hereditary sign of the Rurikids: the trident. The Novgorodians could not fail to recognize it – to them, it meant peace, not war – and they rushed to the shore, to welcome back a prince, whom apparently they had missed during the past two years. No doubt, Vladimir had changed; a rougher life had left its marks on his face, but his expression was as ever 'kind and serene'; it may even have been triumphant when he set his foot, elegantly clad in a green morocco boot with a long curved toe, on the same wharf on to

Gokstad–Viking longship.
(*University Museum of National Antiquities,
Oslo.*)

which he had jumped as a child, eight years earlier. Handsome as he was, he must have cut a brave figure, entering the city at the head of his men, with his brocade breeches, his silk shirt, his dark purple-blue coat hemmed with red at the bottom and with gold at the cuffs, and over it his dark-blue robe bordered with gold and decorated with a ruby clasp, his sable cap crowned with gold, and a thick golden torque weighing heavily on his chest.[45] The people cheered, the *veche* bell pealed, the blood of cattle again sprinkled the statue of the voracious Perun, and the poor received large portions of sacrificed meat. The city had been taken without a blow, and everyone was pleased, except Yaropolk's lieutenants, who wondered what would befall them. It is probable that the mob did not treat them with too much consideration, and they may even have been brought in chains before Vladimir, who immediately ordered that they be set free.

'Go to my brother,' he said – and we seem to hear a catch in his voice as he proudly quotes the challenge his father used to send to his enemies – 'and tell him that I am setting forth against him. Let him prepare to defend himself.' And he gave them a piece of clay stamped with his trident as a safe-conduct.

2   Rogned

Every victor deserves a prize, and Vladimir thought that a new wife would be just the thing. He may also have reflected that a princely father-in-law with estates on the road to Kiev could be a useful ally: Vladimir always liked to kill two birds with one stone. Anyway, having heard that Rogvolod, prince of Polotsk,[46] had a pretty daughter, he decided to ask for her in marriage. If she was, as some sources maintain, already betrothed to Yaropolk, this of course made such a marriage even more desirable: it would be pleasant to thumb one's nose at one's eldest brother before real hostilities began. Uncle Dobrynya,[47] Vladimir thought, would make an excellent ambassador, and so Uncle Dobrynya was dispatched to Polotsk, where he was very poorly received. His nephew, it must be confessed, was in a doubtful position: only the fortunes of war would tell whether he was a rebellious bastard or a legitimate heir avenging the wrongs that had been done to him. Rogvolod's attitude was markedly cool, and his two sons[48] may have made overt fun of the elderly Slavic general who had climbed up through the ranks, not without some help from his not too virtuous sister, and who now represented a prince without a throne. Still, Rogvolod called Rogned into his presence, officially conveyed the offer to her (the very fact shows with what deference Russian women, even daughters, were treated at the time) and asked her what she thought of it.

Rogned stood there, a blond beauty in a light-red dress with wide, loose sleeves, and a gorgeous dalmatic belted with a wide golden band. Golden rings were intermingled with her hair and shone on her temples. A shawl veiled her head and rested on her right shoulder.[49] The proud girl knew that, according to the prevailing custom, a wife would take the shoes off her husband's feet on the wedding night. She looked Dobrynya, Malusha's brother, straight in the eye, and replied: 'Tell Vladimir that I will not draw off the boots of a *slave's son*.' Then she nestled closer to her father and coyly added: 'Now, if it were Yaropolk, that would be another matter.' One can hear the two brothers guffawing in the background. 'You have your answer,' said Rogvolod.

'Go.' An irate Dobrynya travelled all the way back to Novgorod, bitterly chewing on the insult which had been inflicted on his nephew, his sister, himself and all his family. Far from being a slave, Malusha had held the enviable position of housekeeper to a great princess; he, to all practical effects, had been a viceroy in Novgorod; his father, old Malk of Lubech, was an honourable man; Vladimir would soon be Great Prince of Kiev: a slave's son indeed! The uncle did not spare his ward and master any part of the humiliation he had experienced, and he called for revenge. Vladimir's young blood reacted as was only natural. How could he reign over a nation if he allowed himself to be treated with disrespect? He would make an example of Rogned and her family. And if there really were some negotiations in progress concerning a marriage between Rogned and Yaropolk, so much the better: wouldn't it make brother Yaropolk furious to have his fiancée stolen from under his nose! That would give the right tone to the campaign which was about to begin.

Vladimir wanted his first war to end in undisputed victory, and he took precautions. In addition to his Viking retinue, he engaged the services of Novgorodian volunteers, numerous Chuds and Krivichans, and marched off.

Polotsk lay on the right (northern) bank of the Western Dvina. The small tributary called the Polota separated the earliest section, called *Verkhny Zamok* (upper castle), standing high on its headland on the right (western) bank of the Polota, from the more recent section, called *Zapolotye*, stretching out on its left bank. The layout was the usual one: a *Podol* inhabited by craftsmen surrounded the citadel (*Verkhny Zamok*) which towered at the top of its hill; the prince's palace was of course within the citadel. The two armies met in the plain beside the town. The moment when Vladimir's mettle and his luck would be tested had finally arrived. He rose high in his stirrups and cast a last glance at his men.

He may not have been too sure of the Chuds and the Krivichans who might just as well have sided with Rogvolod if he had sought their alliance; the Novgorodians were undoubtedly faithful, but these amateurs had yet to prove their worth; on the other hand, the Viking mercenaries looked good. 'Men with a more perfect physique were never seen. Tall as date-palms and rubicund',[50] dressed in baggy trousers gathered below the knee, woollen hats with headpieces falling over their necks under the helmets, cloaks which covered only half the body so that the right arm should always be free to strike – they stood impassively, accepting warlike discipline as a matter of course, ready to charge forward at a wave of the Prince's hand. They were armed to the teeth. High shields protected their whole bodies; they carried hammers and axes to fell the enemy – they had been nicknamed 'the axe-bearing barbarians' – swords to cut their opponents to pieces once felled (good swords, broad and flat, two-edged and grooved, of a Frankish type, so excellent that Arabs would open graves to steal them), and knives and daggers to finish the work. But for the time being none of these would be used: spears would suffice. Vladimir made a gesture, and they lowered their spears, so that the whole army appeared to be one enormous saw extended at Rogvolod's troops. The Vikings, everyone knew, did not only look good. They were 'the bravest of companions',[51] they would fight to the end, they would die for or with their Prince; surrounded, they would kill themselves rather than surrender. It was a glorious feeling to be in command of such men.

'Forward.'

The saw began to move. With levelled spears, the Vikings advanced, one huge war machine bristling with thousands of spikes. They marched silently at first, as if they would crush any obstacle without even noticing it. But suddenly, as the two armies were about to clash, a frenzied roar rose from the Vikings' ranks, and they rushed forward, transported by the spirit of battle, their red and yellow hair flying in the wind, their eyes bloodshot, their mouths open, their arms thrusting, smiting, slashing and jabbing, first with the spears, then, when the enemy's lines were broken, with axes and hammers, next with swords, finally with knives which they slid adroitly between helmet and breastplate, just a little above the collar-bone. A powerful stench rose from the battlefield. Rogvolod's troops fled and locked themselves in the citadel.

Polotsk's Verkhny Zamok was surrounded by the usual fortifications: a moat; a wall built of timber filled in with earth from the moat; on top of the wall a platform protected by a wooden stockade with embrasures for archers; towers at the corners; a drawbridge across the moat. The defenders, of course, had the advantage, but on that day nothing could stop the attackers; ladders were flung against the walls, and covering themselves with their shields as with a roof, Viking commandos slowly began to climb under an avalanche of arrows and stones. The Slavs followed, anxious to show that they were neither less brave nor less able than the 'mercs'. Many fell into the moat, many were beaten back at the top, but some succeeded in reaching the platform. In a few seconds the archers were exterminated. Dropping to

92

the ground, the commandos threw open the gates and lowered the drawbridge. Vladimir's army rushed into the citadel with wild shouts. The butchery began.

Rogvolod was hiding in his palace, with his wife, his daughter Rogned and his two sons. It would have been better for him if he had died in the midst of his men. The fighting, one imagines, took the whole day, and it was already evening when the palace was taken. The city was being sacked by torchlight. Murder and rape were everywhere, and already the funeral pyres of the Vikings fallen in action were beginning to smoke. The door to the great hall of the palace was beaten down, and at the head of the invaders Vladimir and Dobrynya rushed into the semi-darkness. They were breathing heavily, bespattered with blood, their swords in their hands. They had spent hours killing, and the sombre intoxication of battle, that special eroticism known only to people who have fought with cold weapons, dimmed their eyes. The beaten prince and his family cowered in a corner. 'There she is!' cried Dobrynya. 'She called you a slave's son. Make her a slave's son's slut then! Here. Now. While they look.' The men seized Rogvolod and his two sons and held them. Then, when Malusha's honour had been avenged, they killed them: three more corpses to be added to the already numberless slain that day.[52]

No doubt all this sounds pretty gruesome. The Vikings were not exactly *nice* men, at least in wartime; as to Vladimir, he had won among them the reputation of *fornicator immensus et crudelis*,[53] which could hardly have been achieved by strictly chivalrous behaviour. On the other hand, moral criticism does not come too convincingly from the contemporaries of Auschwitz, Katyn, Dresden, Central Park and the motorcycle gangs. War was war then, and peace was peace, and on the morrow after the battle, Vladimir, who could have given Rogned to his men, took her for his lawful wife. To emphasize that she was his princess, he gave her the Slavic name Gorislava,[54] and nine months later Izyaslav was born, a legitimate Russian prince.

3 Exit Yaropolk

Having dispossessed his two brothers, Yaropolk reigned peacefully in Kiev. According to some,[55] he leant toward Christianity, being of a meek and gracious disposition; he was not baptized himself, but he did not prevent anyone from accepting baptism, presumably from Bulgarian priests, although he may have had Western sympathies. In 973 he sent envoys and rich gifts to Emperor Otto I at Quedlinburg; in 977, he entertained Pope Benedict VII's legates in Kiev. All this may have endeared him to a small minority, but the rest of his people must have objected, and Vladimir was to make good use of the situation.

Straight from Polotsk, he marched to Kiev and entrenched himself in front of the city.[56] What did he feel on catching sight of the place where he had spent his childhood? Here it was, nearly within his grasp, to reign over if only he could take it. It is said that one can never go back, but maybe it is possible, especially if it is to become master where one used to be an insignificant brat. Vladimir gazed at these ramparts, these roofs, these countless orchards, these helmeted men-at-arms showing above the battlements, and thought that if he was successful, all this would belong to him. Here was no foreign city that it would make sense to take, pillage and burn, but his ancestors' heritage, his own future wealth, the living of people whom he already considered as his. The damage his Viking allies were causing in the country they occupied, annoyed him; he felt more like a peasant than like a conqueror when he saw how the villages all around were being ransacked. The Russian soldiers up there might try to kill him today, but they would obey him tomorrow, if he found a way to vanquish them and still to keep them alive. Then, together, they could make of this country one of the most powerful in the world, a rich, prosperous country, good to live in, and feared by Pecheneg, Greek, Bulgarian and Viking alike. To take the city without scarring it, to pluck the fruit without bruising it, such was Vladimir's assignment. Naturally, the stalk would have to be broken, that much was certain.

The great Sveinald, it seems, was dead.[57] Yaropolk had replaced him with another general called Blud. The name is not exactly prepossessing: it reminds one of the German *Blut* (blood), and of the Russian *blud* (lechery).[58] He may have been a friend of Dobrynya's. Joachim indicates that Dobrynya was in charge of the Blud project; this, being in character, may be true. In fact, Blud may have been working for Vladimir even earlier as an influence agent, if, as we are informed,[59] he kept repeating to Yaropolk: 'Prince, your younger brother Vladimir cannot fight against you. Can a tomtit challenge an eagle? Do not bother to gather your troops.' Such foresight and cunning would be quite in Vladimir's manner. Whatever the case, the siege was already begun when Blud received the following message from the enemy's camp: 'I desire your help. You will be my second father when Yaropolk is gone. He was the one to commit fratricide. I armed myself but to save my life.' It is useful in politics to have the appearance of innocence.

By betraying his lord, Blud would seem to dissociate himself from an abominable crime. Blud, who was no fool, replied that he was willing to be Vladimir's second father, and recommended that the city be taken by storm: in that way, he, Blud, would run no risk at all. But Vladimir knew what happened to cities taken by storm, and he wanted to keep his Vikings away from Kiev; this was precisely why he needed Blud. A plan was devised. Blud closeted himself with Yaropolk and 'disclosed' to him some startling intelligence he had just received, presumably from spies or informers: the people of Kiev, he said, corresponded with Vladimir, and were preparing to surrender the city to him. Obviously Yaropolk had no illusions about his own popularity, so instead of investigating the information or attempting a sortie, or even trying to negotiate with Vladimir while still holding the upper hand, he fled.

The devilishly simple plan (whose was it? Blud's? Dobrynya's? or rather Vladimir's?) had worked. The Great Prince had been separated from the unharmed city, which had no choice but to throw its gates open, thus confirming Blud's intelligence and Yaropolk's trust in him. Two birds with one stone, again. On July 11, 978, Vladimir rode into his capital, to the acclamations of his new subjects, who recognized in him the worthy son of Svyatoslav, and anyway were anxious to make a favourable impression. One can be sure that the pagans cheered louder than the others.

The fruit had been plucked in excellent condition, but this was not the end yet. There was still a Great Prince on the run somewhere, and Vladimir knew – or rather felt – what makes monarchies so special: they create nations, whereas republics are created by them. Russia was still an ectoplasm: he and he alone would crystallize it into being. He was to be the sole catalyst. There was to be no sharing. Unity was what it was all about.

Yaropolk had shut himself in the city of Rodnya, a little more than a hundred kilometres south-east of Kiev, at the junction of the Ros and the Dniepr. He had not bothered about stocking up with food, and supplies were cut off as soon as Vladimir had laid siege to the town. Soon the starvation was such that a century later Russians spoke of 'famine like in Rodnya'. Perhaps Yaropolk could still have sallied against Vladimir – the eagle against the tomtit – but part of his army had stayed in Kiev and probably joined Vladimir's ranks; besides, Blud, the trustworthy Blud, had changed his tune: 'Prince, do you see what a large force your brother has? We cannot overcome them. Make peace with Vladimir.' Vladimir, meanwhile, was patiently – or impatiently – waiting. Young as he was, he must have itched to storm Rodnya, but he saw no point in the massacre of soldiers who soon would be his own and whom he would need to protect his realm against many possible enemies, including his present allies the Vikings. A civil war is a bad war: if there are many dead, it will suppurate for generations. A little starvation, on the other hand, will harm a nation only temporarily. So he sealed the city and kept his bloodthirsty captains firmly in hand. Dobrynya, knowing him as we do, was probably in favour of an attack, but Vladimir knew how to say no, even to his dear uncle.

Yaropolk felt that he had let all his opportunities slip through his fingers. Vladimir's mercy seemed the only chance left for him, and, at Blud's advice, he decided to avail himself of it. 'I shall take what my brother will give me,' he said resignedly, remembering that he had been quite willing to let Oleg live after robbing him. But then he did not think like a Great Prince: he had been one only in name, and the reasoning of a nation-builder was quite beyond him. Blud sent a message to Vladimir, frightening in its conciseness: 'I am bringing him.' One faithful servant called Varyazhko tried to warn Yaropolk against such a wretched surrender: 'My Prince, do not go to your brother. They will kill you there. Rather go to the Pechenegs, collect an army and come back to fight.' Vladimir would have done it, but Yaropolk shook his head. His heart heavy with his impending fate, he mounted his horse, and, followed by a few men, including the infamous Blud and the loyal Varyazhko, left Rodnya. He probably expected to find Vladimir at the camp, but discovered that he had gone back to Kiev. What a trip it must have been! As he approached the capital, the defeated Yaropolk must have thought more than once of the many times he had entered it as Great Prince of all Russia, and maybe also of his childhood days, when it had simply been home to him. Behind him, Blud and Varyazhko rode in silence, brooding about the past and anticipating the future. 'Vladimir is kind,' thought Yaropolk. 'He will spare me. We played together as children.'

Finally they reached Kiev. The Great Prince, it is to be presumed, entered the city incognito, at nightfall. He rode up to the palace which had been Olga's, Svyatoslav's and then his. He dismounted slowly and threw the reins to one of his men, Varyazhko perhaps. He ascended the steps with Blud at his elbow, and, at some distance, the others who were of lower rank. Yaropolk went in first, followed by Blud, who immediately closed the heavy door. 'My brother, where is my brother?' In the great, red-slate hall two Varangians stood with drawn swords. Vladimir was nowhere to be seen. Maybe he was showing himself somewhere else, so as to have an alibi in the eyes of the people.

Outside, Yaropolk's retinue was waiting, anxiously milling around. A scream was heard from within. 'The Prince's voice!' Varyazhko sprang to the door. It was locked. Of course he knew what had happened. He jumped on his horse and fled.

4 Aftermath

There are of course many sound arguments against murder, even political murder, and, for some reason, nature especially revolts against the murder of a near relative, as if there was some kind of monstrous incest in kin killing. Be that as it may, and repulsive as Blud's treachery and the use that was made of it can appear to us, peace had been restored to Russia for many years to come, and at what price? Scarcely more than one human life. Kindness and rectitude it was not, but statesmanship it was, and quite elegant in a cynical way: rarely had such great results been achieved with such sparing means. Svyatoslav might not have murdered a brother in cold blood, but he would cheerfully have killed him in the field, plus a few thousand mothers' sons to keep him company; certainly Yaropolk himself would have done nothing of the kind – he killed brothers through clumsiness, not malice – but also how aptly Karamzin's stern formula judges the man and his career: 'The very trust Yaropolk put in Vladimir's honour,' he writes, 'shows a kind, ever unsuspicious heart; but a prince who follows nothing but the advice of his favourites, and is incapable of saving his throne or dying like a hero, *deserves pity not power.*' During the thirty-seven years of his reign, Vladimir would show which of the two he deserved.

His first days still smacked strongly of war: it was victory, not yet peace. When Yaropolk's spoils were brought to him, his brother's widow rated high amongst them. The former nun was still exceedingly beautiful, and his heart missed a beat at the sight of her. Of course there is no proof, but one is somehow prompted to think that he had not forgotten her, that on that first day ten years earlier she had made on him an indelible impression, and had, so to speak, introduced him to the mystery of femininity. Anyway there were also coarser reasons: conquerors have always felt that women were their natural reward; a new paramour with every victory was becoming a habit of Vladimir's; to ravish the widow of a defeated enemy was to defeat him a second time, even more crudely and cruelly. The fact that she was a Christian and a nun, and that possessing her had that faint taste of incest, was also exciting; she was pregnant, but what did Vladimir care? He took her.

Then there was the question of Blud. There is no reason to believe Tatishchev when he says that Vladimir feasted the general for three days as a reward for his service, and then killed him, as a punishment for his treason.[60] As a matter of fact, Blud's descendants, the Bludovs, were later a well known noble family. But it is true that Blud himself disappears from history at this time; no important mission seems to have ever been entrusted to him, and there is certainly no evidence that Vladimir treated him as a second father. On the contrary, knowing the value of faithfulness, the new Great Prince made many efforts to regain Varyazhko's confidence. Probably the son of a Slav engaged in the Viking retinue – at least such is the origin that his acquired name seems to suggest – he joined the Pechenegs, as he had advised Yaropolk to do, and now, to avenge his prince's death, he ceaselessly harassed the Russians with the help of his new friends.[61] This made Vladimir even keener to avail himself of his services. After long negotiations, and a solemn oath from the Great Prince that no reprisals would be taken against him, he returned to his home city. Vladimir kept his word. Varyazhko's fate is typical: no servant of Yaropolk's was ever punished in any way. Vladimir's concern was unity, and he was both astute and generous enough to know how to achieve it.

The Vikings presented another problem. They had occupied Kiev and arrogantly demanded payment for their participation in the campaign. They even hinted at blackmail: 'The city is ours,' they said. 'We want two grivnas per citizen.' This sounded exorbitant to the Prince. It was certainly more than he had promised. The only real battle had been the Polotsk one; the two sieges had cost no lives, or very few. It seemed a pity to pay so dearly for what had been conquered so cheaply. Besides, when Vladimir made those promises, he had considered Yaropolk's possessions as enemy ones, made to be looted; now they had become his, and he saw no reason to ruin his own good city of Kiev to please a few useless foreigners. Ingratitude can be a virtue in a statesman. Vladimir asked for time: he had no money now, the Vikings would have to wait until the autumn, when the taxes would come in; the marten skins would be collected in a month, he explained, and then he could pay up. During that period of grace, he selected the Vikings he wanted to keep, not the troublemakers, but 'the good, the wise and the brave', and made them presents of lands and hamlets, which rooted them in Russia and did not cost the city anything.

When the delay came to an end, the remaining Vikings still wanted to be paid, but they were given to understand that money was not available and would not be, for some time to come. In the meantime, Yaropolk's friends had made their peace with Vladimir, and the Russian army was in control. The Vikings saw that they would have to mend their manners; they probably named more reasonable figures, but now even this was too much. They had been a nuisance; if they were paid, they might be tempted to stay; it was much better to get rid of them. Of course it was a gamble: they might have tried to resort to force. But they were divided among themselves, and they never dared. One wonders at Vladimir's cunning. The Constantinople dream was not dead, and he managed to have the Vikings themselves begging to be sent to Greece *instead of payment*; thereupon he graciously allowed them to depart. Presumably their plan was no longer to attack but to serve the Emperor, and this may have been the beginning of the famous Viking bodyguard in Constantinople. Even so, Vladimir took one more precaution. For the time being, he needed peace, and did not want the Greeks to suspect him of any evil intention against them. So he went so far as to send a letter to the Basileus to warn him of the Vikings' arrival, and to suggest what should be done with the ruffians: 'Do not keep many of them in your city, or else they will cause you much harm as they have done here. Scatter them in various villages, and [most essential point] do not let a single one return this way.'[62] Obviously Vladimir had already nothing to learn from Machiavelli.

One cannot help but wonder if these events are not somehow connected with the undated incidents to which the Icelandic sagas allude when they mention a misunderstanding between Vladimir and his friend Olaf. Calumny, they maintain, forced the Norwegian

Prince, who had successfully fought on Vladimir's side, to depart from Gardariki under a cloud. Conceivably, he did not approve of the way his Viking brothers had been treated. Whatever the case, he did not rise to the Greek bait; instead, he travelled back north and settled for a time in Vinnland (on the Baltic Sea) where he married Prince Burislav's daughter, before engaging in new adventures.

While all this was going on, Vladimir had begun to work on a project which was especially dear to his heart. He had spent the last ten years in Novgorod, where the hated Christian presence was hardly felt, and in Scandinavia, where it was not felt at all. Consequently he had been shocked at the lack of pagan piety among the Kievans, and decided to launch a counter-reform – the more so as he had every reason to be grateful to the gods. And so, while Volos' statue occupied a becoming place in the *Podol* on the very bank of the Pochayna (a small affluent of the Dniepr), among the tradesmen and craftsmen whom he protected, on the hill inside the city a whole pantheon of statues was erected, at whose feet blood ran freely on every suitable occasion. Even children were brought by devout families to participate in the gory festivities.

Seven deities stood there like antennae, attracting upon Kiev the blessings of all natural and supernatural powers: Dazhbog, the sun god, Stribog, the god of the whistling winds, Mokosh, the only Slavic goddess, Khors the mysterious, Sim, spirit of households, Rogl,[63] spirit of harvests, and of course, towering above the rest, Perun, the Striker, the god of thunder and lightning, of oaths and maledictions, the giver of rain, the surfeited State god, who had taken Vladimir under his personal protection (or rather whom Vladimir had taken under *his* personal protection). Perun's statue was the most beautiful of all: the body was made of wood, but the head was silver, with a ferocious golden moustache. He shone when the sun shone, he glittered by moonlight, but to admire him in all his awe-inspiring splendour, you had to see him when a thunderstorm broke. Then, with great rumblings booming from one end of the sky to the other, with rain streaming down from the rending clouds, the invincible Perun would glare out of the darkness at each flash of lightning, as if emitting his own intermittent, livid beams.

CHAPTER FOUR

Prince

1 People

It is fairly easy for the historian to reconstruct events of the past, especially the more spectacular ones which left an impression on the participants, and sometimes even helpful vestiges, such as battlefields strewn with rusting armour, crumbling cities, changed borders, and the like. It is already more difficult to fathom the hearts and minds of historical characters: psychology did not interest our ancestors as much as it does us – and even in our contemporaries, thoughts, tendencies, passions and options can rarely be judged with objectivity. Granted: Nero was a monster, and Vincent de Paul a saint, but what were Napoleon, Cromwell, or, for that matter, Richard Nixon? Still, there is some possibility of inducing motives from actions, some hope of drawing acceptably lifelike portraits, just as painters do who endeavour to give a glimpse of the soul through their treatment of the pose, the features, the skin, the eyes. What really verges on the impossible is to capture the petty details of bygone everyday life – atmosphere, smells, the things that we know so well about our own times, and that are so hopelessly lost a few decades after we are gone, because no one ever bothered to record such minutiae. Yet the attempt must be made, for history is not complete without what the French call 'la petite histoire', and as far as Vladimir's history is concerned, this seems a good spot to pause for a minute and at least try to envisage what kind of world it was

The Cathedral of St Sophia, built in Kiev in 1037, still bears its witness after nearly a thousand years, in a Russia completely transformed.
(*Photo Novosti Press Agency, Moscow.*)

that he made his, and that was destined so radically to change.

First, his city. When, on that eleventh day of July AD 978 (one thousand years ago for the writer and already more for the reader), he rode his horse into Kiev, he was entering a city whose origins had even then been forgotten. Old people babbled about three brothers, Kiy, Shchek and Khoriv and their sister Lybed, who had given their names, respectively, to the city itself, the Shchekovitsa hill, the Khorevitsa hill, and that tributary of the Dniepr which was so convenient for the watering of horses, but there was some argument as to whether Kiy had been a nobleman or a ferryman. Anyway, many cities possess similar legends concerning founding brothers, and no one takes them seriously. The only certainty is that *kiy* means hammer, but who wielded what hammer in Kiev's ancient history will have to remain a mystery now, as it was in Vladimir's time.

On his way toward what would be his capital for thirty-seven years, rising high in his stirrups and breathing in the exhilarating summer air of a homeland which had become doubly his, the young Prince could admire on both sides of the road the rich orchards which girdled the city, and where apples, pears and quinces glistened in the sun. The cherries had already been picked and were drying on the rooftops. Further off, long rows of funeral mounds evoked the protection of forebears whose names had been forgotten, but whose spirits still hovered over their ashes, mixed with the ashes of their wives or mistresses who had volunteered to join them in death.

Soon the *Podol*, where most of the common people lived, opened before its new master, and the military procession wound its way between dwellings of two

109

types: mud huts partly buried in the ground, or more elaborate *khaty*, built of timber filled in with clay, and consisting of one main room with a baked clay oven, a small entrance hall and an unheated shed. Roofs were made of earth; palings or wattle fences separated properties. Women lined the walls waving to the handsome young Prince; street urchins ran after the soldiers, wondering at the Vikings' grim faces and massive weapons; as to the men, they had all repaired to the market-place, which was the pride and nearly the *raison d'être* of the whole city.

Large and square, the market-place was surrounded by shops and storehouses. Booths and stands occupied the space in the middle, under the protection (and in the shadow) of Volos' idol. Here you could buy anything you wanted to eat – salt, wheat, rye, millet, flour, bread, honey, meat, game, fruit, vegetables, fish – or to wear – fabrics and furs, shoes and hats. You could furnish your home with pottery, metalware, wooden bowls; you could acquire wax or frankincense; if you were a builder, you could bargain for timber; if you wanted to stock up your farm, horses, cows, sheep, geese, ducks and chickens were available; if you were a soldier or a travelling salesman, you would have no trouble finding weapons suitable to your needs. Whatever you were buying, you ran no risk of being cheated by a dishonest merchant: the city officials held scales at your disposal, which they would carefully check, and it would cost you only a small fee to use them. Here farmers' fairs were held every Friday (the Slavs used a seven-day week); here thefts were announced; here, if you were really desperate, you could sell yourself into slavery and receive a minimum price of half a grivna (one nogata went to the town clerk for writing the deed).

Here also, or at least in that part of town, the numerous Kievan craftsmen, both high and low, worked, and on that particular day it seems we can hear them cheering loudly but also whispering into each other's ears: 'What is *he* going to be like? It's always the same story with governments: you know what you lose with one, you don't know what you're in for with the other.' Yes, here they are. They have come out to greet the son of Svyatoslav the Prince and Malusha the housekeeper, the illegitimate half-breed who left as a boy, eight years ago, and is coming back bringing his Vikings, a conqueror! Oh! he looks noble enough, his expression is kind and debonair, and his mother was a Slav, and all that, but practically, how will his reign affect them? That is another question. Will he be a great builder, in need of architects, stonehewers, stonemasons, bridge-builders, carpenters and the like? Will he be a warlike lord like his father of blessed memory, and enrich shield-makers, bowmakers, quiver-makers, catapult-makers, saddlers, fortification-builders? Will he encourage the blacksmiths, tinsmiths, coppersmiths, who had a part of the town to themselves? Will he uphold the great Kiev tradition of shipbuilding – Constantinople itself used to order boats from Russian shipwrights, whose work was considered far superior to European standards? Judging from his elegance, he would set a rather dressy style, and that would be good for the spinners, the weavers, the sempsters, tanners, boot-makers, hood-makers, silversmiths and goldsmiths. But what about his father's palace? Would he want to modernize it a bit? Would he be looking for whitewashers, woodworkers, nailmakers, locksmiths, painters, silver-platers, glaziers? And the scribes, those intellectuals who had thriven under Yaropolk, would the young warlord have any use for them? – One feels that many of them looked at the new Prince with one eye, while squinting with the other at Volos: 'May the gods grant that we prosper under this one,' they muttered under their breath between two cheers.[64]

On leaving the Podol, Vladimir approached the ramparts of the older part of the city, the Gora (hill). Later four gates led into it: the Zhidovskie, Lyadskie, Ugorskie and Zolotye (golden). It was probably the same in Vladimir's time, and in that case there is no doubt that he entered through this last gate, which was the main one, and which his son Yaroslav was to fortify with a huge tower of white stone. The tower still stands. On the Gora there were also market-places, among them the Babin Torzhok, but they were much smaller, and only everyday necessities could be found there. The houses became larger and larger as one climbed the hill. The boyars possessed real mansions, tall and ornate, with galleries along the sides and pigeon-cotes on the roofs. Vladimir's great white horse, with his mane left long, Viking style, kept pounding his way up the hill, and soon the palace appeared, Olga's palace where Vladimir had spent his childhood, the only stone building in town.

Its ground floor contained storehouses of different kinds, where supplies were stocked for the inhabitants of the whole citadel. An outside flight of steps led to the first floor; the steps were made of wood, gaily painted in variegated colours and supported by wooden posts. The entrance door opened onto the vestibule, which was directly connected with the great hall, where banqueting and councils took place. The floor was made of bricks; the walls were decorated with red slates, marble slabs, mosaics, frescoes; there were glass and carved ivory

Artist's project for the reconstruction of the
Golden Gate of Kiev. The church is built over
the gate itself.
(*Photo J. da Cunha-Plon. Courtesy of Mme
Zalessky.*)

objets d'art; there were even statues, bronze or silver, gilt with gold dissolved in mercury, representing – a trifle crudely perhaps – men with their hair cut round, wearing embroidered blouses with long sleeves, and trousers down to their ankles. Somewhere around here was the *gridnitsa* (guardhouse). A Russian stove made of bricks, just like the ones still in use, occupied one corner. The furniture was mainly tables and benches, but the Prince was entitled to an armchair. There were other rooms on that same floor, containing high beds and wash-stands, with copper ewers and bowls. Above it towered the *terem*, a beautified loft belonging exclusively to the women. Other structures surrounded the palace itself: cellars, bath-houses, honey-stores and dungeons, the last rather sensibly devoid of doors; a very small window allowed food to be passed inside, but to free a prisoner a ladder had to be used and the timbering of the roof taken apart. This was so much trouble that gaol sentences were not too frequent, but once a prisoner had been confined to one of these oubliettes, it took a foreign invasion to have him liberated – at least such is the story told by one of our bards. When the bogatyr Ilya of Murom displeases Vladimir by helping himself to the sovereign's reserve of wine and by throwing the cellars open to the rabble, the Prince calls out 'in a thunderous voice':

> Hey you, servants, faithful servants,
> Hasten, hurry, with celerity,
> With celerity and with legerity.
> Lock that gallant for me in the dungeons,
> Close him in with an iron grate,
> Cover him with chopped oak on all sides,
> Strew him with yellow sands,
> Let him starve a little and unto death.

All the other bogatyrs, indignant at such harsh treatment for such a petty offence, resign from their posts, and when, three years later, the nomads attack *en masse*, Vladimir deplores his rashness: surely Ilya, the only one who could have saved Russia, must be dead by now. But the little princess, who has been secretly feeding the prisoner, announces that he might still be alive. This time Vladimir shouts 'in a sonorous voice':

> Hey you, servants, faithful servants,
> To the deepest dungeon go,
> Scatter off the yellow sands,
> Put the chopped oak all asunder,
> Pull the iron grate away,
> See if Ilya Muromets is yet living.[65]

Whereupon they find old Ilya in his gaol, placidly reading the Gospel by candlelight – which anticipates a little our story.

Just like the boyars' mansions, the Prince's palace was embellished with carved and painted galleries, and we can imagine Vladimir addressing his people from one of them. No doubt a numerous crowd – Kiev's population at the time is estimated at several tens of thousands – stood there staring and gaping at the new master. Some of the citizens were, one presumes, pressing as close to him as they could get: these were the so-called boyars, a mixed lot; a good number of them had earned that honorary rank by serving the Prince in peace and war; others were tribal lords in their own right; some were of Viking origin, others pure Slavs, many crossbreds. There was nothing exclusive about boyardom, and no privileges were attached to it: whoever was important through heredity, wealth, personal qualities, eminent service or choice of the Prince, was a boyar. Further away from the Prince stood the *muzhi* (upper class), the *lyudi* (at that time, middle class), the *smerdy* (half-free labourers), the *zakupy* (indentured labourers), the *izgoi* (former slaves) and the *cheliad* (complete slaves).[66] There were also, it is to be surmised, women of all ranks. The Viking and the Slavic traditions were in agreement concerning the freedom and dignity of women. They went where they pleased and did mostly what they pleased, not through superior cunning, like in Western Europe, but quite openly. To murder one would cost a man 20 grivnas in bloodwite alone; a married woman was allowed to possess property; if her husband appropriated her hemp, flax or linen, or if he sold fabrics made by her, this was theft, punishable by law; if parents were so unreasonable as to force their daughter to marry a man she did not like and she committed suicide, they were held responsible for her death. This liberal system, by the way, seems to have worked very well, since contemporary foreigners wondered at the 'unbelievable chastity' of Russian women. Chaste as they were, there is no doubt that they were among the first and most fervent admirers of the twenty-year-old sovereign in whose life they were to play such an important part.

2 Wealth

The craftsmen had nothing to fear from Vladimir; he ruled with a firm hand, was conscious of everyone's interests, and all branches of the economy prospered under him.

At that time the Russians were noted for what must needs be called industry, especially for metallurgy, pretentious as the word may sound for a fairly primitive society. The iron ore exploited by the Drevlyans was used to make tools like spades, scythes, sickles, picks, rakes, hammers, ploughs, parts for mills, knives, scissors, and of course weapons. Copper was imported from the Caucasus and Asia Minor for kettles, wash-basins, candlesticks; lead from Bohemia, for seals; silver from both East and West for dishes, bowls, goblets; gold from Constantinople for jewellery, which consisted of ear-rings, necklaces, bracelets, rings, and more originally, enamelled crowns and temple pendants.

Trade was of course one of the greatest assets of the Russian economy. Under Viking influence it could only flourish, and the land and water routes that met in Kiev carried an unceasing flow of merchandise. Casks of heady Greek wines, rolls of gorgeous silks, lengths of stiff brocades, exotic fruit such as peaches and apricots; exquisite jewels and glassware travelled up the Dniepr, coming from Imperial Constantinople. On the Zalozny road, one would encounter caravans coming from Baghdad bringing spices, precious stones, shimmering satins, weapons of Damask steel; droves of fiery Arab horses to be sold on the Kiev market followed the incongruous-looking camels. Along the Kursk road came silver which the Volga Bulgars obtained from mines as far away as Tashkent or Benjahir in Afghanistan. Carts slowly rambling from Cracov or Warsaw, boats sailing swiftly southwards from Novgorod, were loaded with German wares: wools, linens, tinted glass, herring, beer, and the ever-precious needles and salt. But no economy could survive on imports only, and the trains of waggons or barges converging on Kiev met others, just as full of precious goods, on their way out. Down the Dniepr floated boatloads of furs, grains, honey and waxes for the Constantinople bazaars. The Zalozny road carried into the Orient walrus tusks from the Novgorod

Arctic colonies, German linens and cloths, and of course Russian furs, honey and waxes. The Western routes provided Europe with flax, hemp, tow, burlap, hops, tallow, suet, sheepskins, hides, and the inevitable honey, wax and furs. These furs, which the Russians had so consistently used to pay their taxes that the word *kuna* (marten) came to signify a certain amount of money, were in great demand in all markets. There were the pelts of weasels, foxes, lynxes, sables, Siberian squirrels, ermines, martens, beavers, coloured hares, and very special black foxes, which came from Bulgar and for which Arabs would pay 100 dinars apiece to make coats and caps for their old men, since they retained heat better than any other kind of fur.

There was yet another item that the Russians would gladly supply to East and West; in fact it can be said that they held a sort of monopoly in it at the time: slaves. These slaves were mainly prisoners of war, and in times of conflict, when the supply was abundant, you could find one for as little as two nogatas. At other times you could sell a pretty wench for 150 dinars, but if you wanted to obtain a truly talented slave, a musician for instance, or a craftsman, you had to be prepared to pay nearly ten times as much – this seeming to indicate a proper respect for the acquired skills which are the basis of civilization. Trade, it must be emphasized, was very efficiently managed in Kiev; storage services were developed, credit was in regular use, and in cases of bankruptcy, foreign creditors took precedence. Such was the law, and it constituted a considerable encouragement for alien trade agents, Armenians, Arabs, Vikings or Greeks.

Commerce with Constantinople was essential to the Russian economy, and had been strictly organized in

Oleg's time. Every year in June a convoy of boats[67] led by several hundred Russian merchants would leave for the south. On arrival, they would settle down outside the city of Constantinople, near the Church of St Mamant, after presenting to the Greek authorities documents signed by the Prince, identifying them as bona fide Russian businessmen. The Greeks were so afraid of an invasion that they would allow their visitors into the city only in groups of fifty men, under the supervision of a solemn Greek official. One tenth of the goods brought to Constantinople went to pay taxes to the Greek government, but it was that government's duty to feed the Russians during the whole summer, to permit them to use the Greek baths (that was duly stipulated in the treaty) and to provide them with free shipping tackle – anchors, cables, sheets, sails – when, in the autumn, they would board their ships loaded with Greek goods and sail back to Kiev. Generally the system worked to mutual satisfaction, and Kluchevsky has even been able to maintain with some appearance of good reason that wars broke out between the two parties only when some obstacle impeded normal trading relations, and the Russians fought to re-establish them.

One would normally have expected agriculture to be the main occupation of the relatively primitive Russian people, and naturally it did exist, so that the local population could be fed and even some exports managed. Rye, wheat, oats and barley provided the staple foods; peas, lentils, turnips, cabbage, onions and garlic grew in the vegetable gardens; flax and hemp furnished the material for local products such as army tents made of burlap, cordage nets, linen which the women wove, and ropes which the men twisted when they were not busy fulling felt for hats and winter shoes. Horses and oxen were bred, both for field work and – strangely enough – for riding purposes. But generally speaking the inhabitants of the Russian plains had for centuries earned a bad reputation as farmers. Procopius and Leo the Wise criticized their laziness – they simply would not be bothered with tilling lands which are still among the richest in the world – and considered them as semi-nomads. The one speciality at which they excelled was apiculture: true, the beehives were installed in hollow trunks, and since the bees were not domesticated in any way, work was reduced to a minimum and profit expanded to a maximum, which was exactly how Southern Slavs liked their way of making a living to operate. Still, all this was slowly changing, and although it is impossible to determine exactly what part Vladimir played in the transformation, there is no doubt that under his reign an economy which was still extremely dependent on forest and river came to depend more and more heavily on the cultivated field. A nation was being born, and a nation cannot live on wild honey and hunting, like a tribe. Kostomarov comments with great insight on a *bylina* (an epic poem of popular origin) of the Kievan cycle which, in poetic terms, describes the evolution.

It begins with the adventures of the Magician Prince Volgà (no relation to the river) who sends his retinue to capture martens and foxes. The retinue has no success. Volgà transforms himself into a wolf and chases the beasts into his own silken nets. Then he orders his men to catch 'swans and geese and grey duckies and little birds', and again they fail. So he assumes the shape of a hawk, and the swans, the geese, the duckies and the little birds fly away from him straight into the snares that he has set. Same experience with fish: Volgà becomes a pike and all the sturgeon which the retinue could not handle land on their tables. This is interpreted as a picture of a society where hunting and fishing were the main resources, but which could not thrive on them without the competent authority of a prince.

A few more clever impersonations – an aurochs with golden horns, a little bird, a grey wolf, an ant (the list, by the way, suggests expert knowledge of how military intelligence works) – allow Volgà and his men later on to conquer the kingdom of India, where they exterminate all the males, both young and old, but have the good sense to leave alive seven thousand fair maidens, 'for reproduction purposes'. When it is time to share the booty:

> What at the sharing was dear?
> What at the sharing was cheap?
> Good horses went for seven rubles,
> Sharp sabres went for five rubles,
> Steel maces went for three rubles,
> But the female sex went for nothing:
> Old women for half a coin,
> Young women for two halves,
> A fair maiden for a whole coin.[68]

Once again the benefits of leadership appear in no uncertain terms, this time applied to what had been so far the main princely industry: pillage. But now Volgà encounters Mikula the Villager, who is ploughing his field. For two days the Prince runs after the ploughman and finally manages to catch up with him on the third evening, at supper time. They engage in conversation, and Volgà mentions that he intends to collect a tribute from some rebellious towns: will Mikula accompany him on his expedition? Gladly, but first he has to pull his plough from the ground and clean it. The retinue is ordered to do it for him, but even all the men together have not enough strength. Then Mikula pulls it out himself with one hand, and negligently throws it behind a bush. Thereupon he joins forces with Volgà, to whom he explains the pleasures of a farmer's life. He is prosperous and enjoys respect from his neighbours. On arrival in town, the rebels refuse payment, but they are soon brought to reason by Volgà and Mikula who give them a hearty thrashing:

Hey, you clowns, take this for your foolishness![69]

'Thrice be cursed whoever rises 'gainst such gallants!' exclaim the chastened seditionists, rubbing their backs. The scene ends a little like in *War and Peace*, when Nicholas, single-handed, quenches a revolution on Princess Mary's estate; but here Mikula and Volgà operate together, and that is the main point. The 'clowns' are forced to submit to order, and this order, recognized as a necessity both by the plundering invader and the native provider, is founded on a compromise between Volgà's warlike, looting, aristocratic Viking tradition, and Mikula's unbreakable, earthy, plebeian Slavic strength. Such a compromise, or better such a fusion, is exactly what happened essentially during Vladimir's reign, although Olga had inaugurated the process with her system of taxation, and Yaroslav would crown it by proclaiming his set of laws known as The Russian Truth.

3 Power

The history of the origin of power in Kievan Russia can be synthesized as follows:

1   natives invite foreign princes to Russia in order to ensure exterior protection (Rurik)
2   a) foreign princes usurp overall power (Igor)
     b) by so doing, they create a national framework and ensure interior peace (Olga)
3   natives enjoy benefits of peace and legitimize usurped power by accepting it (Vladimir and 'Mikula').

A question could be asked here. Did this third stage happen before or after the christianization of Russia? In other words, where does the encounter between Mikula the Villager and Volgà the Magician take place: in a pagan or in a Christian world? (The fact that the composition of the *bylina* is subsequent to Vladimir's time being of course irrelevant.) – The present author's contention would be that the question is not being asked in proper historical terms. The components were already there before christianization: intermarriages, trade enthusiastically practised, taxes more or less willingly paid, common interests, common aims, common enemies, a general settling-down of the forest-roaming Slavs as well as of the seafaring Vikings, all that made co-operation between foreign usurpers and local labour desirable for both parties, and maybe even inevitable in the long run. Yet it is doubtful whether it would have 'jelled' as (and when) it obviously did, if a favourable catalyst had not been introduced into the mixture. This was the Christian idea that no power is of earthly origin and, conversely, that all princes are responsible to a higher Prince. The Father complex, if you will. There is no disputing the fact that the Father complex was often abused by evil-intentioned – and sometimes even well intentioned – potentates, but that does not weaken in any way the following observation: by accepting

124

baptism, Vladimir and his people would eventually transform their relationship; before baptism, he had just happened to be the strongest man in the community, and it had been advisable to obey him or else; after baptism, he would have to recognize that he had been given his strength by one stronger than he, to whom he was accountable for the way he used it; on the other hand, the people would have to believe that it was not by accident but through God's will that this man was their lord. Christianity transformed power into authority. What, without baptism, would have been a productive concubinage, was to become, through baptism, a sacred marriage. For better or for worse.

That would happen in a few years. In the meantime, we might as well have a look at the Prince's organization in Kievan Russia.

Hereditary tribal chieftains had already disappeared in Vladimir's time. Whatever effective power the local lords exercised they held officially or unofficially from the Prince, by a kind of recognition or confirmation or toleration of its importance. Also stemming from the Slavic background, there were local elected governments, with *veche, posadnik* and *tysyatsky*.[70] The traditional working unit had been the *zadruga* (extended family), but it was yielding to a more modern, more professional one, called the *verv* – one imagines the psychological problems involved – comparable to a guild of workers related by specialization rather than by blood.

The self-administration of towns and unions seems to have worked smoothly enough. So long as taxes were paid, the Prince did not meddle in local business: only Christianity would give him enough authority to do that. The taxes were levied per plough in agricultural districts and 'per smoke' (per hearth) in non-agricultural ones. There were city customs offices situated on bridges and embankments; there were tolls, taxes on store-houses, taxes on market-places, taxes on taverns. Two thirds of the monies finally collected by the Prince went into the State exchequer; one third, as in older times, into the Prince's privy purse, for the upkeep of his family and retinue.

Besides the State, of which he was gradually becoming the head, the Prince found himself at the helm of two main bodies. One was his personal estates, with administrators to take care of them: a general manager or bailiff, a master of stables, a chief of shepherds, village elders in towns and ploughmen's supervisors in the field. The other, and far more important one, was his *retinue* – the word traditionally, and not very satisfactorily, used to translate the Russian *druzhina*, in itself an elusive and often contradictory concept. Here philology can help us a little. *Druzhina* (from *drug*, friend) means 'a gang of friends', something like 'house' in 'House of Capulet' or 'House of Montague', but more equalitarian in concept and even bloodier in results. A *druzhina* is composed of senior members, each one of them called an *ognishchanin* (*ogon*, fire), sharing the Prince's fire with him, and of junior members called *detsky*, the ones whom he feeds and whose normal place is the *detinets* (keep). With some differences of rank, they can be called *gridy* or *otroki*. Note that in modern Russian *deti* means children, and *otroki* adolescents: the same shift of meaning happened in Latin (*puer*, child or servant), in Greek ($\pi\alpha\tilde{\iota}\varsigma$), and even in English where 'boy' can have both meanings. Among the *ognishchane* are counted the *koniushy* (master of the horse), the *tiun* (steward), and the *podiezdnoy* (adjutant). Vikings or Slavs, noblemen or commoners, these are all prince's men, and they form his *druzhina* in the narrow sense of the word. In a wider sense, the *druzhina* is a group of professional soldiers, not mercenaries but career men, who are also paid by the Prince, serve him as police force and bodyguard, and in wartime form the core of yet another *druzhina*, the whole army, composed, in addition, of the city militiae under the orders of their respective *tysyatskie*.

It would be a mistake to imagine that, thanks to his *druzhina*, the Prince ruled the country as an absolute monarch or even as a feudal lord. Quite the contrary. Not only did the members of the retinue freely express their opinions, which the Prince was obliged to take into consideration, but the people also were represented through the Prince's council, which consisted of two circles: the outer one, including all the men of importance in the realm, which was called the Boyar Council, and the inner one, composed of three to five 'foremost lords' (*muzhi perednie*) among whom was the elected chief of the Kiev militia (*tysyatsky*). The outer circle held deliberations in special circumstances, the inner one every day. Another major difference from the West can be found in the administration of justice. Whereas in a Christian kingdom like France, the principle of justice resided in the very person of the King, who held not only the sceptre and the orb but also the Hand, in pagan Russia the Prince did little more than administer it and profit by it. A murder, for instance, was sanctioned by law and necessitated the payment of a wergeld (compensation to the relatives) but also of a bloodwite (fine to the Prince). The amount was – very sensibly in the author's opinion – calculated in proportion to the victim's usefulness to society: the murder of the master of the horse would have cost you twice as much as the murder of a cook (no doubt the French would have reversed the ratio). To simplify, 40 grivnas of wergeld, 40 of bloodwite, was what you were expected to pay for polishing off a middle-class citizen (*lyudin*). A slave could be assassinated without fine, but you would still have to disburse a wergeld of 5 to 12 grivnas. If you were so foolish as to trifle with the life of a Prince's man, in bloodwite alone you would have to part with 80 grivnas.

Not founded in justice, not yet founded in religion, not founded any more in the crude right of the conqueror, somewhat shakily founded in heredity, the Prince's power in Vladimir's time found the confirmation it needed in the waging of wars, whose main objectives were the opening of roads and collecting of tributes. In the seven years which followed his accession to the throne, Vladimir led seven (or six) campaigns, all of them completely victorious except one, and even that he managed to conclude with an honourable peace, while he still held the advantage.

As early as 981, presumably as soon as the difficulties with the Vikings and Yaropolk's partisans had been ironed out, Vladimir struck first one powerful blow to the West, and then one to the North-east, as a man would push crowding neighbours with his elbows, left and right, to give himself some breathing space. In the West, he wanted free access to the Vistula basin,[71] and the best way to obtain it was to control the territory of the Lyakhs, in particular their cities of Cherven and Peremyshl. So he appropriated the territory and the cities. In the North-east, the Vyatichans were conveniently forgetting to pay the son the silver piece per ploughshare that they had promised to the father;[72] so he reminded them. They submitted – at least so it seemed until the next year, when no silver pieces appeared in

Kiev, and the independent-minded Vyatichans rose in arms. They had to be crushed again:

Hey, you clowns, take this for your foolishness!

This time (982) they learned their lesson.

So far it had been one punch to the left, two jabs to the right. It was the left's turn. In 983, Vladimir found that the Yatvingians, who held the Niemen basin, stood between him and the sea. Besides, they threatened his old and new possessions on the Vistula. So the Yatvingians were beaten and their territory seized. All Western routes were now open for trade, and Russia's border had been pushed back at least three hundred kilometres – maybe as far as the Baltic shore, since, according to the Icelandic chronicler Sturleson, all Livonia (today Esthonia and Latvia) belonged to Vladimir.

It was time to think about the North-east again. In 984, one of Vladimir's generals, nicknamed Wolf's Tail, defeated with great ease the Radimichans.[73] They agreed to pay a tribute, and faithfully fulfilled this obligation for many years. The sly Southerners found the event very funny, and for centuries teased the Radimichans: the tail of a wolf was enough to terrify them!

In 985, feeling secure at home and on his borders, the Great Prince decided to launch his most ambitious offensive. So far Fortune had smiled on his every attempt, and he must have thought it was time for him to show that he was as great a general as his father had been. Economic and territorial imperatives had decreed his previous expeditions: this one would be a real war of conquest. He did not embark upon it without taking all necessary precautions; whereas up to now he had fought alone, or had even entrusted his army to a

Wolf's Tail, this time he felt that the best possible advice might be needed: he summoned his uncle from Novgorod.

Yes, Dobrynya, who had made himself so popular in the northern city when he served there as counsellor to the viceroy, had become a viceroy himself. One should put aptitudes and affinities to good use. Besides, young Vladimir may have felt more comfortable on his throne in Kiev with his mentor kept busy a thousand kilometres away. There is no reason to believe that Dobrynya was not successful in whatever he undertook in Novgorod, but the only undertaking we know anything about is his participation in Vladimir's pagan counter-reform: whether acting on instructions or on his own initiative, the uncle erected a new idol in the northern capital as the nephew had done in the southern one, and organized lavish sacrifices at its feet. There is, one feels, something faintly comical in this haste shown by the old and experienced opportunist to imitate the whims of his brilliant but youthful kinsman. Now, feeling that for his new campaign he would need all the financial, military and intellectual resources he could muster, Vladimir offered Dobrynya a tankard of mead and said: 'Uncle, let us have a go at the Bulgars.'

Historians are not in agreement about which Bulgars he meant, but it seems more than probable[74] that it was the Volga or Kama ones, known as the Silver Bulgars. This – as a look at the map will show – was quite an expedition, and not exactly in Vladimir's line: he was a unifier, not an empire-builder. Nevertheless a number of successes were obtained. The Torks became allies, the Khazars got a thrashing, and many Bulgars were captured. 'Look at the prisoners,' said Uncle Dobrynya. 'Have you seen those boots they are wearing?' 'What

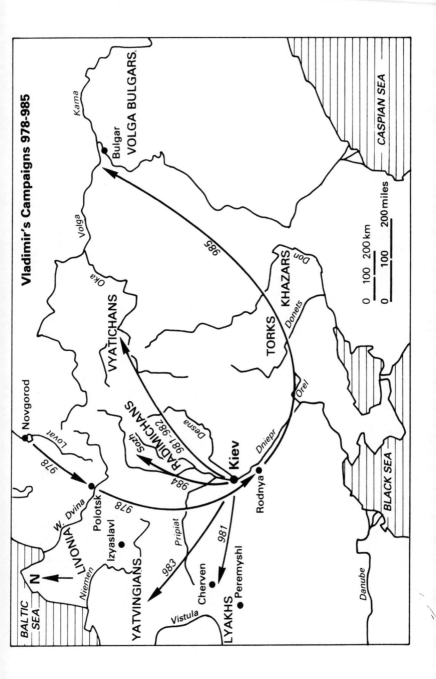

Vladimir's Campaigns 978-985

about those boots?' asked Vladimir. 'People who wear
such boots do not pay tributes: they collect them,' said
Dobrynya. 'Vladimir, my boy, let us rather look for
enemies with bast shoes.' The anecdote may not be authentic, but it is meaningful: it refers to the old difference
between the man of the sword and the man of the tool,
expressed in cobbler's terms. Once again, one can only
marvel at the young Prince's moderation and wisdom.
How he must have wanted to prove his old uncle wrong!
But he felt he was too far from base; even if he could beat
the Silver Bulgars, the prize would not be worth the
price; he graciously offered peace. It was gratefully
signed by the Bulgars who could fight if they had to, but
preferred to sell silver and keep their beautiful boots out
of the battlefield mud. 'May peace prevail between us till
stone floats and straw sinks,' was their imaginative oath.
Victor of himself only, but having lost nothing,
Vladimir returned to Kiev at the head of a still un-
defeated army, and made his usual prodigal sacrifices to
the ever-hungry Perun.

One year – *The Chronicle* says it was in 983, and
Vladimir had just completed his momentous campaign
against the Yatvingians – he felt that Perun deserved
some special mark of gratitude consonant with the general counter-reform that was in progress. Maybe it was
on catching sight of the grey waves of his ancestral
Baltic Sea that he vowed to renew the good old Viking
tradition of sacrificing to the gods not only dumb
animals but, on official occasions, men as well. Really,
there was nothing very unusual about it even in Kiev.
Sorcerers could hang more or less whomever they
pleased, so long as it was for religious reasons.[75] Svyatoslav had offered human sacrifices when he was in a desperate plight in Bulgaria.[76] Three years later, Hakon of

Norway would slaughter his own son Erling, to propitiate the goddess Thorgerd before a difficult battle. But
how much more delicate to offer the supreme gift in
thankfulness instead of supplication! It *would* have appealed to Vladimir to do the right thing by the gods.
Lots were drawn, and it happened that a young Christian
boy called Ivan[77] was designated to die.

How fair the drawing of the lots was, we do not
know. It seems an interesting coincidence that a
Christian should have become an accidental victim of a
pagan cult. Maybe there had been no pagan candidates,
maybe this was the first (and last) attempt at organized
persecution. Anyway, messengers came to the boy's
father, a Viking named Theodore according to Church
tradition, and said: 'Since the lot has fallen upon your
son, the gods claim him as their own.' 'Gods?' contemptuously retorted the father, who had lived a long
time in Greece. 'Manufactured dolls, you mean, or
maybe devils. I will not give up my son to the devils.'
The messengers went back to the people – it seems
Vladimir was too wise to take an active part in the
conflict – and reported the father's obstinacy. There was
an uproar. The men armed themselves, broke through
the stockade that surrounded Theodore's house, and
found him standing with Ivan on the porch. Ivan is
described by the chronicler as being 'fair in face and in
heart'. 'Surrender your son to the gods!' thundered the
pagans. The father replied: 'If they are gods, they do not
need you; they will send one of their number to take
him.' On hearing such blasphemy, the people hurled
themselves at the two Christians and tore them to
pieces. So it was under Vladimir that the first two
Russian saints, Theodore and Ivan, received the crown
of martyrdom.

4   Life and death

When he was not fighting or sacrificing to the gods, Vladimir knew how to enjoy life. He was a builder and he transformed the city of Kiev so that foreigners wondered at its beauty. Among other edifices, he built a summer palace outside the city, at Berestovo,[78] where his recreation was the hunting of birds with nets hanging from trees, and another palace at Vasiliev. He also loved parties, and his hospitality made him famous. Whether at eleven for dinner or at six for supper, he would heartily attack his grilled or boiled beef or mutton, poultry or game, his whole swan or his fish baked in honey. His vegetables he would consume either boiled or sometimes raw. After that, he would cut with his knife into a big chunk of corned meat or cured ham. He might gobble up a pie or two, and, like any good Russian, he would swallow considerable quantities of a variety of porridges, to which he would help himself with a silver spoon. His bread would be white wheat; his desserts, curdled milk and *kissel* (a kind of semi-liquid jelly) and cakes with honey and poppy-seeds. All this he would wash down with mead, grain beer, *kvas* (a kind of rye cider) or, being a Great Prince and something of a sybarite, with Greek or even Italian wine. This carousing and gormandizing could go on for hours; indeed, according to the *byliny*, it seems that Vladimir scarcely did anything else; dinners and suppers were relative concepts, and obviously often fused into one gigantic meal. With a good deal of poetic exaggeration but not without historical grounds, the drinking feats of his retinue are described as follows:

> You would think a golden trumpet blowing,
> Or a silver pipe intoning:

It is Prince Vladimir[79] speaking,
Shouting in his loudest voice:
Hey you, servants, faithful servants,
Fill a cup of green wine,
Fill a cup of strong beer,
Fill a cup of sweet mead,
Pour all three cups into one cup,
And present it to the gallant
Young Dobrynya, Nikita's son.[80]
The good servants have obeyed their Prince,
They have filled a cup of green wine,
They have filled a cup of strong beer,
They have filled a cup of strong mead,
They have poured all three cups into one cup.
Now the cup holds a pail and a half,
Now the cup weighs sixty pounds.
They present it to the gallant young Dobrynya,
And Dobrynya grips it with one hand,
And Nikita's son drinks it at one breath
To the health of Prince Vladimir.[81]

Which, by the way, goes to prove that, contrary to general belief, cocktails were not invented by Yankees, but at Vladimir's court.

Music and shows were constant ingredients of those feasts. Professional musicians were invited to perform on tambourines, psalteries, wooden pipes; strolling dancers, often comic and sometimes masked, would execute ballets to the musicians' tunes; Byzantine actors would travel all the way from Constantinople to Kiev to present their acts. Sometimes noble visitors would themselves take a psaltery, run their fingers down the golden strings and play a mournful dirge or a jolly ballad composed on the pentatonic scale.

It was not absolutely necessary to have a reason to indulge in such festivities, but it helped, and there is no doubt that all pagan occasions were made good use of. It was not enough to have a merry wake when a man had just died; the first anniversary of his demise was also celebrated with generous mead libations over his grave. The two yearly holidays dedicated to Lad, god of love, the celebration of Volos, and the happy cycle of seasons provided regular opportunities for dancing, singing, eating and imbibing. The winter solstice was acclaimed as the rebirth of the sun; next, the spring, personified as a young girl, had to be welcomed; then the *russalki* (river mermaids) would come out of the rivers and wander on the shores for a whole week: fiestas would be held in their honour; the Great Day of the Dead would come next, another good chance to get somewhat bacchic, and the summer solstice would follow, a mysterious night when ferns bloomed, treasures were found, animals spoke in man's language, and young couples, their heads decorated with wreaths, danced around huge bonfires and, hand in hand, jumped over them. The funeral of the sun took place after that, and then the first Thursday after the first autumn storm would be a particularly holy day: it was dedicated to Perun himself, and probably marked by especially plentiful banquets in the afternoon, following exceptionally bloody sacrifices in the morning.

Still, Vladimir's greatest delights were derived from satisfying – or at least trying to satisfy – his tremendous sexual appetites. The Viking that he was through his male ancestry revealed itself shamelessly in carnal lusts. *The Chronicle* must be exaggerating when it states that he had three hundred concubines at Vyshgorod, three hundred at Belgorod[82] and two hundred at his summer palace of Berestovo, to which the *Nikon Chronicle* adds three hundred at Rodnya: eleven hundred in all, plus, according to *The Chronicle*, five wives – Rogned, two Czechs, a Bulgarian and the Greek nun, plus numberless married women whom he seduced and unmarried girls whom he violated. This does seem a little too much of a good thing: the concubines were more probably slaves among whom he chose temporary bedfellows rather than honouring them all in alphabetical order, and as to seductions and rapes, history does not recall a single one after Rogned's. Vladimir was no Tarquinius, and the excellent chronicler in all likelihood got carried away by his rhetorical comparison between Vladimir and Solomon. And yet Thietmar's testimony is there, and the 'immoderate and cruel fornicator'[83] must have reigned over quite a seraglio, daily demanding of the flesh something it was not in its power to yield.

With all his cynicism in such matters, Vladimir did run, at least once, into a problem which could have been fatal to him, but which he solved with his customary elegance and efficiency. Busy with his concubines, he had little time left for Rogned, and settled her in a palace on the Lybed with her son Izyaslav, more or less forgetting about her. One imagines that, like many a neglected wife, she was making a nuisance of herself, thereby originating the vicious circle of estrangement and spite. More fortunate than most husbands, Vladimir could afford to act as if she simply did not exist. One night however, maybe in a moment of tenderness and nostalgia, or maybe just because he had been hunting west of Kiev and found it easier not to ride as far back as Berestovo to get his quotidian pittance of love, he decided to pay a visit to his second wife.[84] She received her lord graciously enough, and he fell asleep in her arms. The sense of danger that comes to all who lead an adventurous life woke him up. He opened his eyes and saw

Rogned pointing a knife at his throat. He gripped her wrist not a second too soon, and angrily asked the obvious question: 'Why?'

Rogned had a passionate heart: the proud girl who refused to pull off a slave's son's boots had come to love the slave's son, and was ready to kill him because he did not love her in return. 'I am bitter,' she said, 'because you have killed my father and conquered my land, all that because of me, and now you do not love me any more, neither me nor my child.' Vladimir arose. He was not touched. Here was a woman whose life he had spared, whom he had married, whose son he had made a prince, and she lifted her arm against him? 'Put on your wedding dress,' he ordered. 'I shall return and kill you, my wife, with my own hands.' He strode out, to the gallery maybe, to get a breath of fresh air, maybe also to add solemnity to the expected execution. When he came back into the room, Rogned, sparkling with jewels, was sitting on the high bed, and a little boy, not more than seven years of age, his eyes still clouded by sleep, stood in his way, blinking in the candlelight and offering him a naked sword. 'Father,' he said, 'did you think you were alone here?' It was his son, Izyaslav. Vladimir recoiled. His answer – if chroniclers are to be believed – has been preserved, and one detects in it both testiness and a hint of shame: 'Who would have thought you were here?' . . . What Izyaslav had just told him was this: 'You can kill my mother if you want to, but I shall be her witness.' A moment went by during which the man and the wife and the son exchanged fearful glances: everyone, Vladimir included, must have been afraid of what he might still do. Finally he threw the sword to the ground and left.

The next morning, the Great Prince gathered his

boyars, and although this was scarcely an affair of State, asked their advice. The fact in itself throws an interesting light on the relationship between a Russian prince of the tenth century and his people, or rather his *friends*. The boyars consulted among themselves and came up with the following piece of wisdom: 'Do not kill her, on account of her child [a Rurikid!]. On the contrary, restore her appanage and give it to her and to her son.' Vladimir meditated for some time and concluded that he could only gain by making their opinion his own. Generosity always appealed to him. Besides, wouldn't it be nice to get rid at one stroke of an importunate wife, of a possible murderess, and of a son whose face would, from now on, always awake unpleasant memories? And all that with an air of doing the handsome thing. And finally, didn't he need someone to take care of the new lands conquered from the Yatvingians and Lyakhs? An outpost out there would be quite the thing, and a strong-willed mother taking care of it for her son would be the most efficient of *posadniki*. Vladimir had destroyed Rogvolod's Polotsk; he built Izyaslavl and he set Rogvolod's grandson to reign over it, under the supervision of Rogvolod's daughter, but for his, the Great Prince's, benefit: again Vladimir's signature, two birds with one stone.

In spite – or perhaps because – of his incontinent life, Vladimir thought much about death, and when he looked at all his women, the fair and the dark ones, the willing and the unwilling, the virgins and the mothers, he must have wondered which one of them would answer the fateful 'I' when his funeral was being prepared and his sons and boyars went and asked them: 'Who among you will die with him?' For, by the time he died, he hoped that all this Christian nonsense would have come to an end, and he would receive a glorious

140

old-fashioned funeral complete with the Russian suttee, which foreigners admired so much . . . For ten days he would lie in his grave, and during that time mead would flow freely, orgies would be held, the girl who loved him enough to die with him would sing and drink, getting with each day more and more intoxicated on honey and music. A ship would be hauled up on shore, and a birch scaffolding erected, on which the ship would be poised, the only proper coffin for a Viking. Underneath, wood would be stacked. On the ship, a couch covered with Greek brocade would be laid out by an old woman he knew, or by another one who would have taken her place: no matter, she would be an expert in such things, and they would appropriately call her the Angel of Death. Over the couch, a canopy would be suspended and draped with style. Then they would dig Vladimir out of his grave – it would be winter, he imagined, and his body would still be intact – and they would dress him in gorgeous clothes – furs and brocades – with golden buttons. They would carry him with respect to the couch on the ship, prop him up with embroidered cushions, give him his weapons, and lay fruit and plants at his feet, also bread, meat and onions. Then they would take his favourite dog, cut him to pieces, and put the pieces beside the fruit. They would do the same with his horse, and with several cows, and with cocks and hens, filling the ship with flesh and with blood, as if he had been Perun himself.

Meanwhile pavilions would have been built around the ship, each one belonging to one of his kinsmen – sons they would be, he hoped: old Dobrynya would have been long dead by that time, and Vladimir had no other relatives, but surely sons would not be lacking. The girl who loved him would then go from one pavilion to the other, and they would take her, each one in his turn, proclaiming after each sacred ravishment: 'Tell your lord Vladimir that I have done this for the love of him.' The next day, the girl would be taken to a wall, and the men would lift her above it for a short time, her feet placed in their palms. 'Behold!' she would cry. 'I see my father and mother.' They would lift her again and, ritually, she would cry: 'I see all my dead kin.' When, for a third time, she was raised above the wall: 'I see my lord seated in Paradise,' she would exclaim with passion in her voice. 'Paradise is green and beautiful. Vladimir's servants are around him. He calls me. Oh! take me to him.' So they would bring her to the ship where the old woman would be expecting her. The girl would take off her bracelets and rings and give them to her: 'Here, take these.' Now the men would surround her, coming closer and closer, holding shields and sticks in their hands. They would give her a last drink, and she would sing a last song, a long one perhaps, if she had begun to regret what she was doing: Vladimir had seen some of them, drunk as they were, quail at the last moment; fortunately the shields could be clashed together to cover the unseemly cries. But no! His woman would be in a hurry to join him. Here she is already, ascending the ship by walking on the upturned hands of the men. They hand her a hen, and she tears its head off and throws the body into the ship. As soon as she is on board, the warriors begin to strike their shields with their sticks, raising a rhythmical, deafening din. Six of Vladimir's sons jump on the ship, and there, under his closed eyes, on the couch bespattered with blood, they unite a last time with the girl to pay a last homage to him. As soon as they have staggered back, the old woman appears again. She lays the exhausted girl beside her beloved lord, seizes her

142

veil, loops it around her neck and holds out its end to two of the men who start twisting; two others hold the victim by the hands, two by the legs, and the Angel of Death herself plunges a broad-bladed dagger between her ribs, plunges it and pulls it out, and plunges it again and again and again . . . Then she leaves the ship, followed by the men.

Vladimir's closest kinsman – it would be his eldest son, Vysheslav – hiding his nakedness from behind with one hand, kindles the stacked wood. After him, all the people run up with torches that they have prepared and throw them into the wood. The flames rise. If Stribog is favourable, a strong wind blows, fanning the fire. Flamelets fly into the canopy, the pyre roars, the ship is engulfed in the conflagration, its planks crashing asunder, its ribs exposed. The roasting meat smokes and smells, everything is ablaze. Vladimir's immortal self, secure in the destruction of his familiar objects, so that no sorcerer can enslave him by bewitching them, accedes to an eternal Paradise, where he will be a great Prince and enjoy for ever the favours of his eternally beautiful companion. What a noble, virile, Viking way to end one's life![85]

CHAPTER FIVE

The Light on the Road

1 Situation

And then something happened. There was a ray of light on the road and all symbols were changed as in an algebraic equation.

Vladimir's conversion has been a stumbling block for most of his biographers. Those addicted to hagiography have seldom resisted the temptation to paint him blacker than the devil before that fateful event in order to make his subsequent whiteness even more dramatic. At the other extreme, well-meaning agnostics have raised doubts concerning his sincerity: according to them, he would have become a convert to Christianity exclusively for political reasons. Between these two, superficially shrewd customers are ready to believe in the conversion but not in the transformation in behaviour which followed, although what the one would have meant without the other remains obscure. In short, it seems necessary, before we go into Vladimir's conversion, to ask and try to answer a few questions about conversions in general.

That such phenomena exist or rather happen is not disputed even by atheistic psychologists, who interpret them as yet another aberration of the psyche. Conversion to Christianity was the main mode of recruitment used by that religion until the time when Christian education took over. For centuries numberless missionaries throughout the world have had no purpose but to convert members of other religions, and in

145

modern times some of the greater philosophers, raised in atheism, later became Christian converts. As a matter of fact, *con-version* is what Christianity at its beginning was all about: μετανοεῖτε, says John the Baptist to his followers (Mark I, 13, Matthew III, 2); μετανοεῖτε, says Jesus Christ himself to his (Matthew IV, 17), and μετανοεῖν means not only to repent, but also to change one's feelings, to turn in another direction. The latin verb *converto*, from which comes our own *to convert*, expresses the same idea of turning away and toward, just like ἐπιστρέγω, which it translates, and which is used seven times in the Gospels and twelve in the Acts – scarcely a coincidence at a period when numerology was a philosophy in itself. Historically, the Church owes its survival to Constantine's spectacular conversion under the ramparts of Rome, and if some are tempted to discard it as suspicious, there is little doubt that for its very existence the Church of the Gentiles is indebted to another famous conversion on the road to Damascus: a flash of light causing temporary blindness, a voice expressing mild reproach, and one of the fiercest persecutors of the new religion became its most effective champion.[86] In short, a conversion is not exactly – or not only – a miracle: many have been observed, and they brought about radical changes in the lives of those who experienced them.

From a Christian point of view, there exists a whole theology of conversion in which we need not delve in depth, especially as not all theologians agree on their findings, but some points of reference should be established here and now. There are, we are told, three main motives for conversion: the search for truth, the desire for moral perfection, or an emotion, often a collective one. There are gradual conversions and there are sudden ones; the first tend to be of the intellectual, the second of the emotional type. Theologians distinguish between the transitive and intransitive aspects of conversion. To simplify, what the convert does himself is intransitive, but what God does to the convert is transitive. St Thomas Aquinas, for instance, maintains that the initiative necessarily belongs to God and that man is only obliged to co-operate with him. As to the Council of Trent, it flatly declares anathema 'whoever would be of the opinion that a man without inspiration and previous help from the Holy Spirit might believe, hope and love or repent as he must to obtain the grace of justification'. But even in such a rigid framework there is some latitude for dispute as to what are the proportions of the transitive and intransitive aspects in conversion in general and in every conversion in particular. This is not as futile as it may sound to some: everybody grants that conversion is impossible without grace, but grace seldom strikes an unprepared subject, and who is responsible for the preparation: another grace or the subject himself? So, another distinction is made between internal grace, the one which allows for the preparation of the ground, and the external one, which affords the opportunity for the actual jump from the old state of mind into the new. For instance, in St Paul's case, at the very time when he was persecuting the Christians, some kind of work may have been going on in him through internal grace, but when suddenly the light shone and the voice spoke, he was conquered through external grace. Vladimir's spiritual adventure was, as we shall see, different: either internal grace or his own volition caused his intransitive quest for truth, which was finally rewarded by a transitive illumination, with records allowing some doubt as to external grace being present in any visible form.

Such, very briefly summarized, is the theologian's viewpoint. The historian, on the other hand, has to take a few other factors into consideration, and among them the fact that conversions generally go in batches: there are periods in history which seem to agree better than others with potential converts. Vladimir's interest in Christianity started in 986, and it definitely belongs to such a batch. Several tribes of Baltic Slavs had accepted the new religion between 942 and 968; prince Mieszko of Poland had been baptized in 966; King Harold of Denmark followed suit in 974; Olaf's conversion took place some time around 976, and Duke Geza of Hungary became a Christian in 985. This batch was the last one of a series that had lasted in Eastern Europe for a century: the Danube Bulgars had been christianized in the second part of the ninth century, while the Khazars were accepting Judaism, and just after, the Volga Bulgars had turned to Islam. Paganism, it seems, was no match for the expansion of monotheism, and, at the end of the tenth century, the only question was to which of its three varieties the last pagan nation in Eastern Europe, i.e. Russia, would adhere. Vladimir, as we know, made the choice, and an obvious question arises here: how much of a choice had he? Was it not inscribed in the nature of things that a Slavo-Viking state had to side with the West and not with the Orient? Even if Vladimir had tried to adopt Islam or Judaism, would it have worked, or was the rolling wave of progressive, white, Aryan Christianity so strong that Russia would have been overrun by it in spite of her Prince's will? This, we have to confess, could be argued both ways, but since, generally speaking, ifs make good arguments but not very good history, it seems more sensible to stay with facts, and the facts are simple: Vladimir did turn toward

Christianity and Christianity did fulfil his people's spiritual needs. A subsidiary fact is that Vladimir undoubtedly could have chosen the Roman form of Christianity, but that he chose the Greek one, and that his people followed him.

So much for generalities. Let us now turn to the circumstances of Vladimir's historical decision.

As we well know, he was not the first Christian of his race: his grandmother Olga had been baptized – whether in Kiev or in Constantinople is not essential here – and her new beliefs had brought great joy to her.[87] She had shocked her family by insisting on being buried according to Christian rites, and there is reason to believe that her example did play a more or less important part in Vladimir's decision. In fact, in the midst of his pagan counter-reform a doubt must have lurked in his mind: 'The wisest of all women would have disapproved of what I am doing.' But Olga's example was not the only one. Christianity was definitely present in Kiev in Vladimir's time; to what extent remains to be determined.

According to a tradition dating back to the third century and Eusebius of Caesarea, Russia was evangelized by St Andrew, the First-called of the Apostles of the Lord. 'Scythia fell to Andrew,' he says, and is upheld in this in the fourth century by Epiphanius of Cyprus. St Jerome writes: *Scythica frigora fervent calore fidei*, 'The frosts of Scythia are hot with faith.' Eucherius of Lyon (fifth century) mentions that 'Andrew mollified the Scythians with his word.' There is a Kievan legend to the same effect. According to it St Andrew blessed the hills of Kiev with these words: 'See ye these hills? So shall the favour of God shine upon them that on this spot a great city shall arise, and God shall erect many churches therein.' After leaving a cross to mark the sacred place, he travelled northward and was appalled at the way Novgorodians flogged themselves with birches in their steam baths – no doubt one more dig from the Kievan wags at their northern rivals. Nevertheless the tradition was taken seriously enough by the Russian Empire, whose highest decoration was the Order of St Andrew, created in 1698 by Peter the Great, and whose navy sailed under St Andrew's cross.

Another story associates Russia's early evangelization with a disciple of St Paul called Andronicus, and there is some possibility that Pope St Clement I, third successor of St Peter according to the Roman Catholic reckoning, was martyred in Cherson.

After that nothing is known of Christianity in Russia until, in 866, Patriarch Photius writes in his famous encyclical:

It was not only that people [Bulgarians] who rejected their old godlessness for the faith in Christ, but this was also done by a people mentioned and glorified by many. I mean the Russians, who, having conquered their neighbours, became arrogant and, thinking well of themselves, took up arms against the Roman Empire. Today they have themselves discarded their impious heathen superstition for the immaculate Christian faith and hold us in esteem and friendship, although only recently they harried us by raids and outrages.

This came six years after Askold's fleet had been scattered in the port of Constantinople by a storm (which Photius believed to be an answer to his prayers to the Holy Virgin,[88] and is contradicted by other evidence to such an extent that some historians think that Photius' eulogy should be applied not to Kievan Russians, but to another Viking settlement, probably in Tmutorakan. This seems a little far-fetched. It is more probable that some sudden conversions, spectacular but limited in number, fired the good Patriarch's optimism: wishful thinking is not unheard of in missionaries and their chiefs. Or maybe the holy storm struck the Russians' imagination and they appeared to have converted for a few days, before relapsing into their previous errors, as is indeed suggested in one of Vladimir's *Lives*. Approximately at the same time, a legend tells us, a Greek bishop converted some Russians by throwing his New Testament into a fire which refused to destroy it, and it has been argued that this was Michael, Bishop of Corcyra. Whether these Russians were from Kiev, Tmutorakan or some other place is unknown. In brief, evidence provided by the Byzantine writers Scylitzes and Cedrenus, by the *Nikon Chronicle* and by the anonymous *Life* of St Stephen of Surozh (in the Crimea) which recounts, in legendary terms, the conversion of the Russian Prince Bravlin (?), added to Photius' testimony, seems to indicate that some Russians had become Christians in the second half of the ninth century, no more than that: they certainly were not as numerous and influential as some historians would like to believe.[89]

Fortunately *The Chronicle* throws some light on the matter by reproducing the texts of different treaties signed by Greeks and Russians during the tenth century. The present consensus of historians is that these texts are authentic. The interesting point is that, whereas the Greeks always swear to observe the treaties by the Gospel or the Holy Trinity, there is an evolution in the terms of the Russian oaths. In 907, under Oleg, the Russians swore by their weapons (which bound the Vikings) and by Perun and Volos (which bound the Slavs). In 911, still under Oleg, they swore 'according to their religion', and they seem to have had only one, paganism. In 944, under Igor, things had changed. At the beginning of the treaty horrendous maledictions are invoked upon the heads of those Russians who might transgress it: 'As many of them as have been baptized from the land of Russia, may they be punished by God All-powerful and condemned to perish in the next world; and as many of them as have not been baptized, may neither God nor Perun help them, may their shields not protect them, may their own swords and arrows and other weapons cut them to pieces and may they become slaves in this world and the next.' Later it is stated that 'our Christians from Russia swear according to their faith, and the non-Christians according to their religion', and the text ends with some more information as to how these oaths were taken: non-Christians would put their naked swords, shields and other weapons on the ground, before the statue of Perun, and Christians would swear by the church of St Elias, which stood in Kiev, not far from the Prince's palace.[90] In 971, things had changed again, and Svyatoslav swore friendship with the Greeks in clearly defiant tones: 'by the god [sic] in whom we believe: Perun and Volos, god of cattle'. No mention of any Christian oath was made, although Olga's trip to Constantinople (957) had already taken place and we know that Svyatoslav had at least some Christians in his retinue.

What is to be deduced from these elements? That there was a Christian party in Kiev, and that it had its ups and its downs; that at times it was powerful enough to be officially recognized by an un-Christian Prince; that it possessed a church dedicated to a prophet traditionally associated – just like Perun – with thunder, and that we have no earthly way of knowing how numerous that party was. *The Chronicle* mentions incidentally that there were 'many' Christians among the Vikings, which may be a way of saying that there were none or few among the Slavs, as should be expected, since the Vikings were the mobile, progressive part of the population. The word 'many' is obviously ambiguous: a strong minority – maybe 25 per cent – seems like a reasonable assumption; if they had been more than 50 per cent *The Chronicle* would rather have said that there were still many pagans among a predominantly Christian retinue. That is all, and there is no point in milking the sources for more than they can produce.

So far so good, there were some Christians among the Russians, mainly among the Vikings, rather than the Slavs. But where did their Christianity come from?

A small part of it, in a more or less indirect manner, may have come from Rome, as a few religious Russian words of Latin origin seem to attest; a larger part came from Constantinople, where the Vikings were frequent visitors, on warlike or commercial missions; a fair amount must have come from Bulgaria. There are even some historians who have tried to prove that all Russia's Christianity, including Vladimir's brand, was of Bulgarian origin.[91] Without stretching the facts so far, some points should be recognized. Bulgaria had been evangelized (in the 860s) by one of the greatest missionaries of all times, St Cyril of Thessalonica, otherwise known as Constantine, in all probability the inventor of the cyrillic alphabet, and by his brother Methodius. This is not the place to study Cyril's mission, but one of his strokes of genius must be mentioned. Whereas Western nations had to wait for Luther and the Renaissance to have access to the Bible in their own languages, Cyril, in spite of some Greek opposition, translated it into a vehicular language based on a Macedonian dialect which could be understood by all Slavic tribes, and not only has it remained to this day the official language of their churches, but it has also provided patterns, structures, discipline and vocabulary for the evolution of their respective secular tongues. 'I had rather speak five words with my understanding, that I might teach others also, than ten thousand words in an unknown language,' said St Cyril in St Paul's spirit, and wrote the following poem:

> Now with your understanding hear,
> Thus hear, you Slavs,
> The Word which feeds the soul of man,
> The Word which strengthens heart and mind,
> The Word prepared to fathom God.

Constantine's work, executed in the best practice of Orthodoxy, was appreciated by the converted Barbarians, and Metropolitan Hilarion summarized their feelings when he stated that 'new faiths demand new tongues, just as new wine requires new skins'. So, linguistically speaking, the ground was broken, and the Word was definitely coming from Bulgaria, in a language which was familiar both to Slavs and Vikings, the latter, as already seen, being quite prone to adopt local tongues. In addition to this linguistic aspect, the collapse of the first Bulgarian Empire (972) may have had some influence on the subsequent events, the exodus of Bulgarian priests to Kiev[92] lending support to the Christian party, which seems to have flourished moderately under Yaropolk and to have been cut down to size by Vladimir upon his accession to the throne.

Thus, according to our scanty information, was the stage set. Now, for the main character.

We have seen Vladimir fiercely attached to the old

heathen gods. That makes sense. Many a saint, beginning with St Paul, was violently anti-Christian before
his or her conversion, as if to illustrate St John's reference to God's disgust with the lukewarm (Revelation III,
16). We also have seen Vladimir as a frantic lecher and a
grim warrior. That again is not unusual. Even without
referring to Jesus' apparent partiality for courtesans and
centurions, it is quite clear from the history of the
Church that starting with a fiery temperament is not, in
spiritual matters, a handicap. And a closer look will
show us that a new mood was coming over the twenty-
five-year-old Prince. Between 981 and 985 he led at least
one campaign a year, and then, suddenly, until 992, not a
skirmish (with the exception of the very special Cherson
expedition). Yet there was no scarcity of enemies
around, and if Vladimir had wanted to pick a fight, he
would have had no trouble finding an opponent. Richly
endowed natures, however, tend to dispose of one interest fast and then turn to another. Concerning his private
life we have one parallel indicator: no new marriages are
mentioned for the period directly preceding the conversion. One might be accused of fancifulness if one
asserted that Vladimir had been looking for something
in women that they could not give him and that at last he
realized he ought to look elsewhere, but surely everyone
will agree that a harem of several hundred must have
produced in the long run an impression of monotony, if
not the humbling effect of sheer exhaustion.

So what we have before us is a twenty-five-year-old
Prince – but let not his age fool us: at twenty-five he has
drunk more fully from the cup of life than many a
modern adolescent of forty – replete with success and
beginning to suspect that the activities in which he has
spent his energies so far have yielded so many free satis-

factions that there must be something superficial in them: sex, war and paganism have proved to be gratifying as far as they go, but life could not be so childishly straightforward; there must be something beyond the endless repetition of the same violent pleasures and rites. Vladimir's metaphysical mind is groping for deeper truths than those on which he has thriven so far. It is not that he is, like some romantic petty bourgeois, dissatisfied with his lot; on the contrary, he has used his lot to the bone, and now the whole world appears empty to him because he has outgrown his own. There would really be nothing strange if the young Barbarian should turn to another, richer civilization to try and compensate for the poverty of his.

But here another point appears, and it would be a serious mistake to underrate it. It is difficult for us, having been raised in the gentle Christian tradition, to realize under what drab, squalid colours it must have appeared to pagans, and especially to warlike pagans like the Vikings. They found the doctrine hideous, disgraceful, unworthy of the lowest of men. Theirs was a culture entirely built on values like pride, courage, violence, what it is now fashionable to call machismo. But there is no machismo in Christianity, quite the opposite. If, to quote St Paul, a crucified God was 'unto the Jews a stumbling block and unto the Greeks foolishness', unto the Vikings it was ignominy. True, Christians did not always behave meekly – and this, some might argue, is precisely what saved Christianity, since it is doubtful whether it would have survived without the help of sword and stake; worshipping the Lamb did not prevent the Greeks, for instance, from being very effective wolves at times; basically however, and whatever useful exceptions can be found to the rule,

Christianity is a religion of forgiveness and humility, the two most contemptible words in a proud man's vocabulary. The trauma of breaking away from a world founded on manly virtues was shattering. To become a Christian was simply to lose one's self-respect. Moreover, who wants to be a traitor, even for the sake of truth? 'Adore what you used to burn, burn what you used to adore,' said St Remy to Clodovicus the Frank when he baptized him, and there undoubtedly is something shocking in that crude but apt formula. A convert is, among other things, a turncoat, and, if he repudiates a code of valiance to replace it with a doctrine of submission, he must appear a coward into the bargain. Therefore, whatever hesitations Vladimir may have had at several points in his conversion, they are easily accounted for, especially since what was hard for an individual must have been immeasurably harder for a prince whose ideal and *raison d'être* could only be might and glory, before Christianity attempted to replace them with paternal justice.

In a beautiful poem, not always historically accurate but full of profound and humorous insights into the psychology of his hero, Aleksey Tolstoy puts the following words into Vladimir's mouth:

> Aye, I want to be humble, but not to lose face.

This definitely was one of Vladimir's preoccupations even after he had bowed before the truth of Christianity. And to bring him to that dramatic point, in spite of the psychological obstacle we have just examined, something more than boredom, disappointment or political convenience must have been needed. In theological terms, this was internal grace ensuring the transitive aspect of Vladimir's conversion. The intransitive one was expressed not only by a certain lull in his activities, but also, paradoxical as this may seem, by his passionate attachment to paganism, his building of pantheons, his human sacrifices, his deep, unswerving conviction that the riddle of life has an answer, and that this answer can be found in religion and nowhere else.

2 Quest

Concerning the actual fact of Vladimir's conversion, we possess for once a variety of sources, somewhat contradictory but mostly complementary. The matter is of importance, and a comparative study seems indispensable.

Jacob the Monk, to begin with him, attributes the event to Olga's example, and goes on to express in a somewhat muddled way the convergent effects of internal and external grace: 'His heart having been influenced by the Holy Spirit, he desired holy baptism. As God saw the desire of his heart and espied his goodness, God, the Father, the Son and the Holy Spirit, sent from heaven his mercy on Prince Vladimir, He who probes hearts and bosoms, God the righteous, who knows everything beforehand, enlightened the heart of the Prince of the Russian land, Vladimir, so that he received holy baptism.' In other words: 1 – internal grace, 2 – Vladimir's desire and moral qualities, 3 – external grace, 4 – baptism.

The author of the *Life of Boris and Gleb*, Vladimir's two martyred sons, traditionally known as 'Nestor', expresses himself as follows: 'There was in those times,' he writes, 'a prince by the name of Vladimir who ruled over the whole Russian land. He was a righteous man, and merciful toward the poor and orphans and widows [this testimony is essential: whereas *The Chronicle* and the *Lives* have been accused of distorting Vladimir's portrait before his baptism, 'Nestor' recognizes moral qualities in him at all times], but [this 'but' is a whole piece of history – and metaphysics – in itself], *but* a pagan by faith. God sent upon him a certain hindrance and made him become a Christian, like Plakida in ancient times.' The hindrance remains unspecified, but the reference is to a 'righteous and merciful man, *only* a pagan by faith' to whom Jesus Christ appeared during a hunt in the guise of a deer. Plakida fell on his knees and said: 'Lord, who art Thou and what dost Thou command me, Thy slave?' The answer was: 'I am Jesus Christ, whom unknowingly you adore. Go and be baptized.' Which Plakida did, with his wife and children, before eventually becoming a saint under the Christian name of Eustace (second century). The passage ends with the words, 'And with this Vladimir also God's apparition did that he became a Christian.' Hindrance, apparition . . . According to 'Nestor' there seems to have been a definite incident when God's external grace was made manifest, so that the sequence of events is as follows: 1 – Vladimir's moral qualities, 2 – external grace, 3 – baptism.

The *Prologue Life* is even less explicit but points in the same direction. God, it says, 'breathed the grace of the Holy Spirit' into Svyatoslav's son. He, who had at first 'followed his father's custom and shown much veneration for idols', 'was awakened from sleep' and, 'having inquired into all nations' religions', discovered 'the holy Greek faith as a candle in a candlestick': 1 – grace, 2 – quest, 3 – illumination, 4 – baptism.

Metropolitan Hilarion adopts a different attitude. Whereas the others stated Vladimir's desire and God's intervention as plain facts, he marvels at them in a moving passage of his *Discourse on Law and Grace*. Curiously enough, it is he who insists least on the action of the Holy Spirit and emphasizes most Vladimir's personal merit.

How didst thou believe? [he exclaims] How wast thou kindled with Christ's love? How didst thou enter a wisdom, higher than the wisdom of earthly sages, a wisdom which consists in loving the invisible and concerning oneself with heavenly things? How didst thou begin to love Christ? How didst thou thyself go up to him? Tell us, who are thy servants, tell us, O thou our teacher, whence thou didst inhale the fragrance of the Holy Spirit, whence thou didst drink the sweet cup of remembrance of a future life, whence thou didst conceive and perceive how good the Lord is? Thou hadst not seen Christ, hadst not followed in his footsteps: how didst thou find thyself his disciple, and, not having seen him, how didst thou believe in him? Verily did the blessing of the Lord Jesus spoken to Thomas – Blessed are they that have not seen and yet have believed [John XX, 29] – come true with thee. Therefore we dare confidently call thee blessed, since the Saviour himself called thee so; blessed art thou for thou didst believe in him and wast not offended in him, as he truthfully said: blessed is he whosoever shall not be offended in me [Matthew XI, 6]: those who knew the law and the prophets crucified him, and thou, who hadst read neither law nor prophets, didst pay homage to the crucified. How did thy heart burst open? How did the fear of God penetrate thee? How didst thou cleave to his love? Not having seen an apostle come into thy land and by his poverty and nakedness and hunger and thirst incline thy heart to humility; not having seen devils being cast out by the name of Christ, the sick in good health, fire transformed into cold, the dead rising, not having seen all these things, how didst thou then believe? O amazing miracle! Other kings and rulers who had seen all this happen at the hands of holy men did not believe and only inflicted more passion and tortures upon them. But thou, O blessed one, without any of these didst run to Christ, only through good thinking and intelligence, having understood that God is the only creator of visible and invisible, heavenly and earthly things, and that he has sent his beloved Son into the world as its salvation. With these thoughts thou didst enter the holy font . . .

Some scanty information can be gleaned from this admirable address: first, there were no inspiring missionaries in Kiev; second, Vladimir's intelligence brought him to Christianity. Some more is provided by another passage of the same *Discourse*. After a few laudatory remarks about Vladimir's parentage, personality and rule, which was both firm and peaceful, Hilarion adds that 'having lived in his time and tended his land with truth, courage and sense, he was visited by the Highest; the All-merciful eye of the God of goodness took notice of him and wisdom shone in his heart so that he understood the vanity of idolatrous fraud and began to search for the only God who created all creation, visible and invisible'. This would give the following sequence: 1 – Vladimir's moral qualities, 2 – grace, apparently internal, 3 – disillusionment with paganism, 4 – quest, and to add from the preceding passage, 5 – becoming kindled with Christ's love.

Before going on to other sources let us summarize the results obtained so far. All four biographers recognize the transitive aspect of Vladimir's conversion; one indicates clearly that external grace was used in the form of a 'hindrance'; another hints at some direct enlightenment; two mention a quest for the true religion. The motivations suggested are: Olga's example; Vladimir's moral qualities; his intellectual capacities; his disenchantment with paganism. The conversion seems to have been of the gradual, intellectual type, but at some point 'an illumination' happened, which 'kindled' the love of Christ. To these considerations modern historians have added, besides possible political designs, the influence of some of Vladimir's Christian wives, of whom one, according to *The Chronicle*, was a Greek, one a Bulgarian and two Czechs.

Supplementary, obviously unverifiable, information is provided by one of the Icelandic sagas. Olaf Tryggvison, whom we last saw leaving for Vinnland in rather bad humour,[93] lost his Polish wife, resumed his travels and decided to visit the friend and patron of his youth. The event is undated, but it could just as well have happened around 985 as at any other time – if indeed it did happen. Vladimir's hospitality was, as usual, boundless, and Olaf spent the winter in Kiev with his retinue. He was already a Christian, but had not yet been baptized. A vision sent him to Constantinople, where he was to receive Christian instruction as well as holy baptism. This having been duly taken care of, he immediately began sharing his newly confirmed faith with voluntary and involuntary candidates. His zeal for propaganda was such that in later days he was to send the following message to Jarl Sigurd in the Orkneys: 'Get baptized directly or I shall kill your son whom I hold hostage.' In his own Norway, he was to show even more energy, albeit not without humour. On finding the Trondhjem aristocracy opposed to his programme of christianization, he announced to them that he was quite willing to return to pagan ways and would start by sacrificing to the gods not vulgar slaves or criminals, but eleven local chieftains among the noblest. That was the end of the Trondhjem opposition. He then proceeded to Moere where his reputation had preceded him and the

Christian faith was received with instantaneous enthusiasm. Fortunately – mainly for him – he did not attempt anything so drastic with Vladimir, but, having returned to Kiev as the forerunner of an otherwise unknown Bishop Paul, he was content with preaching not so much *pro* as *contra*: 'I hope, my liege,' he would say, 'that through your wisdom you will learn to believe in one true God, the creator, who made heaven and earth and all things visible and invisible, rather than wander in such darkness as to believe in false idols who can be of no help to anyone, especially as they cannot move unless people carry or pull them, as I used to remark to you when I yet had no real notion of God.' At first he was utterly unsuccessful with the Prince, but his wife *erat facilior* (which wife? Maybe Olava, who already had patronized the handsome Olaf in Novgorod?) and according to some versions Vladimir's mother prophesied that Olaf's undertaking would finally meet with success. This would imply that Malusha had followed her son to Kiev: what a triumph it must have been for her! The arrival of 'Bishop Paul' from Constantinople clinched matters and the Russian *Konung* and his people were happily baptized.

This of course is nothing but a legend, but the presence of a Greek emissary at Vladimir's court is interesting because it confirms *The Chronicle*, and there is nothing impossible in Olaf's exercising some influence on his friend's mind, if only by his persistent affirmation that the wooden gods were no good and that a more real God had to be sought elsewhere. As a matter of fact, this source, doubtful as it is, is the only one to throw some light on the negative aspect of Vladimir's conversion, i.e. on his abandoning beliefs to which he had been so passionately attached. Can it be that, among other arguments, Olaf used the unsuccessful 985 campaign against the Volga Bulgars to demonstrate the idols' ineptitude?

The bulk of the information we possess concerning other aspects of the event is provided, as usual, by *The Chronicle*. Curiously enough it picks up the tale *in medias res*, with emissaries from different churches and countries flocking to Kiev in 986.[94] Had Vladimir invited them to a series of religious seminars? Had they used their sixth sense, the missionary one, and perceived that here was a brilliant young prince whose land was large and prosperous, and whose pagan faith had begun to waver? *The Chronicle* does not say, but it is not necessarily a coincidence that the first ones to call were sent by the Moslem Volga Bulgars. Better than anyone else, they knew that for once Vladimir had no reason to be particularly pleased with his own gods, and they may have hastened to take advantage of this opportunity, or he may have desired to know what kind of religion ensured such opulence – and such beautiful boots. Anyway they came with their turbans and full eastern attire, and he sat back in his armchair in the banqueting hall and inquired what they had to say.

They knew all the salaams: they bowed and they touched their foreheads and their chests, and they began their speech with elaborate flattery about Vladimir's wisdom and good sense. He listened. He was not to be taken in so easily. He sensed they had come to the point when they respectfully added that he really did not know much about religion and would be better off adopting theirs. He asked tersely: 'What is it?' He had always had an interest in religions, and as a pagan he had no objection to foreign gods. He would have been happy to recruit a few more for his pantheon if they were to prove useful. But the Moslems stated that they believed in Allah: one God over the whole world. Henotheism was implicitly contained in Slavic paganism, and Vladimir must have felt that radical monotheism is philosophically more tenable; it did not really contradict what he knew already – that there was one god, Svarog, who was above the others – it merely deepened his knowledge; it rang more like the truth.

So he suggested that they proceed, and they explained that they revered Mahomet, which again made sense: if there is to be a revelation, there has to be a revelator. Vladimir became more and more interested and took a whole course in Islam. Some things pleased him, such as polygamy and immortality in one's own rank: it confirmed what he already believed. A curious point was made here by the Bulgars: 'After we die,' they said, 'Mahomet gives each of us seventy beautiful women; he chooses the most beautiful of the seventy and transfers on to her the beauty of all the others; she then becomes our wife.' The symbolism is clear, and although the chronicler missed it completely, it may be that Vladimir dimly discerned the meaning of this myth about the Only Love which is more beautiful than all the others and whose beauty it mystically shares. Between that one woman, who was as beautiful as the seventy put together, and the pagan girl who chose to die with her beloved, there was a mysterious resemblance, and it began to look as if there was some meaning after all in that search Vladimir had so frantically pursued among his hundreds of lovers . . . He may at this time have had an inkling of Goethe's *Das Ewigweibliche zieht uns hinan*. One is unavoidably reminded of the curious passage in the Public Library manuscript quoted by Shakhmatov, which, without any mention of Islam, reads thus: 'Vladimir committed many acts of lechery, and finally he was attracted by a wife and finally found the grace of God.'

But other tenets of Mahomet's law displeased the Great Prince. Restrictions on pork seemed ludicrous; circumcision frankly disgusting; as to teetotalism, it was out of the question: Vladimir would listen no further. It probably happened when, hospitable as ever, he offered the muftis a drink; they refused and explained why. Then he pronounced his famous and jolly 'For Russians drinking is their joy; we cannot be without it.' The Bulgars left in high dudgeon, and if one were to subscribe to Pascal's individualistic concept[95] of history, one would have to say that if the Ottoman Empire did not annex Europe five centuries later, it is because a Russian prince was a little too fond of his cup of mead.

Knowing Vladimir's crafty mind, there is of course a temptation to think that the carnal response was but an only too credible pretext. Either his negotiations with the Moslem King of Khwarezm about his joining Islam were not proceeding satisfactorily; or he felt that such a meticulous religion would not be practical in Slavic terrain; or even – if he had already had a private revelation of Greek Christianity – he was just making a good show of investigating all possible religions, so as to lead his people into a readier acceptance of it. Attractive as this last hypothesis may be, there is nothing to confirm it, and it is much more likely that Vladimir was conducting his search in all objectivity and that his reaction was sincere. Whatever the case, this was not yet the end of the Moslem proposition, as will be seen later on.

Next to appear on the stage were Germans representing the Roman flank of Christianity. They may have been, as *The Chronicle* has it, emissaries of the Pope; they may have come on their own initiative. Russia was a choice morsel and it seems there was some kind of a contest between missionaries as to whose prize she would be. It is not surprising that the Germans, who had so witlessly missed the boat in 959, were anxious to repair that mistake.[96] All went well so long as they explained their beliefs: 'Our faith is light; we adore God who created heaven and earth, the stars, the moon [for some reason the sun is missing, a copyist's negligence probably] and everything that breathes', but once again no agreement was reached as to the way of life recommended by the priests of Rome. *The Chronicle*'s text is biased[97] and anyway corrupt, but it would seem that Vladimir objected either to Western Christian fasting habits or else to oily manners. Be that as it may, the holy visitors packed and departed.

Now it was the turn of the Jewish Khazars to come and plead their cause, which they did with a great show of superiority: 'The Christians,' they contemptuously remarked, 'believe in him whom we crucified.' In our time of Judeo-Christian ecumenism, it is hard to realize that for centuries the blood of the carpenter from Nazareth separated the Christians and the Jews more than any other two sects: it was not only the Christians who could not forget who had immolated their God to the acclamations of the populace, it was also the Jews who despised the Christians for adoring a common criminal who had perished at the hands of justice. Once again monotheism agreed with Vladimir, and if he was not obliged to worship someone who had let himself be nailed to a cross without putting up a fight, so much the better. So he directly inquired into the commandments of the Jewish faith. This is very like him, for he was a practical man and wanted to know if he could live with his beliefs to be. The rabbis mentioned pork and hare as

167

forbidden (he frowned), circumcision as necessary (he scowled) and observing the Sabbath (he relaxed). 'And what,' he asked, 'is your native land?'[98] They answered: 'Jerusalem'. He went on with his cross-examination, and the very form of the next question – if it is the least bit authentic – suggests that he knew the answer (but then, of course, the chronicler did, and he must have rewritten the dialogue): 'Is your homeland still there?' They looked at each other, fumbled with their shaggy beards and confessed that God had grown angry with their forefathers, scattered his People throughout the world for their sins and surrendered their land to the Gentiles. If Vladimir could not do without a drink and a hearty meal, he certainly would not risk losing his land. The retort flew at the honest rabbis as from a well stretched bow: 'How dare you teach others, when you yourselves are rejected by God?' And the irate Prince added: 'If God loved you and your faith, you would not be scattered through many lands. Or do you want the same to happen to us?' *Exeunt* the rabbis. Enter the Greeks.

If *The Chronicle* presents the events in the order in which they happened, and if they were not engineered by Vladimir to happen in that order (which, on the whole, is not likely), it is worth noting that the Greeks, who won the contest, were, in the best tradition, the last to arrive. Olaf's saga mentions a Bishop Paul, *The Chronicle* quotes at length a nameless 'Philosopher' – which, a century earlier, was Constantine-Cyril's nickname – whom later chronicles call Constantine or Kyros, and, as we shall see, the Greeks did dispatch to Vladimir a nameless envoy entrusted with a secret diplomatic mission (although not before 987). Are all three the same? Or is 'Paul' an imaginary figure and are the other two different men, as the timing seems to indicate?

This last hypothesis seems the most likely one, and we shall be content to call 'Philosopher' the man who evangelized Vladimir, even if he was also a bishop *in partibus* and maybe something of a confidential negotiator.

The Philosopher then, as missionaries sometimes will, began by discrediting his colleagues and competitors. First he had a go at the Bulgars, and what he had to tell about them brings an unexpected confirmation of the authenticity of the quest. Quite undeservedly, one assumes, the Bulgars had, during the Middle Ages, a worse than ambiguous reputation. From the word *Bulgar* comes the French *bougre* (a homosexual) – this could of course be ascribed to French xenophobia, but there is no doubt that the Bogomils sprang from Bulgaria and that some of them indulged in strange excesses. There definitely was a connection between them and the French Cathars; there also was one between the Cathars and different gnostic movements of the first centuries; some of these gnostic groups, whatever their philosophic and even religious virtues, strove to attain the highest aims through the strangest means, including, in particularly esoteric circles, the consumption of sperm. Now this is precisely what the Philosopher intimated the Bulgars did, among other abominations including coprophagy. It may be, of course, that the Philosopher was just ascribing to the Bulgars – the Volga Bulgars at that – the nastiest traits that crossed his mind, but the coincidence is at least worth noting, especially since there is a Moslem form of gnosticism which might have lent itself to calumny of this sort. Anyway the objective was reached, for, on hearing the loathsome imputations, Vladimir 'spat on the ground and said: How disgusting!'

Having thus slyly disposed of Islam, the Philosopher,

who made a point of showing he was well informed, mentioned that the Germans' visit had not escaped his notice. He had nothing so interesting to impart about them – after all they also were Christians, rivals rather than adversaries; even the schism would not be consummated for another sixty-eight years – but he criticized their way of administering Holy Communion, in the shape of hosts rather than bread. The technical aspect of the question did not interest Vladimir too much, and he changed the subject to the Jews, who 'had stated that the Germans and the Greeks believed in one whom they had crucified'. If the remark was a trap, the sleek Greek did not fall into it: neither did he deny the fact, nor did he attempt to explain humility, kenosis, non-resistance to evil and the like, which the Viking Prince would scarcely have understood at this stage. Instead he replied in quite earthly terms:

Yes, we believe in him, for some prophets have foretold that God would be born, others that he would be crucified and buried, that he would arise on the third day and ascend into heaven; but they beat those prophets to death and others they sawed with saws; when the prophecies were fulfilled, God came down to earth, was crucified, and after his resurrection, he ascended into heaven. There he awaited their repentance for forty-six years, but, as they did not repent, he set upon them the Romans, who destroyed their cities and scattered them into different lands where they still live in servitude.

The story made sense to Vladimir, with one exception, the obvious one: 'But why', he asked 'did God come down upon earth and endure such passion?' The Philosopher offered to explain everything from the beginning. And Vladimir, already under the charm, settled down more comfortably in his armchair and said: 'I would be glad to hear it.'

The scene may be entirely apocryphal. In that case, the chronicler, who sometimes hides his talent exceedingly well, suddenly unleashes it here, for nothing could be more probable and to the point than its whole unfurling and in particular the questions Vladimir is supposed to have asked. Not that he necessarily asked those very questions in those very words, but his trend of thought is so remarkably true to life and, so to speak, in character.

The first question the Philosopher answers by summarizing the whole of the Old Testament. After that Vladimir asks two more, and they show good sense and a critical mind. Having understood the fundamental paradox of Christianity, Vladimir addresses himself, with a Viking's fondness for prophecies, to the question of their fulfilment: 'Has all this happened or is it yet to occur?' Whereupon the long-winded Philosopher recites the New Testament, and Vladimir, impressed by the inner cohesion of the Christian *Weltanschauung*, tries to get a still clearer picture of it. He has grasped that everything is in the symbols and he asks: 'Wherefore was he born of woman, and crucified on wood, and baptized with water?' The Philosopher then discloses the mystical imagery of the *apokatastasis*: Jesus Christ was born of woman to compensate for the first woman's sin; he suffered pain on the tree so that the righteous might taste of the tree of life; as to water, it is the primary element, it was used to destroy a sinful mankind in the time of Noah and now will be used to wash its sins away; besides, the Spirit of God hovers 'over the face of the waters; thus men are now baptized with water and the Spirit'.

There is a sharp contrast in *The Chronicle* between the Orthodox disquisition on the redemption of man, and the petty limitations and restrictions exposed by the representatives of other religions. It may be that the Philosopher was a better orator than his competitors, or that the chronicler, knowing the result, gave him better lines, but the fact is that his speech does create an impression of plenitude and depth. After all, theology *is* above all Greek, and there is in the Eastern Church a traditional emphasis laid on the spiritual, rather than the moral, aspect of Christianity. It is significant that the Philosopher does not even mention the ascetic aspect of Orthodoxy and the demands of a Christian way of life: for him faith comes first, the rest will follow. But he does not hesitate to apply the great medieval argument, retribution, which is his *coup de grâce*. To conclude his speech, he dramatically displays a canvas on which is depicted the Last Judgement, and, with his finger, he points out the righteous on the right, marching joyfully toward Paradise, and the sinners on the left slinking away to hell.[99]

Crude as the image may seem to us, it was undoubtedly an improvement on the pagan concept according to which everything would go on in the next world as it did in this one, and Vladimir was impressed. Was it at this moment, while he was peering askance at the frightening canvas, that he met his 'hindrance', that he saw his 'apparition', in other words that external grace struck him, as some would like us to believe? It does not seem so. He had always wanted to stay on the right side of his gods, whoever they were. He sighed, says the chronicler, and thoughtfully commented: 'It is well for those on the right, but woe to those on the left.' The Philosopher thought he had won; he tried to press the advantage: 'If you want to stand on the right with the righteous, be baptized!' he exclaimed in his missionary zeal.

But the Great Prince shook his head. He had made a

mental note of everything he had heard and seen, but his was not a trustful nature, and he would not be taken in so easily. Besides, he needed more information. At this point he saw Greek Christianity as a possibility, perhaps as a probability, that was all. 'I shall wait just a little more,' he said,[100] and rose. The audience was at an end. The Philosopher received generous gifts, all kinds of honours, and was courteously asked to leave Kiev. The search for a new faith was only beginning.

3 Investigation

It was already 987 when Vladimir called a meeting of the Outer Council, boyars and elected city elders together, to study the matter. He reported to them on his conferences with the religious representatives of the Volga Bulgars, the Germans, the Khazars and the Greeks, all Russia's neighbours. The Danube Bulgars were not represented because they believed like the Greeks; the Poles, because they believed like the Germans. The Greeks, Vladimir observed, criticized all other faiths and commended their own. Their envoy knew the history of the whole world from the very beginning and told it at length. He was an eloquent fellow and it was delightful to listen to him – which did not prove him right, the Great Prince implied. The Greeks believed in an eternal life, but only for those who had adopted their faith: all others would be consumed by fire in the next world.[101] According to the Viking tradition, the Prince was the religious leader of his people, responsible, so to speak, for their salvation, and it was his duty to present the facts for the council's consideration.

The response was full of sagacity and wariness: 'Prince,' they said, 'you know that no man condemns his own possessions.' But it was also surprisingly objective. The matter, they felt, deserved deeper investigation. It would be a good idea to send Russians abroad to get inside information about different religions rather than to be guided by hearsay. How sensible! How wise! How well some of our contemporaries would do to imitate the Russian boyars and to verify how foreign ideologies work abroad before blindly adopting them! Seldom has such openness allied with such circumspection. And how brilliantly the result justified that alliance!

By that time the cat was out of the bag and the common people knew about Vladimir's endeavours to find the right faith. They concurred with the council, and as Vladimir also liked to be informed, it was in full accord with his people that he created an *ad hoc* committee, made up of four[102] good men and true, presumably respected but somewhat sceptical pagans.[103] Their duty it would be to go and check the foreigners' propaganda. Quite a civilized and thorough way of doing things.

The Khazar Jews had eliminated themselves at the first hearing and were excluded from the inspection tour, but the Germans and the Bulgars were not, and it is quite characteristic of Vladimir that, although he was obviously inclined to believe the Greeks, he still did not take their allegations on trust. And it appears that, on second thoughts, if Islam were proved right, he was prepared to consider giving up mead.

It was quite a trip through plains and forests, east to Bulgar, back to Kiev, west to Germany, south to Constantinople and then back to Kiev again. The journey took at least several months, and one would like to know what the travellers talked about on the road, what souvenirs they brought to their wives and children. To Vladimir they brought a unanimous and conclusive report. The Moslem cult as practised by the Bulgars they did not like, partly because the rite was not explained to them, partly because they saw *no joy* among the faithful – again, Olga's theme: joy – partly because the mosques stank a trifle too much. That was that. In Germany they were treated as tourists, and although they viewed many Western ceremonies, they were disconcerted by the coldness of Romanesque churches, by the restraint of Gregorian chanting. 'We saw no beauty there,' they said, which was, doubtless, unfair, but not, as some might think, irrelevant. Joy and beauty should accompany God's worship, because it should mirror his own beauty and joy: anything less can be interpreted as misleading and even insulting. The committee's touchstone, however clumsily used, was in itself perfectly valid: they discarded the Western variety of Christianity because they had been bored in German churches, which is, in a deep sense, not at all a frivolous but on the contrary a respectable reason: churches were not invented to be bored in. What an idea of the Kingdom it gives! And that, again, was that.

Now for Greeks. No doubt the committee's impartiality was slightly dulled by the reception they got in Constantinople. The Emperors Basil and Constantine did not repeat the mistake of their predecessor who had managed to hurt Olga's feelings.[104] On the contrary, as soon as the Russians had arrived, Basil received them in the Sacred Palace, inquired about their business, rejoiced at hearing their news, showered them with gifts and attentions. The next day the Patriarch, Nicholas II Khrisobergos, received a message from the Basileus, instructing him in the way the Russians should be treated. The Patriarch himself was no fool: he knew his business and his interest. Everything was assembled

to impress the Barbarians with the heady beauty of the
Greek liturgy. The magnitude of Hagia Sophia – whose
architecture is a treatise on theology and which had
already stood there for nearly five centuries, i.e. twenty
generations – the magnificence of the pontifical service –
the Patriarch officiated in person – the splendour of the
holy vessels, the shimmering vestments, the golden,
jewelled mitres and crosiers, the hovering of the
deacons, all that glimpsed through perfumed mists of
incense while alternate choirs thundered ethereal music
from invisible galleries, how could the unsophisticated
Kievans have resisted such a heavenly conspiracy? Place
was made for them in the middle of the church, explanations provided, every mark of respect shown. It was a
seduction scene and it worked.

But not all seductions are meaningless. The sentence
which the envoys used to describe their impression
when they were explaining to Vladimir what had happened to them – and which is, by the way, quite a cliché
of Greek religious folklore – was an apt summary of
what Orthodox liturgy is all about: 'We knew not,' they
said, 'whether we were in heaven or on earth.' That was
precisely the point and they had got it. The concept may
appear bizarre and, who knows, even blasphemous to a
puritanical mind, but it is the very heart of Orthodoxy,
in which the whole world strives for transfiguration,
while some elements of it have already attained their
Mount Thabor and bask in its unearthly light. The
censing, the chanting, the rigidity of the vestments, the
petrified order of the service – in Vladimir's time, none
of these had changed for five centuries, and they are all
still approximately the same in ours – are not the expression of a stilted formalism or a mere appeal to the senses
(although it is true that Orthodoxy casts no discredit on

St Sophia, Constantinople: this is where
Vladimir's emissaries 'knew not whether they
were in heaven or on earth'.
(*Lithograph-Photo Roger Viollet.*)

the body and expects it to participate in prayer and grace); on the contrary, far from partaking of the mortiferous influence of the letter, the ritual is composed of vivifying symbols of eternal Life. As God created man in his image, men use images to reach back to God. The Church herself is an icon, and nowhere is she more pure than in her music and ceremonies, from which all individual preferences are excluded, and in which tradition – i.e. the closest possible imitation of transcendency – prevails. At one of the most solemn moments of the liturgy (the *Cherubikon*), the mortals sing that they 'mystically represent the Cherubim', while the angels themselves are supposed invisibly to accompany the priest as he brings out the Holy Gifts. At another moment (the *Epiklesis*), the priest calls upon the Father to send down the Spirit, and it is believed that the Spirit actually becomes present in the church, not only in the souls of the faithful but in the very substance of the rite, understood not as a celebration but as a re-enactment of the sacrifice and resurrection of the Lord. 'Liturgy,' writes Fr Damian Hart,[105] 'is a reflection of theology . . . The fullness of faith is all in Orthodoxy *and its form of worship.*' Mathematically it could be said that liturgy is a model of the Kingdom; therefore it is quite legitimate to judge the Kingdom by the liturgy.

And so the envoys stood there, in the great banquet hall, before Vladimir and his boyars, humbly confessing that they did not know what to say about the religion of the Greeks. Why so? 'On earth there is no such splendour or such beauty and we are at a loss to describe it.' These four had witnessed something that most people in the audience could not even imagine. It was as if they had come back from another universe. Their eyes were still fixed on a vision they could not communicate because it had become an interior one, which they shared amongst themselves and could share with no one else. 'We cannot forget that beauty,' they said, standing in a row and exchanging timid glances of understanding, because the seed was sprouting in them, and they knew of things of which their listeners did not conceive.[106] How does one report a mystical experience to one's superiors? They were trying their best, and they feared they could not find the appropriate words, and yet their words are strangely appropriate: 'The only thing we know,' they said, lamely yet brilliantly, 'is that there God dwells among men.' No more effective way could have been devised of expressing the inexpressible. The Prince and the boyars felt that something had happened to the envoys: they were changed, they literally were not the same men, they were new men, as St Paul would have put it. They partook as brethren of the great secret. Vladimir observed them with awed curiosity and his astonishment grew when they confessed they had become strangers in their own land. They were dazzled, they were bewildered. 'When a man has tasted something sweet,' they said simply, 'he does not want anything bitter. Therefore we will not remain here any longer.'

Their straightforward decision to leave the country if it was not baptized, or rather the impossibility of continuing to live in a non-Christian land, was the strangest thing the boyars had ever heard. It shook them. They had lived contentedly in paganism, but now they were wondering. What was this 'something sweet' without which one could not survive once one had tasted it? The example of Olga suddenly loomed large in their memories: she also had spoken of an inimitable, irreplaceable joy . . . There were mutterings and asides, and emphatic head-shaking. Finally one of them, expressing the general opinion, turned to the Prince and said: 'If the Greek religion had been bad, your grandmother would not have adopted it. She was the wisest of all human beings.'[107] The tide was mounting. Vladimir did not need any longer to lead his people toward a new faith; they preceded him, they pointed the way. There was no voting. No one even cried: 'Let us become Christians!' Vladimir only asked – always the man of action: 'So, where shall we be baptized?' They believed that he would settle everything for the best: after all he was their prince and it was his job. 'Where you please,' they replied, happy to leave the arrangements in his hands.

At the point we have reached in *The Chronicle*, its discrepancy with other sources is manifest: Vladimir has accepted the principle of baptism, although he has not yet made up his mind concerning questions of time and place, and he still has not been the object of any illumination; internal grace may have inspired him, but without his realizing it; in fact his evolution *appears* to have been 'intransitive', taking the form of an objective comparison of religions after some unknown disenchantment with his own. It may of course be argued that the disenchantment itself was inspired by God, but there is no doubt that other sources lead us to expect something more spectacular, an external phenomenon comparable to what had happened to St Paul, or at least to Vladimir's own envoys in Hagia Sophia. This observation may help us to understand better what follows.[108]

4   The deal[109]

It is now necessary to move the calendar back a few days

to August 14, 987,[110] and to adjourn to one of the numerous audience rooms of the Sacred Palace of Constantinople, where the Basileus, sitting on a golden throne under a pillared canopy with purple curtains, has just been hoisted up into the dome by a block-and-tackle mechanism, while the Russian envoys, having reached the third porphyry inlay in the floor, are making their third obeisance to him, surrounded by warbling golden birds perched on golden plane trees, by roaring golden lions and hissing golden griffins engineered to impress the crude Barbarians with the wonders of Byzantine civilization.

Basil II looks down from the ceiling with the impassivity of an idol. Since his brother and co-emperor Constantine VIII cares only for pleasure and is content to leave him all the actual power and the bother that comes with it, he is the absolute master of what is still known as the Roman Empire. His court counts twenty thousand specialized officials, including several sworn sole-ticklers, who are addressed by sonorous titles like Your Sublime and Wonderful Splendour or simply Your Admirability, and in whose garments gold has been worked in in proportion to their nearness to him. He lives in a fairy-tale palace where the walls are porphyry, the pillars jasper and onyx, where the chandeliers hang from jewelled chains, and where all the pots and pans, including special spoons to remove wax from his imperial ears, are solid gold. He is purple-born and entitled to wear the hyacinth tint of purple, whereas dozens of other shades are reserved for less exalted members of his family. His secular grandeur is nothing to his spiritual significance: he is 'the King of the Romans, the Delight of the Universe, the Incomparable Commander, the Guardian of the World', he is 'Beloved

182

Basil II, surrounded by angels, stands in
triumph over his enemies.
(*Photo Giraudon.*)

by God, Guided by God, Safeguarded by God', 'his arm sustains the balance of the world', he is a Wise Hero of the Faith and the Bulwark of Christendom, he is Isapostolos King of Light and Incorporation of the Logos. Next September he will be a remote reincarnation of Dionysius, tasting and blessing the new wine; last Easter he assumed the role of Jesus Christ, kissing old beggars' feet on Holy Thursday and appearing clad in white cerements on the day of the Resurrection; his closest associates are eunuchs, because eunuchs are more like angels than whole men. When he enters a room, people veil their eyes with their sleeves, like the Seraphim in the presence of the Lord; his mission is quite simply to see that in the life of men reign 'the same order and the same rhythm which the Demiurge has introduced into the universe'.[111]

With all that, at the climax of Byzantine power and prosperity, the Basileus Basil II perched on his mechanical throne is in deep trouble.

The short, round, ruddy young man with the big whiskers has been Basileus in name for twenty-four years already, but until the age of eighteen he has had to do the will of his mother, then of her second husband, then of her lover. After that, it has taken him nine years to get rid of his kinsman, chamberlain, prime minister and namesake, Basil the Eunuch. This was only two years ago, and already the finally independent Basileus has managed to displease the aristocracy, to antagonize the Church, and, for his first military initiative, on August 17, 986, to get the Greek army trounced by the Bulgars as it has never been trounced before. In three days it will be the first anniversary of the battle: how could the Basileus help brooding over it? Especially a gloomy character such as Basil. Ascetic, tough, ignor-

185

ant, avaricious, unclean, he will develop with time into one of the most effective rulers of the Empire. Historians will call him a military genius, and schoolchildren will shudder at the story of his capturing fourteen thousand Bulgar prisoners and putting out the eyes of ninety-nine in every hundred, leaving the one hundredth one eye to guide his fellows back to their prince. Two of his sayings have reached posterity and they paint the man: when he dispossessed a monastery of its income he wryly remarked that he had turned the monks' *refectory* into a *reflectory*, as they would now be wondering where their bread would come from; when his empire tottered around him he wrote pathetically – and, no doubt, sincerely enough – that of the afflictions a man could know he was familiar with all, of the joys, with none.

Such is the man before whom the Russian envoys have bowed to the ground, and in addition to all his problems, there is one that lies particularly heavy on his mind. Its name is Sclerus.

The noble Sclerus is an old hand at rebellion. In 978, nearly ten years ago, he already rose against his imperial master. Basil the Eunuch shrewdly used against him another nobleman, Phocas, who defeated him in single combat, but now, seeing the young Basileus is not putting on too good a show, Sclerus has decided to try and give him one more push. There is no real feeling of legitimate descent in Byzantium; whoever is anointed by the Church *is* the Basileus, and the Church always anoints the most powerful man, for 'there is no power but of God' (Romans XIII, 1). Therefore old Sclerus hopes literally to step into the Basileus' red boots, and a good part of the army is with him. Use Phocas again? It is the obvious way, because it will split the aristocratic party in two; Phocas is a good general and popular with his men, but that is exactly why he might prove an even greater risk than Sclerus: intelligence reports indicate that Phocas himself would not mind being a Logos Incarnate and a Morning Star for a change. So of course they will have to be played the one against the other very carefully, for what the method is worth. If the worst comes to the worst,[112] Basil can always count on his Russian Viking guards: splendid fellows they are, with their hair worn long, their arms bare except for silver clasps, their ruby ear-rings, the red dragons embroidered on their jerkins and the double-headed axes in their hands. It is known that they fight well and will kill themselves rather than surrender. Still, they are a bodyguard, not an army, and in the near future an army might be needed, very strong and very faithful. With the Greeks, you never know. They might remain loyal; they might also go over to Sclerus or to that Phocas . . . After all Basil II could scarcely forget by what bloody means his own ancestor Basil I had acquired the throne.

When he came to think of it, the visit of the Russian Barbarians could prove to be a happy coincidence. Constantinople had been at peace with Kiev since 971; there was even an alliance clause to the treaty Svyatoslav had signed: not only would he never have any evil intentions against the Greeks, but if any other foe threatened them, he swore to become his enemy and fight him. Originally the plan had been devised to use the Russians against the Bulgars, but Svyatoslav's death had prevented it from being carried into action. There was no way in which murderous young Vladimir could be pressured into executing a treaty which he had never signed, but he could be asked to provide some more of these Vikings who fought for the best reason: money. Of course he would expect to be compensated himself, but that was no problem: the wealth of the Basileus was inexhaustible. Vladimir had shown commendable feelings in that secret letter received seven years ago.[113] Maybe he could be put to good use again. Now what did these four Russian characters want?

They wanted to investigate the religion of the Greeks.

This opened up two new paths of thought, both hopeful ones. If Russia were to become Christian, and through Constantinople, not through Rome, this would please the Patriarch very much, and God himself was behind the Patriarch. A century ago Photius had cried victory too soon, but now, thanks to the successful mission of 'the Philosopher', it might be that the Russians would indeed show themselves ripe for truth. That was good. And what was equally good was that if Russia were to be baptized by the Greeks, she would *ipso facto* enter the sphere of Greek influence, not only religious but also political. Better still, the Prince of Kiev would become a vassal of the Basileus, and through the use of a few gallons of holy water the Empire might suddenly be stretched out to the Arctic Sea, encircling Bulgaria and jostling the Western Empire from the flank.

It was not sure to come off, but it was worth a try.[114] Hence the instructions sent to the Patriarch – Basil knew how to seize an opportunity – hence the gifts and honours showered on the uncouth travellers from the North. They were probably invited to dine with the Basileus in the Hall of Nineteen Tables (with twelve reclining guests each); they received special overalls to wear over their clothes, and when the master of ceremonies had sworn by the Basileus' head that no food provided at the feast would be forbidden by their religion, they were treated to all the Byzantine delicatessen cooked in fish-brine, caviar, olives, ginger, rolled in on dinner-trolleys, and to wines flavoured with pitch, resin and gypsum. As honoured guests they may even have been invited to partake of certain dishes the Basileus himself recommended, while organ, choirs, Indian jugglers and Chinese acrobats alternated with readings from St John Chrysostom. There is something nearly humorous – and maybe providential – in the fact that the uncouth travellers from the North were not overwhelmed by the secular splendours they were shown, and that it was the liturgy they witnessed the next day which converted them, not to the cause of Caesar, which it was covertly supposed to serve, but to the cause of Christianity which it served both on the surface and in depth.

Some theological interest lies in the fact that this liturgy was held on the day of the Dormition. Although there is no Assumption dogma in the Eastern Church, the whole concept of the transfiguration of the Mother of God this side of death is a central one in Orthodoxy: it brings, among other things, a promise of *apokatastasis* for creation as a whole, Mary being, so to speak, its forerunner in the Kingdom. The cult of Mary is deeply engrained in Orthodoxy in general, but in Russian Orthodoxy in particular, with the icon of the Theotokos of Vladimir (the city, not the saint) playing an important part. It would be meaningful to many Orthodox Russians to realize that the evangelization of their people began under the sign of Mary's accession to the Kingdom.[115]

The Russian envoys left Constantinople well pleased with their reception, and Basil sent them on their way well pleased with the possibilities suggested by them. There had been no mention of a military pact, but project Conversion had started right, and the practical advantages which could be derived from it would probably come in due time.

The next week brought bad news to the Basileus. The very day the Russians went to Hagia Sophia to find their Light, Phocas started his own rebellion in Asia Minor. Basil had foreseen this and was not disconcerted. The question now was whether he could set the two noble rascals by the ears or if they would conclude an alliance against him. In any case reinforcements would come in handy. An emissary was dispatched to Kiev with a secret mission (there was no point in creating a panic): ask Vladimir to send in some more of his troublesome but efficient Vikings. There is no reason to believe there was any direct relationship between the religious deputation of the Russians and the political delegation of the Greeks: project Conversion was a long-range undertaking; it could wait; anyway it was primarily the Patriarch's responsibility, not the Basileus'; what the Basileus wanted was men, and he was ready to pay for them the required amount of gold solidi.

In Kiev Vladimir was still deliberating when and where he would close his search for truth by accepting baptism. He knew that throwing a budding nation from one religion into another could not be done haphazardly, but on the contrary, required prudent steering and forethought. Political as well as religious implications had to be considered. Besides, we detect no enthusiasm in his attitude; he had been convinced rather than converted, and was still waiting for favourable circumstances. He had one stone in his hand and one bird in sight: this was not the kind of deal he was used to. After all there was no special hurry. He had made inquiries and he knew that leading a Christian life would not be all roses. In particular he would have to dismiss his harem, and although these women may have begun to bore him, to be satisfied with one could scarcely appeal to the *fornicator immensus* in him. As to 'making arrangements with Heaven' so as to keep a few concubines on the sly, that was not Vladimir's style: if he was going to reform, he would do it with a vengeance, like a true Russian![116]

The tale told by his envoys had set him dreaming once again about Constantinople. He was mature enough now to know that he would never sack it as his father had intended to do and as he, still a little boy, had imagined himself doing. On the contrary, some kind of deal would have to be made with those progressive Greeks, but a cautious deal: their greed, their guile, had been known since Antiquity.[117] There was no doubt that they would try to get a hold on Russia under the pretext of evangelizing it. That would not do at all. Teachers, yes; masters, no. Some kind of gauge would have to be obtained that would allow Vladimir to control their ambitions. What gauge? This remained to be seen. The Great Prince was in this state of mind when Basil's emissary arrived: he had a message for the Great Prince's ear only.

Vladimir betrayed no emotion, but his heart must have beaten faster when the emissary formulated his request. It corroborated other information according to which the Basileus was in dire straits. Here were the favourable circumstances Russia had been expecting. It was Basil who was in need of military help, not Vladimir who would beg for religious instruction.[118] We all have 'our' situations, such that we can exploit to our personal advantage better than any one else, and Vladimir recognized this as one of his. Not only was profitable bargaining in the offing, but even more appealing to the Great Prince, here was the second bird for his stone. No need to plunder Constantinople to become master of it. The childhood dream would come true in an unexpected way. Vladimir would reign over a Constantinople of his own, with churches, cathedrals, monasteries, civilization, riches, order, harmony, schools, a crowned, anointed Basileus – and, naturally, a crowned purple-born Basilissa: no Empire would be complete without her.[119] And the Basilissa would be the indisputable, irreversible, irretrievable gauge.

We have no information about Vladimir's intelligence service, but it is a fact that he was generally apprised of whatever could be used for his interest. There is little doubt he knew Basil's plight as well as the Basileus knew it himself, even to have dared suggest what he did. 'Viking reinforcements?' he said. Certainly, he would be pleased to provide Viking reinforcements. Of course they would have to be paid handsomely. No argument about that? Good. What did he want for himself? Gold? Silks? Pearls? Wines? No, he wanted neither gold, nor silks, nor pearls, nor wines. He wanted . . . The sophisticated Greek emissary was wondering what ludicrous wish the Barbarian was going to express . . . The Barbarian wanted to marry a purple-born princess, namely Anna, the twenty-five-year-old sister of the Basileus.

Diplomatically, the diplomat tried to explain that this was completely out of the question, but Vladimir was adamant: no princess, no Vikings. Basil had better understand that such was the deal. The unfortunate emissary had to travel back with the ridiculous ultimatum to be delivered to the Basileus. How he must have coughed and squirmed and apologetically giggled when, received in the Sacred Palace, he gave the impertinent message to the Delight of the Universe perched on the throne! Even to utter such words seemed both a blasphemy and a crime. The Delight of the Universe listened in silence. He had received more bad news from Asia Minor: Sclerus and Phocas had joined forces, then Phocas had arrested Sclerus and proclaimed himself Basileus. Even now, already wearing the imperial red boots, he was marching westward, toward the sea. All that did modify the accepted hierarchy of values, if only a little.

The accepted hierarchy of values was clear. For a purple-born princess, daughter of a purple-born Basileus, to marry a Barbarian was *inaudita res*, unheard of. It was not quite unheard of for a prince to marry a foreigner: it had happened to Leo IV who was the spouse of a Khazar princess; it was not unheard of for a princess, the granddaughter of a man of nought, to be given in marriage to a Christian Tsar: it had happened to Maria Lecapena, granddaughter of Romanus I, who gave her to Peter of Bulgaria; but even such derogations were sternly criticized by Constantine VII the Purple-born, an authority on matters of etiquette, who took care to caution his son against succumbing to such shameful temptations. Emperor Otto's suit, which had taken place twenty years before Vladimir's, is especially worthy of note. He wanted a Greek princess for his son Otto II, maybe the very same Anna, who was five years old at the time. He was the first Emperor of the Holy Roman Empire, King of Germany, King of Italy, master of Rome, and his son was co-emperor: scarcely a mis-alliance, one would think, even for a Porphyrogeneta, and the Basileus Nicephorus Phocas did not say no: in the Byzantine tradition, he started playing for time. The irate Otto invaded Apulia and laid siege to the city of

193

Bari, in the hope of blackmailing Nicephorus. His troops failed and he had to resort again to diplomatic means: Liutprand, Bishop of Cremona, was dispatched to Constantinople in the rank of ambassador, to resume the wooing. After a very cold reception, Liutprand got the following answer: 'There is no precedent for anything of the kind. Never has a Porphyrogeneta of a Porphyrogenetus, that is to say the daughter born in the Purple Chamber of a Basileus born in the Purple Chamber, been bestowed upon a foreigner in marriage. Still, since you ask for so high a favour, it will be granted *if you will give in return, as would be proper, Ravenna and Rome and all the lands that lie between here and there.*' Otto did not surrender Ravenna and Rome; instead, after Nicephorus' death, he accepted for his son Princess Theophano who was definitely not Purple-born, being but a kinswoman of the usurper John Tzimisches. And Vladimir, that princeling from obscure Scythia, would presume to call Basil and Constantine brothers-in-law? Preposterous.

But what was not quite so preposterous, given the turn that events were taking in Asia Minor, would be once more to gain time, to obtain the desired reinforcements in exchange for flattering promises, and then to forget all about the unacceptable match. Vladimir would be too happy to have even been considered for a short time as a possible fiancé. And so the shocked diplomat was sent back to Kiev with a tantalizing message: yes, the Purple-born Princess might become the Viking's umpteenth wife, but a Christian could only marry a Christian. Surely he could understand that? Now the ball was in his court. Meanwhile, would he please send those mercenaries? Six thousand would be an appropriate number.

When, one day in the autumn of 987, that communication was delivered to him, Vladimir smiled in his beard. Basil did not know that Vladimir was quite ready to accept baptism. The Basileus probably thought that he imposed a condition which, for the time being, could not be realized. As a matter of fact no provisions for the actual baptism seem to have been offered. But Vladimir would surprise him: why, yes, of course, he would gladly be baptized, and all his people after him. As to the six thousand . . . well, obviously the Great Prince could not put his own army at the Basileus' disposal. But there were enough Vikings around who would go and fight for the devil himself, if he would pay. They were doing nothing, just spitting at the ceiling, as the Russian saying goes, and hoping for a war, any war. If more were needed, one could always send for more to Scandinavia, if one had the right connections. It was just a question of recruiting, organizing and delivering them to Constantinople. Since the recruitment would take a few months and anyway the Black Sea could not be crossed in winter-time and the Bulgars held the Danube, a rendezvous was arranged for next spring at the mouth of the Dniepr. There the exchange would take place: the six thousand men for the baptizing party, the Princess included. The delay was necessary to Vladimir and quite acceptable to Basil: the situation was still far from being desperate, while Phocas was busy taking possession of Asia Minor; there was no need to meet him face to face until he reached the shores of the Bosphorus. As to the secrecy in which the negotiations were wrapped, it was essential to both rulers, since the one intended to go back on his promise and the other, half expecting him to, did not want to look like a fool if he could not prevent it. So Vladimir did not disclose why he was mustering an additional six thousand men. What they knew themselves is a matter of surmise; it may very well be that they learned where they were going only after they were on their way. As to his own people, Vladimir announced to them that he was going down to the Dniepr cataracts, on the pretext, one imagines, of giving a good fright to the Pecheneg nomads who were always making a nuisance of themselves in those parts.[120] The real object of the expedition was probably known to a few boyars, no more.

In the spring of 988 the Great Prince set out by water at the head of an army which can be evaluated at a minimum of twelve thousand: six for the brothers-in-law, at least as many to face any eventuality that might arise. To complete the ordinary retinue and to replace those Vikings who would normally have been added to it but who were going to Constantinople, Slovenes, Krivichans, even Bulgars had been recruited, and not only professional soldiers, but also common men.[121] There may have been some horses (properly equipped with saddles, stirrups and bridles) for reconnoitring Pecheneg territory, but mainly it was infantry armed with axes, one-metre-long double-edged swords, knives, spears, bows and arrows. Some three hundred Russian boats were put afloat. They were approximately fifteen metres long and three metres wide, monoxylons made of giant trees from the Russian forests, and they carried up to forty armed men each. Twenty oars and one sail per boat were put to work when the current was not helpful enough.

> One boat rides before the others,
> Like a hawk he[122] flies before the others.
> All the boats are garnished-varnished,
> All the boats are furnished-furbished,
> But the hawk-boat best of all.

196

High he holds his handsome head,
Prow and stern are like a bison's,
Ample flanks are like a beast's,
Oh! how well adorned is our little boat!
He has eyes set with precious stones,
He has brows grown of foreign sable,
His moustache is made of two steel blades,
His two ears are winter ermines,
Oh! how well adorned is our little boat!
For a mane two foreign foxes have been nailed on,
For a tail two polar she-bears have been hung on,
Oh! how well adorned is our little boat!
His fine sails are of dear brocade,
Rustling brocade, shimmering,
His thick sheets are of seven silks,
His sharp anchors are of steel,
And the anchors' rings of silver,
And the anchors' flukes are gilded,
Oh! how well adorned is our little boat!
In the middle of that hawk-boat
Stands a little cabin all emblazoned,
With its ceiling cloaked in velvet,
With its wainscots clad in sable,
Martens-foxes hanging all around,
Yea, expensive furs from foreign countries!
In the cabin there are benches to be sat on,
And who sits on them but a handsome lad,
Young Vladimir, son of Svyatoslav.[123]

Even if Vladimir's boat was not quite as fancifully decorated as the one described by the bard, it was more elaborate than the rest, being the flagship, and the hereditary trident flew high atop its mast.

It took the army ten days to sail down to the cataracts. Vladimir had reached them three years earlier, but he had never crossed them. Menacing cliffs, nearly ninety metres in height, converged on the river and choked the broad stream into a torrent which flowed six times faster between broad ledges projecting into the current and around huge rocky boulders where eddies formed and spray flew. Vladimir stepped ashore. Some of the men were sent to occupy the hills, to avoid being surprised by the Pechenegs; others stripped and jumped into the shallows, towing the boats with cables, pulling them with their hands, pushing them with poles. Thus they crossed the first cataract called Essupi (Do Not Sleep), the second named Ulvorsi (Island Rapid) and the third one, to which the Vikings referred as Gelandri and the Slavs as Zvonets, meaning that the falls made a ringing din in the gorge. The fourth cataract, Aifor (Portage Rapid) to the Vikings and Nenasytets (Insatiable) to the Slavs, was the largest one. The boats had to be dragged out of the water and then rolled or carried for six miles. The cavalry roved around on the alert, but the Pechenegs were too wise to show themselves, and that first day ended peacefully, the Russian army pitching its camp under the stars.

The next morning Baruforos (Wave Rapid) and Leanti (Seething) were crossed without too much trouble; the men had to disembark but the goods could stay on the boats and the boats in the river. Finally, by taking every precaution, the army reached Strukun (Fast Current), which was the most dangerous, not because of the waters, but because with its width, its ford and its high cliffs, it lent itself best of all to ambushing on a large scale.[124] Old soldiers came up to Vladimir and showed him where his father had died. He looked, and remembered, and tough as he was his eyes may have become misty at the thought that by becoming a Christian he was somehow disowning his father, who had been so

198

brave and had suffered so much. The memory of his own pagan days must have tugged at his heart as he reflected on Svyatoslav's feelings toward Christianity. But times were changing, truth was dawning on the world, and there was no escaping it.

At the end of the day the convoy reached Khortitsa Island, a big three-sided bluff which looked like a ship and where the custom was to rest for a day, while repairing whatever damage the cataracts had caused to the boats. Another custom was to sacrifice cocks before a huge oak which grew on the top of the island: this was to thank the gods for a happy crossing, for oaks were sacred trees, dedicated to the gods, so much so that St Constantine (Cyril) felled one in the Crimea, in order to destroy the worship attached to it. 'It was an enormous tree, its girth twice as large as a man could embrace . . . Spreading out a canopy of sappy dark-green foliage, it stood rapt and slightly trembling in the rays of the evening sun . . . Through the hard, ancient bark, even where there were no twigs, leaves had sprouted . . .'[125] Somebody handed a live cock to the Great Prince and he took out his knife . . . He was, after all, but a catechumen, and no striking event had happened in his life to make him discard for good the superstitions to which he had been so devoted. His army was composed of a vast majority of pagans and they were waiting for him to draw the first blood. No vow bound him yet to the Church, and he may have wished to bid a symbolic farewell to the ways of his youth. He did not believe in idols any more, and could afford to toast them once before declaring on them a merciless war. Maybe he did plunge that knife into that cock's throat, at the feet of the huge green oak; maybe he refrained. Anyway it was the last time the question arose in his mind. From then on he prayed only to the Christian God.

Four more days took Vladimir to the place appointed for the exchange: the estuary of the Dniepr. Would the Princess be there, and the bishops in their golden chasubles, with their golden books and their smoking golden censers? Would his new life begin there and then?

To his disappointment – and perhaps, at least partly, to his secret relief – it did not. The Princess and the bishops were absent. Probably there were some high-ranking officials with flamboyant titles, who made flowery excuses: the Princess and the bishops would come a little later. A Purple-born was not to be transported like a sack of goods. Proprieties had to be observed. If only the Great Prince would condescend to wait a few days? One morning, soon, he would espy silken sails in the distance and hear incomparable Greek chanting coming to him over the waters; he would smell incense mingling with the sea air: let him then prepare himself to receive his bride. In the meantime, those six thousand . . . Grimly, Vladimir nodded. Yes, he would wait a little more, there was nothing else he could do. As to the mercenaries, they were here, at the Basileus' disposal. It would have been impossible to keep them kicking their heels at the mouth of the Dniepr; they had to be fed and paid, and Vladimir had certainly no intention of doing that at his own expense. So the six thousand hopeful braves sailed away, and Vladimir stayed there, on the edge of the Black Sea and of the greatest gamble in his life.[126]

This was June 988 and Basil was in serious need of Russian help. Since the end of 987, Phocas had been in possession of the whole Asiatic part of the Empire. His huge army, split in two, occupied the two ends of the Sea of Marmara and prepared to take Constantinople in a vice. He himself settled temporarily in Abydos, on the east bank of the Dardanelles, but his vanguard, under Kalocyr Delphinas, had appeared in Chrysopolis (now Scutari) just across the Bosphorus from Constantinople. From the windows of the Sacred Palace Basil could see the fires of his enemy's camp at swimming distance from him. Although the Empire extended west as far as Italy, there was no counting on a strategic retreat followed by a comeback: whoever held Constantinople was Basileus. The only question was whether to wait for Phocas' two-headed onslaught or to forestall him, cross the straits, and attempt to destroy him piecemeal. Without the Russians, this was out of the question, but with six thousand fresh devils anxious to earn their pay, it began to sound like a good idea. Basil lacked neither decision nor courage. One day, as the rebels were 'not prepared to fight but rather busy drinking',[127] the Russian Vikings took them by surprise and cut them to pieces, killing 'not a few' and scattering the others. Phocas' vanguard had been thrown head over heels. With his usual clemency, the Bulwark of Christendom took Kalocyr and his two lieutenants and had them crucified and impaled for good measure. Having established a beachhead on the eastern bank, Basil now had to face Phocas himself. Things still looked sombre enough, but decidedly not as sombre as a few days ago, and there was no point at all in sending Anna to Vladimir, the Beauty to the Beast: if Basil was victorious, he would not need the Prince of Kiev any more; if he was defeated, he would need him still less. Meanwhile the Prince of Kiev could wait.

And wait he did, although not quite as patiently as Basil would have liked. He waited through the end of June and through July and through the middle of August. He was not, however, as inactive as he seemed.

He was gathering intelligence concerning Greek possessions within his reach. If the Princess did not show up, he
would take a leaf out of Emperor Otto's book and try to
seize a Greek city.[128] It would not be a perfect gauge, it
would not constitute an absolute hold over the Basileus,
but it would be a healthy reminder of what could be
done behind his back while he was turned the other way.
Even reinforced by the Vikings, Basil had his hands full
and the threat of an attack from the rear would make him
think twice before he would openly forswear his part of
the deal. But it had to be a good, convincing threat, not
braggadocio. As to the religious aspect of the question,
everything in its good time. Vladimir was not yet
baptized, and killing a few Greeks was still a permissible
recreation. Around August 15, 988, when there was still
enough summer left for a short campaign, Vladimir,
recognizing the fact that the Princess was not coming,
gathered his troops and set sail.

5   Siege[129]

Cherson was a small but wealthy Greek colony in the
extreme south of the Crimea. She had stood there, looking north, in the bay of Sebastopol, perched on her rock
over her well protected harbour, for fifteen hundred
years. Although she guarded carefully her fishing rights
and scraped some grain from the neighbouring rocky
land, most of her riches came from commerce. She
traded both with the mother country and with the
inhabitants of the hinterland. In the tenth century, these
were Slavic tribes known as Ulichs and Tiverts, and
also, of course, the powerful Russians from Kiev, who
were felt to be so dangerous that a treaty prohibited
them from wintering in the Dniepr estuary. Some of the

Slavs were absorbed into the city, as well as some Vikings, who traded with her or fought for her, depending on circumstances. Whatever their origin, the Chersonians – some ten thousand of them – were independent-minded people, who would sometimes rebel against the Basileus and always stand firmly for their rights. Strategically, Cherson was but a pawn; yet a pawn correctly used can make all the difference. The coast of Asia Minor was not much more than three hundred kilometres away; the sea breeze in the daytime, the land breeze at night, allowed a ship to make the crossing in twenty-four hours. This was especially important at a time when all Asia Minor was in rebels' hands. The fact that of all Tauridian colonies Cherson was the closest to Constantinople must also have carried some psychological weight. In short, Vladimir could not have chosen better than he did.

Having obtained from merchants, travellers, fishermen and adventurers of all kinds, information concerning topography, fortifications, availability of water and natural resources, and making good use of a fresh breeze from the north-west, Vladimir sailed one morning into Cherson harbour, the oarsmen rowing furiously, the soldiers shouting and knocking their shields together to frighten the citizens, the helmsmen holding the boats as far from the city walls as possible, in order to keep out of range of bows and catapults. The fleet – some one hundred boats – was soon protected from enemy blows and from their view as well as from all winds; it anchored at the farthest end of the cove, and the men landed without a hitch. Rushing up the hill, they discovered the city lying at their feet; they could see its double ramparts, houses, palaces, hovels, streets, churches, monuments, statues, patios; they could observe its inhabitants running to and fro like disturbed ants and preparing for defence. Vladimir knew already that the two towers and the curtain wall closest to him were also the weakest of the whole system, and he may have tried to exploit the surprise effect and storm them then and there. If he did, he failed and had to resign himself to a siege. He pitched camp behind the hill, at a place where wells were numerous, and began organizing the blockade.

At that point in his life, Vladimir had taken at least five major towns: Polotsk, Kiev, Rodnya, Cherven and Peremyshl, the first by storm, the two last we do not know how, the two others by trickery, after a successful blockade (at least of Rodnya), but not at the end of a skilfully conducted siege. The truth of the matter was that he had neither an engineer's expertise nor the right machinery, and that Cherson, defended by stubborn and intelligent citizens, was going to prove a hard nut to crack. The more so as Vladimir was in a hurry to gain possession of it, for reasons of personal pride, of politics and of . . . religion. It was the first time he had given his new God a chance to help him, and he prayed to him earnestly and childishly, although maybe not without the shadow of a doubt at the back of his mind: 'O Lord God who art master of everything! I ask this of Thee, that Thou wouldst give me this town, so that I might take and bring to my own land Christian men and priests to instruct the people in the Christian religion'.[130] This was another, an even more crucial deal that Vladimir was making, and his partner in it was the Christian God Himself: a town for a nation. Consciously or semi-consciously Vladimir must have thought: 'If he cannot or will not give me this town, what is the point of worshipping him?' It was not really a sign he was requesting, but rather encouragement. Many of us are

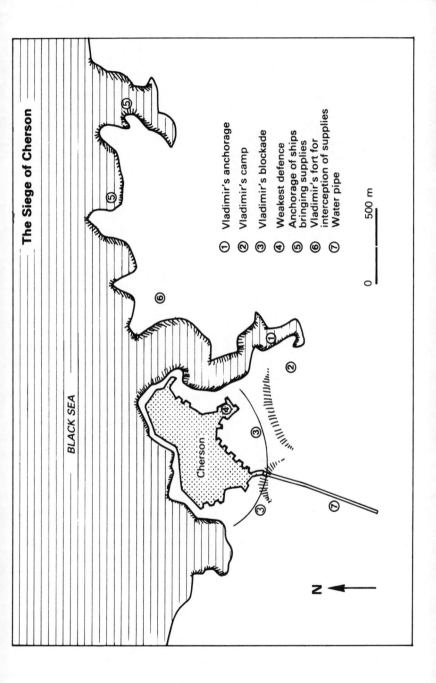

The Siege of Cherson

BLACK SEA

Cherson

① Vladimir's anchorage
② Vladimir's camp
③ Vladimir's blockade
④ Weakest defence
⑤ Anchorage of ships bringing supplies
⑥ Vladimir's fort for interception of supplies
⑦ Water pipe

0   500 m

N

guilty of the same kind of bargaining with Heaven, although in smaller matters, and Vladimir had extenuating circumstances: he was surrendering an old contract to take up a new one, he felt entitled to make some profit or at least to break even. The paradox in his case was that he, still a pagan, was asking the Christian God to deliver to him a Christian town. But why not? God had so many other towns, and this one meant so much to Vladimir.

The blockade did not begin under favourable auspices. The harvest had been garnered in June, and the Chersonians were not ready to begin starving yet. Autumn was approaching fast; the retinue had nothing to do, besides boring guard duties; food was getting difficult to procure: the besieged ate better than the besiegers. It was an unnerving situation for a Prince used to speedy victories, and who had never needed one as much as he did now.

The news from Constantinople did not mean much: the battle at Chrysopolis had been brilliantly won, but Phocas was still master of Abydos and nearly all the east bank. Six months went by and nothing had changed: Princess Anna was still a resident of the Sacred Palace, and the Patriarch still seemed in no hurry to send his bishops, obviously because Vladimir would be in a better position to demand the Princess as soon as he had been baptized. Of course he could have ordered any local priest to baptize him and that would have been that, but a cheap baptism was not at all what he had in mind. Anyway the city had to fall first, such was his deal with God. And fall it would, 'even if I must sit here for three years!' he grumbled through clenched teeth. The Chersonians only shook their heads: the city could not be taken and it would not surrender. There was for that one very good reason: Cherson was secretly receiving supplies by sea.

One day when Vladimir was standing behind a mantelet peering at the enemy's ramparts, while his men and the Chersonians exchanged, as was usual, abuse, threats, jibes and a few ineffective arrows, some of which carried attached messages, mostly obscene, one of his Vikings picked up such an arrow and brought it to him. 'What do you want me to do with it?' asked the Great Prince, who was losing patience. 'Prince,' replied the soldier, 'this message is for you. Read it.' 'How do you know it is for me?' 'The archer who shot the arrow shouted that we should bring it to you.' 'And the Chersonians did not prevent him?' 'He shouted in Norse. I was one of the few to understand him, even among us. To his comrades he said he was making fun of us in our own language.' 'Then he must be a Viking?' He was a Viking: he had signed his name, Zhdbern.

Zhdbern presented himself as a wellwisher of Vladimir's. What his motives were is uncertain: either, although his home was in Cherson, his heart was with the Rurikid Prince rather than with the Greek shopkeepers, or else he believed Vladimir's promise to sit there for three years and he wanted to be on the right side on V Day. In any case, his message was to the point. Some ships, it ran, probably coming from other Greek colonies, anchored at night in the small coves east of the harbour. The crews conveyed all kinds of supplies overland, to a point where daring Chersonians expected them. The Chersonians took charge of the jars, barrels, sacks and packages, loaded them on to their own small boats and, under cover of darkness, silently crossed the harbour back to the city, under the very nose of the Russians, who stayed in the farther end of the cove. Quite some fortunes must have been made this way by the Greek Rhett Butlers.

On reading the message, Vladimir's hopes grew. The solution was really very simple. A strong detachment was sent to build a small fort on the heights east of the harbour and to man it day and night. Now the blockade was sealed and the Chersonians finally began to suffer from the hardships of the siege. But they had made reserves and still did not show the slightest intention of surrendering. On the contrary, Vladimir's retinue was getting discouraged and he more and more impatient: an operation that was supposed to dazzle the Basileus with its velocity was entering its second half-year.

Something had to be done. Little prepared as it was for building earthworks, Vladimir's retinue, under the protection of shields and mantelets, began to erect a ramp between the outer low wall, which the Chersonians could not defend, and the rampart proper. Earth was shovelled into baskets, baskets were carried to the point which had been chosen, and emptied there. It was tedious work, but it had to succeed: when the ramp reached the top of the rampart, the Russians would pour into the city. The Chersonians would be helpless before such an onslaught. It was just a question of heaping earth and waiting a little more.

The men heaped and heaped, Vladimir waited and waited, and the ramp, having at first risen fast enough, ceased growing. Thousands of basketfuls of earth were thrown on it, and they seemed to melt into thin air. More soil was brought and more disappeared. The ramp had attained a certain height and would not get any taller. The superstitious Russians began to wonder what charm the Greeks were using. The charm was nothing but a tunnel they had dug under their own wall. While Russians were piling earth on the ramp, Greeks were stealing it from underneath and scattering it inside the city, so that the ramp sagged continuously. Simple but clever, and there was no way to prevent them from doing it, even when the trick was discovered. The deal with the Christian God was not working out too well.

It was April 989 – the siege had begun in September 988 – when, on the seventh day of the month, which was a Saturday, a terrifying sight shook the minds of both Russians and Greeks: in the middle of the night, on the northern horizon, appeared pillars of fire which gave a reddish hue to sky and land. Men ran out of their houses and crawled from under their tents to stare at the aurora borealis: what could it foretell? A catastrophe, no doubt. But for whom?

At this point a mystery man[131] enters the stage. He was called Anastas, which is a Greek name, and he lived in Cherson, which he was to betray to Vladimir. Some think he was a layman, some a priest, some a bishop. The evidence presented is inconclusive in each case. In subsequent years he was to become a sort of *éminence grise* of the Great Prince, and later to leave Kiev with Boleslav of Poland much as he had left Cherson with Vladimir of Russia. An unscrupulous careerist? A professional Judas? Zhdbern's motives were probably uncomplicated ones, not so Anastas'. He may have counted on a reward, he may have objected to starvation, he may have had higher inspirations at which we can only guess. Here the historian must retire on tiptoe and bow in the novelist, who cannot help being tempted by an idealistic Anastas, a priest maybe, yes, a forerunner of the Society of Jesus, both an intriguer and a fanatic, but basically sincere, who felt that one of the great opportunities of history was slipping past him and could not refrain from poking a finger at it to push it in the right direction. One might maintain that, if Anastas had done nothing about it, a defeated and disgusted Vladimir would have raised the siege, interpreted his lack of success as a punishment from Perun and sailed back to Kiev, firmly decided to have nothing more to do with the ungracious, ungrateful Christian God. Certainly Anastas might have reflected along these lines, supposing he knew about Vladimir's intention to accept baptism if he took Cherson, which is likely since there is no indication that Vladimir made a secret of it. Therefore Anastas had a choice: either he remained faithful to his city or he did a good turn to his Church. For a man to betray his country for ideological reasons is not uncommon, as Graham Greene has stressed, not without some sympathy, in his preface to Kim Philby's autobiography. And so one day Father Anastas, having received some instruction in archery from a relative or a neighbour, took a bow and a quiver, tucked up his cassock, climbed on the rampart and shot a few arrows at the Russians. Being a born plotter, he probably made an elaborate display of patriotism: 'Even I, a priest, want to participate in the defence. Death to the heathens!' A message was attached to one of the arrows. It contained a piece of information so secret that the Viking Zhdbern had had no access to it: it revealed whence came the very blood of the besieged city, i.e. water. *Springs behind you. Water flows down pipe. Dig and cut.*

Someone found the arrow, picked it up, brought it to Vladimir, without realizing, of course, the historical importance of what he was doing. At the sight of the message Vladimir's heart leapt. He lifted his eyes to heaven and cried: 'If this comes true, I shall indeed be baptized.'

One look behind him showed the Prince the only place where the subterranean pipe could reach the city: it was under a ridge abutting onto the ramparts. How had he not thought of it before? 'Dig!' he ordered feverishly.

211

They dug. One metre from the surface the picks struck stone. Vladimir himself was standing over the diggers. Two or three had jumped into the trench and were using their axes on the thing. Yes, it was a pipe, and yes, it broke under their lusty blows, and yes, fresh water gushed out, drenching the soil. For nine months, the time it takes to bear a child, Vladimir had been walking over it without suspecting its presence! He heaved a deep sigh. The Christian God seemed to have made up his mind to abide by his side of the deal. The axes struck again. Water was running freely in the trench. On the city side the pipe was stopped with mortar, so that no infiltrations would relieve the Chersonians' thirst once their cisterns were dry. Vladimir strode back to his tent with the feeling that finally the tide was turning: the pillars of fire had predicted Cherson's downfall, not his. That meant he would be baptized . . . but not before the Basileus had kept his word.

A few days later the parched city surrendered. A triumphant Vladimir entered it at the head of his men, and, most extraordinary feat for that period, speaking perhaps for his humanity, probably for his sense of bargaining and politics, but without any doubt for the unbelievable control under which he held his men, he did not sack the place. To the inhabitants' intense surprise and relief, not one prisoner was killed, not one home was plundered, not one woman was raped. The captive city, with its gates open, lived on, uncertain as to its ultimate fate, but, for the time being, unmolested. The conqueror went further; he consoled the defeated defenders and assured them of his goodwill.[132] This was unheard of for a Christian, let alone for a pagan. Anastas must have felt that he had accomplished the best of deeds when he shot that treacherous arrow.

On the other hand, the huge army was not disbanded. Vladimir did not know yet if the war had ended or if it was just beginning. That would depend on his future brothers-in-law's decision.

6   Illumination

One brother, in the meantime, seemed to have got out of trouble. The other, Constantine, had condescended to forget for a short time his jolly life in Constantinople and had joined Basil outside Abydos. Basil himself, 'having let his beard grow and acquired experience',[133] led his army, including the Russian contingent, and, after some manoeuvring, the battle took place on April 13, 988, a few days after the 'pillars of fire' had been seen. The battle was furious but, for a long time, not decisive. Finally, Phocas in person rushed at the Basileus, and might have killed him in single combat if, by an incredible quirk of fate, he had not himself fallen from his horse, struck dead by a fit of apoplexy. Apoplexy carried the day. Phocas' army took to its heels and was cut to pieces. The Emperors returned victorious, the younger to his revelry, the older to his politics. Something, Basil thought, would have to be done about that upstart Vladimir who was still helplessly besieging Cherson, as a ludicrous method of wooing the Princess. Baptized or not, he would have to be taught a lesson. Marry Anna indeed! Pshaw! The fellow must be crazy.

Then, suddenly, everything changed once more. Not only did Cherson fall, which was annoying – still, what could you expect with pillars of fire in the northern sky? – but the Bulgars, led by their Tsar Samuel, once again on the warpath, took Verria and threatened Thessalonica. A panic resulted. Worse followed: the fire

213

of rebellion, which Basil thought he had stamped out, was rekindled with renewed force: Phocas' widow had set the arrested Sclerus free, and the old general, uniting the remnants of two armies, his own and Phocas', including the dead man's own son, put Constantinople under greater peril than it had been a few months before. If only there were peace with Bulgaria . . . or if only Sclerus would give up . . . But while Sclerus was sharpening his teeth in the East, Samuel was clicking his in the West. To make matters even more tragic, on July 27 a comet appeared and hung over the Empire, announcing calamities and terrorizing the people. How could Basil have guessed that what the comet had in mind was an earthquake to take place on October 25, and not any political development? In the midst of all this trepidation two Russians arrived: Oleg, otherwise unknown, and Zhdbern, who, as a reward for his services, had been promoted to Governor of Cherson and Ambassador Extraordinary.[134] Their message was crude and to the point: 'Prince Vladimir says: if you do not give me your sister in marriage, I shall do to Constantinople what I have done to Cherson.'

Basil and Constantine exchanged glances. 'He is bragging,' said Constantine. 'He is a good soldier,' said Basil. 'Ridiculous,' cried Constantine. 'He spent nine months taking Cherson and he would attack Constantinople?' 'He could not take it,' agreed Basil, 'but neither could we afford a third front.' 'It would be hard but maybe we could,' hoped Constantine. 'Not with half an army,' observed Basil. 'For heaven's sake, brother, what do you mean?' exclaimed Constantine. And Basil, 'who had grown a beard and acquired experience', shook his head and said: 'Who knows what the six thousand would do?'

214

Perhaps in a last effort to gain time, very courteous deputies were sent to Cherson to accept Vladimir's terms, but to request that he be baptized first. How they must have hated bowing and scraping before the Barbarian! The Barbarian replied he wanted nothing better, since the Greek faith and liturgy were after his own heart. But where was Anna? He had been expecting her for nearly a year. They replied, as they had been instructed to, that the Purple-born would come to Cherson as soon as he had been baptized. But Vladimir had been hoodwinked long enough. This time he was going to insist. Why make two expeditions when one would suffice? He wrote back to the Emperors: 'Let those who come with your sister baptize me.'

So, very sadly, the two brothers went to see Anna and told her that they had tried to spare her but that there really was no other way: she was to marry the brute.

Anna, born on March 13, 963, was twenty-six at the time, and unmarried for the simple reason that there was not in the whole world one single Christian who would be a decent match for her. We know nothing about her character, but there is no doubt that, like other Byzantine noblewomen, she was used to delicate ways and a sophisticated style of life. She would drink no heavy wines, partaking instead of perfumed water, she would take daily vapour baths followed by showers, she would be massaged several times a day, she would be used to all sorts of compliments and gallantries from the most important personages, as, for instance, when the ministers of state, in slashed and billowing costumes, their wrists and knees bedecked with ribbons, would dance in her honour by torchlight, accompanied by a flute mingling its music with the gurgling of the fountains in the Sacred Palace. To marry the Scythian from

215

Kiev was to her a captivity worse than death, and she said so again and again, pleading with her brothers, begging them not to send her away from a home where she would die rather than live in the barbarous North. To give an idea of her plight: would a dainty Victorian aristocrat have merrily married some cannibal chieftain from the colonies, with bone needles in his cheeks! And that improper proposal! Who had ever heard of a prince marrying without first organizing a beauty contest, at which each of the young ladies with the proper measurements could at least hope to receive the golden apple from the hands of the bridegroom? And at what time would Anna be crowned? Before the marriage, as was the custom in Constantinople, to emphasize the sacred rights of the Basilissa, or after, as any common princeling's wife?

No, decidedly death would be sweeter than such disgrace. No doubt, said the brother, but death would not help them out. Had Anna no religious feelings at all? Did she not see that God had chosen her to turn the land of Russia to repentance, for His greater glory? Would she refuse to fulfil His holy designs for her? It was her duty as a Christian, said one, to go to Vladimir and make him abide by his promise. It was her duty as a Greek, said the other, to save her country, as she alone could do. With Vladimir to help against the Bulgars, Sclerus could probably be pacified. But she had to understand that it was impossible to fight in all directions at once. If Vladimir joined forces with the rebels or with Tsar Samuel, Constantinople itself would totter. 'Our dear sister Anna . . .' She resisted for many days. Vladimir's personal reputation was far from encouraging; his very insistence on a highly unsuitable marriage had frightening connotations; he had raped Rogned before her

216

father's eyes: what would he do to Anna? Finally, she surrendered.

A great ceremony was held in church, which the imperial family attended in state. Tearfully the two brothers prayed to the Virgin: 'O holy Mother of God, you to whom we owe our true God Jesus Christ, let not that pagan defile our sister your servant, but let him accept baptism!' 'And if he doesn't?' whispered one brother to the other. 'Then God help us!' was the reply. So bad was the situation. At least, to coax the Barbarian into good behaviour, they would ply him with honours and gifts, surround him with princes of the Church, send to him, repugnant as it was, the sacred insignia of a real Basileus, in short – since, willy-nilly, he had to be received in the family – do it right and try to civilize the churl. After all, great benefits, both spiritual and political, could be derived from the Russian alliance. If the price was a little too high . . . well, the inevitable should be accepted with good grace. With tears and sobs Anna finally boarded the ship which had been prepared for her. She kissed her brothers for the last time in her life, and, her eyes turning incessantly toward the cupolas of Hagia Sophia, amid much religious singing and censing, left her native Constantinople. She was never to see it again.

In Cherson, Vladimir was, once more, waiting. One sunny morning in the summer of 989, sails were sighted in the offing: the sea breeze was bringing in the Greek ships with the double-headed eagles flapping from the masts. Vestments shimmered, crosiers gleamed, mitres sparkled in the early morning light. In one sense it was the first morning of Holy Russia. Gangplanks were thrown over the water. Vladimir stood expectantly on the pier, radiant and masterful, arrayed in all his barbaric

217

finery; cloak and torque and pointed morocco shoes and ruby ear-rings. One more victory, one more woman: things were still in order in the world.

Anna appeared at the gangway. She wore a white dress,[135] simply cut, fastened with a plainly made, fantastically valuable clasp, and over it a cassakin of gold brocade. Long purple veils fell straight from the golden net which enclosed her carefully waved hair down to her white sandals done up with strings of gold braid. Vladimir was not exactly a cowboy himself, not even a Napoleon Buonaparte rushing to meet Marie-Louise at Compiègne, but he must have been stunned by the inimitable simplicity of the attire and the supreme nobility of the lady who wore it. She was nothing more and nothing less than the first bride of Christendom – and she was his. While the courtiers and bishops and priests and deacons were landing in a glittering and perfumed procession of robes and golden uniforms, Vladimir stood divided between awe and lust. At the same time, he may have felt the first sign of a disease that was to attack him in an unexpected, maybe a providential way.

We are treading here on delicate ground and it is impossible not to take the reader into our confidence. As already mentioned, most sources hint at a decisive incident which turned Vladimir into a Christian, but *The Chronicle* has so far described only a systematic research which convinced rather than converted him. Now it is going to compensate by presenting us with nothing less than a miracle. When Anna arrived, it says, Vladimir lost his sight. All remedies were of no avail. Anna told him that to be baptized was the only cure. He complied, and as soon as the bishop had laid his hand upon him, he began to see again. 'Now,' he cried, 'I have seen the true God.'

Some observations may be made about the story: first,

the loss of sight seems to be reminiscent of what happened to St Paul, to whom St Vladimir is often compared; second, the remark about seeing the true God might indicate that Vladimir's blindness should be interpreted symbolically: such, according to Karamzin, was the opinion of the Orthodox Church in his time; third, Anna's advice, to be baptized with all speed, shows some reluctance on the part of Vladimir.

The *Prologue Life* recounts the same events, specifying that Vladimir was blind in both eyes and ending with these words: 'Having entered the holy font, his eyes were opened and he was as if he had never been ill; having recovered his sight, he gave praise to God, and having been illuminated he was joyful in soul and body.'

The ordinary *Life* tells a shorter story. Vladimir was ill (no details are provided) and there was a miracle: as soon as the bishop laid his hand on him he was cured from his *yazva*, which means ulcer, sore, wound, plague, but can scarcely mean blindness.

The *Special Life* (Pliginskiy version), without mentioning Anna's intervention, gives the following information: 'Prince Vladimir wanted to commit a faithless act, and for his lack of faith he was soon struck with blindness and covered with scabs, and when he entered the holy font and immersed himself three times the scabs fell like fishscales and his face shone and he was cleansed.' The *Special Life* (Public Library version) reads somewhat differently:

And orders were given to prepare the holy font. Prince Vladimir came up to the holy font but still wanted to commit a somewhat lawless act, and immediately he was covered with scabs and a great fright seized him – then Prince Vladimir hurriedly repented and immersed himself three times in the holy font and received at holy baptism the name of Basil, and

219

immediately the scabs fell from his body like fishscales and his face shone like the sun, and the force and grace of the Holy Spirit fell upon him and he was quite sound.

The only points on which most sources agree are the illness and the cure. Jacob and Hilarion are silent about the incident, but their testimony is far from irreconcilable with such an event. Granted that miracles were in fashion at the time, and that some of the sources may be quoting from each other, it does not seem fair – or even objective – to reject the health theme *a priori*. In addition, the information according to which Vladimir was about to commit some faithless or lawless deed, or both, would explain the gingerly fashion in which the specific incident which converted him is treated in terms of 'hindrance' by those who refer or allude to it. Finally, if we find it difficult to believe in miracles, Vladimir did not, and any happy coincidences which might have occurred would instantly have been interpreted by him and his contemporaries as a visible, 'external', intervention of God. His reply to Anna's advice: 'If this happens, then the Christian God is really great' rings true: it had just the right blend of hesitation and hopefulness: once committed to the God who had already given him Cherson and the first bride in Christendom, Vladimir would gladly welcome any supplementary sign of his power and goodwill.

For all we know, the miracle may have been an authentic one, but even if the cure was not as spectacular as chroniclers and hagiographers make it, it would seem that another, no less meaningful miracle, did indeed happen at the holy font, 'wondrous and glorious' as the *Life* has it, but one that can be explained both in theological and psychological terms: it was the miracle of conversion, and Vladimir emerging from the water was indeed 'cleansed' of his former carnal and primitive conception of the world. To quote from Metropolitan Hilarion, 'With the clothes of the old man, he threw off the decay of faithlessness, and entering the holy font, he was born of the Spirit and of water, was baptized into Christ and clad in Christ, and came out regenerated, the son of immortality, taking for all centuries and generations the name of Basil, the one inscribed in the book of life, to be used in the heavenly city and the imperishable Jerusalem.'

Vladimir took his baptism seriously; he showed it later by radically changing his way of life. He really believed that he was being born again at the very minute his head disappeared under the water. Scabs or no scabs, no wonder 'his face shone like the sun', since he had indeed 'seen the true God'. At the very least he had, without a doubt, rejected the scabs of sin and been illumined by the desire to be good.

What probably happened, and what seems to conciliate most sources without shocking modern common sense, is this.

When he saw the Purple-born sister of the Basileus coming down toward him on the gangplank, all gold and perfumes and royal simplicity, the Viking in Vladimir was sorely tempted. She was in his power, to do with as he pleased. He could be baptized and marry her, he could take her and leave her, he could smile and send her back to Constantinople. The people of Cherson rushed forward to meet her, their Princess, slightly less than a goddess. She hastily retired to the palace that had been prepared for her – there her only consolation was to repeat thousands of times the famous and humble prayer of Jesus[136] – and he was left wondering what he *would* do because he *could* do anything. It was not so much Anna; it was the old man in Vladimir recoiling before his imminent destruction. Baptism, matrimony, continence, moderation, humility, salvation . . . All this was not unavoidable. The Princess could still be had, and Cherson could still be sacked, and the merry life of the past years could go on. The fact that recently it had not been so merry faded before the fear of losing it. In his mind, Vladimir was pretty sure – but not quite – that the Christian God was the only true God, and personally he had no complaints against Him, on the contrary. But bidding farewell to one's former self is never easy, and at some points all pretexts seem good so long as they encourage the *status quo*. How often do we painfully push Sisyphus' stone to the top of the hill and then secretly wish it to roll back? Vladimir was in just such a mood, and, as everything finally seemed to be playing into his hands, he wavered. Embodied in the desirable Anna, Christianity, which had been pretty abstract so far, had suddenly become disquietingly real. Not that he did anything wrong – if he had, tender-hearted history would undoubtedly have kept a trace of it – but, for a few days, he did nothing. Did not get baptized. Did not get married, but waited for one of those winds of the soul which have to rise in us before we dare set sail for shores unknown.

'By divine agency', as *The Chronicle* has it, or otherwise, he fell ill. That happens. Since, in the Middle Ages, no one believed in such an irrational concept as chance, he could not help but put two and two together and conclude that his malady was somehow connected with his tergiversations. Doctors could do nothing for him – nothing unusual in that – and Princess Anna, who had every reason, religious, political, personal, to point out that only baptism could cure him, did so. [137] Moreover she was probably sincere: this was a time when all good things were believed to lie in one direction. And even nowadays what Christian Scientist, for instance – and perhaps what Christian, whatever his denomination – would deny that spiritual purification is good for health? So, finally, he called in the priests and said: 'Have it your way. Baptize me.'

Then – is this so surprising? – what ought to have happened actually did happen. A short time before, Vladimir was writing to the Emperors: 'My soul thirsts for holy baptism.' His temporary recoil carried no weight against the thirst on the one hand and the effectiveness of the rite on the other, even without mentioning grace, which had every reason to descend on the head of this fundamentally good man who had led a life of murder and lechery and was freely renouncing it for ever. The bishops, the priests, the deacons, the chanters, the singers and – yes, why not? – the angels surrounded Vladimir the servant of God when he was systematically exorcized, thrice immersed in holy water, and then confirmed in his new faith and anointed with sacred chrism. On his forehead, his eyes, his ears, his nostrils, his lips, his breast, his hands and his feet was thus affixed 'the seal of the gift of the Holy Spirit'. He rose a new man, 'resplendent as the sun', feeling none of the symptoms of his former illness (as who would in such circumstances?), and, since there is no real conversion without repentance, he may well have exclaimed as, according to Jacob the Monk, he really did:

Lord and kind Sovereign! Thou hast remembered me and hast brought me to Light and I have known Thee, who art the Creator of all creation. Glory to Thee, God of all, Father of our Lord God Jesus Christ! Glory to Thee and thy Son and the Holy Spirit! How merciful Thou hast been to me! I was in darkness, I served the devil and the demons, but Thou through holy baptism hast illumined me. I was like a beast, much evil did I do as a pagan, and I lived like a brute, but Thou hast tamed me and taught me by thy grace. Glory to Thee, O God, glorified as the Trinity, Father, Son and Holy Spirit, O holy Trinity! Have pity on me, put me on thy path and teach me to do thy will, for Thou art my God.

On beholding their Prince healthy and joyful – Olga also had stressed the joyful aspect of Christianity – many of his companions demanded to be baptized too. There may have been some dedicated courtiers among them, but one should not forget that joy is contagious, that religious emotions in particular tend to communicate themselves to crowds, and so it seems, on the whole, more realistic to suppose that most of these neophytes were sincere.[138]

The wedding ceremony followed. Vladimir kissed his wife and 'loved her without measure because she was pleasing to God', writes one of the chroniclers[139] with a mixture of delightful naïveté and deep understanding: if subsequent events are to be taken into consideration, it appears that Vladimir really loved Anna as a wife, in the Christian sense of the word, whereas all his former spouses had scarcely meant more to him than his concubines. But there is no reason to believe that other considerations did not help: Anna was young, refined, she may have been beautiful, she was Greek – and we have already played with the idea that a Greek woman was for Vladimir the first embodiment of the Eternal feminine – she was a Purple-born Princess, and everybody knows that princesses are more attractive than other women, in short the strict monogamy by which Vladimir henceforth abode need not be met with too much compassion: he was approximately twenty-eight, he had sown his wild oats – a lot of them – it was time for him to attempt a new adventure, the adventure of settling down.

The streets of Cherson were all revelry. To the popular jubilation which generally accompanies royal marriages was added this time one very sound reason to rejoice: Vladimir announced that he was giving Cherson back to the Basileus, *without a ransom*. Not in contempt, not in arrogance, but as the gift it was customary for a Slavic bridegroom to make to his in-laws. The gesture was royal – a whole city in the bride's basket – and made a lot of sense: Vladimir could not have kept Cherson if he had wanted to: it was too far from base. He could have looted it, yes, but that, for higher reasons, he did not want to do. Was not returning it, as a gift to a lady, the most elegant way to dispose of it? Once again a case of several birds and one stone.

Among all the festivities which took place in Cherson, Vladimir found time to entertain a mission sent by Pope John xv. This is interesting on two counts: it shows how alert Rome was to all new developments in Christendom: it also shows that, baptized by the Greeks, Vladimir took the first opportunity to show that he did not in any way recognize their suzerainty, and would entertain the best relations with the Bishop of Rome if he felt like it.

At the same time, he erected in Cherson a church dedicated to St Basil, the patron of the Basileus and his own, which was appropriate and polite. *The Chronicle* says the church stood on the soil which had been removed from the ramp he had tried to build, which, if true, was both humorous and profound. After a surfeit of feasts – and we can imagine what they were like, offered by either the ever hospitable Vladimir or by the deeply relieved Greeks – the Great Prince decided to travel back to his capital, with the new Basilissa. Cherson remained untouched. Vladimir took nothing with him but holy icons, sacred vessels, the relics of St Clement and his disciple Phoebus,[140] and two bronze statues and four bronze horses which he liked so much that the Greeks gave them to him. Those Hellenic horses riding up the cataracts (the Seething, the Insatiable, the Do Not Sleep) must have been quite a sight, and the inventory itself, half religious, half artistic, strikingly summarizes the specific features of Greek-born Russian civilization.

Even before the cataracts were reached, the fleet sailed past Khortitsa Island. There, on the top of the bluff, stood the sacred oak. But now it was autumn and, with the leaves gone, one could see that 'some of the branches had been broken and the bark scarred. With its enormous ungainly limbs sprawling asymmetrically, and its gnarled hands and fingers, it stood like an old, grim and scornful monster.'[141] Vladimir, one imagines, scowled at the 'rigid, misshapen' form. 'Why do you frown so, my lord?' asked Anna, who was doubtless still a little afraid of the great and loving man she had so unwillingly married. He answered nothing and only looked the other way: how could she, born a Christian, with Truth deposited in her cradle, understand that he was taking leave of his past, his youth, his vices, his mistakes, and, in a sense, of his very self? For from then on it would not be his life, but 'Christ's in him'.[142]

CHAPTER SIX

Basileus

1 Joy[143]

In the poem in which Aleksey Tolstoy recounts the baptism of Vladimir[144] he describes in particularly perspicacious terms the hero's return to Kiev, the hereditary city which he has now learned to love in a more meaningful way:

> What I thought to possess by the strength of the sword
> Has now taken possession of me.

The Russian boats have crossed the cataracts. They are approaching home. The religious chanting of the priests alternates with the oarsmen's war songs. When Kiev appears with its Shchekovitsa hill – we can visualize the wooden towers, the earthen walls, the people pouring out to meet their once more victorious Prince – the singing ceases, silence falls over the waters, Vladimir, filled with 'the sense of new beginnings', rises from his princely seat, and

> a new vision is opened to him.
> Like a dream his past life by him flies,
> He senses the truth of the Pastor;
> His first tears have rushed forth from his eyes,
> And for the first time, as it seems, he descries
> The city which calls him her master.

Poets are sometimes the best historians, and the idea that on his return Vladimir had the impression of seeing Kiev for the first time is a profound insight not only into the

227

psychology of the princely neophyte, but also into the historical meaning of the event. So far he had been nothing but a hereditary dictator – a beneficent one because he happened to be born kind and shrewd – and he had 'possessed' the city, inasmuch as he had wrought his will over her. Now he was going to rule over her 'by divine right', i.e. he would confess to being her master only inasmuch as he himself recognized a higher master to whom he would be responsible for the use he made of his power over her. In Russia the concept of legitimacy was born on that day, and although it was to be often abused, misused, misunderstood, there is no doubt that it signified progress over the law of the jungle which had prevailed so far. The city spread out on its three hills was at Vladimir's mercy just as Anna had been on that gangway a few months before, but Vladimir was not to be bothered by any more alternatives or temptations. Just as he knew that he had become a new man, he knew that this was not going to be the old Kiev, the seat of pleasure, power and mistaken worship: it was to be a new Kiev, purified of paganism, sanctified by baptism, and treated from then on not as an heirloom but as a trust. To possess this new city, ruse and might would be of no avail: the only key to its gates was the truth of God.

The people waited, the people cheered. On the very edge of the water, Tolstoy describes an ecstatic contingent:

> The Christians were coming from cave and from wood,
> Roofless outcasts, shy wanderers, they stood
> And praised their Creator and Saviour.

Then Vladimir turned on his retinue a gaze which had become 'peaceful and meek' and said to his brothers-at-arms:

Your swords and your axes, my friends, will no longer
Be our only allies in the field,
For the time has arrived, and the strength we now wield
Will make us exceedingly stronger.

With all the solemnity the occasion required, Vladimir ascended now the very pier on which, as a child, he had played at taking Constantinople. If he was to rule over a new city, the people had to understand that they had a new lord. He would let the Vikings go on calling him *Konung* (King) and the Slavs *Knyaz* (Prince) or *Kagan* (Khan), but, although he never insisted on the title, the Greeks would properly address him as Basileus, and it would be as well for the people to observe at once the sacred insignia that came with that sacred name. We have to imagine him stepping on to the wooden embankment clad in a black chasuble, a huge purple mantle embroidered with gold, and the famous red boots. On his head he was wearing the crown sent by his brothers-in-law. It consisted of a golden circle studded with pearls, adorned on the sides with pearl pendants, covered with purple silk and surmounted by a cross set with four big pearls. In his right hand he held the golden sceptre, scintillating with gems and also symbolically surmounted by a cross. At the present time, only the ceremonial attire of Orthodox archbishops can give an idea of the hieratic magnificence of the ensemble.[145] Perhaps it is not the hood that makes the monk, but when the monk is any good, the hood makes him better. Vladimir was worthy of the imperial costume. He had twenty-six years left to reign, and he would make the best of each one of them.

The first measure of his new reign was to settle his accounts with his famous favourites, the pagan gods. There and then he thundered his orders: the idols were to

229

be burned, slashed, hacked down to small chips. Volos, the god of cattle and commerce, was thrown into the Pochayna. And then, when nearly all the Pantheon had gone – Mokosh, and Dazhbog, and Stribog, and Sim, and Rogl, and the mysterious Khors – it was the turn of Perun of the insatiable appetite. Ladders leaned against the huge wooden body; ropes were tied around the silver nose and the golden moustache. With crude jokes men hoisted and hauled. The colossus which had been an object of worship a few minutes before shook and squeaked on his base. Vladimir stood there, screwing up his eyes at the downfall of the false master to whom he had addressed so many prayers, sacrificed so many lambs and bullocks. When the great mass came crashing down and the splinters flew, he did not wince. He hated the lie he had loved for so long. 'Tie him to a horse's tail.' They tied him. 'Flog him.' The servants took sticks and began flogging the cheat. 'Dump him into the river.' Whips cracked, horses reared, oaths and cries resounded, and the blows still rained on the defenceless carcass as it was dragged down the Borichev stream and thrown into the Dniepr, in an orgy of contempt and ridicule. Kiev was well rid of the thing, but that was not enough. The whole Russian land had to be cleansed, and this could not be achieved if by any chance the current drove the idol ashore. So a special party of twelve men was sent to accompany 'the father of lies' downstream, in order to push him back into the water whenever needed, until he had reached the cataracts and been smashed against the rocks. *The Chronicle* states that this did not happen: after crossing the cataracts without mishap, the idol was finally thrown by the wind on to a beach at the foot of what came to be known as Perun's Hill. This would easily suffer a symbolic interpretation: the old pagan

Vladimir as Basileus. Coin minted under Vladimir.
Hermitage Museum, Leningrad.

stock, it might be said, was not completely eradicated from Russia; one could even maintain that it flourished again after one thousand years, but for the time being Vladimir's victory seemed complete.

To us, who have not known the dark evils of paganism, so much indignity heaped upon the fallen god, such a passionate desire not only to destroy but also to humiliate, may seem exaggerated; already the chronicler felt the need to explain that the idea was not to make the huge wooden doll suffer, but 'to affront the demon who had deceived us in this form'. It must be remembered that early Christians did not doubt the existence of pagan gods: they saw in them the embodiment of fiends whose purpose was to delude mankind and against whom simple, credulous souls had to be protected. Vladimir's imaginative execution of Perun was meant to demonstrate the weakness of the devil when confronted with the true God, and so to convert idolaters to Christianity. No doubt it may also have expressed an angry reaction against his own religious mistakes. Finally, it expressed the jubilant triumph of the Church Militant over the forces of darkness and death, a triumph which seems to have been somewhat worn out by the centuries, but of which St John Chrysostom gave an unforgettable verbalization in his Paschal Epistle. Hell, exclaims the great orator 'is spited for it is erased; it is spited for it is made a mockery; it is spited for it is annihilated; it is spited for it is in chains . . . O death, where is thy sting? O Hell, where is thy victory?'

As the grotesque, once so dear, figure, was pulled down, dishonoured, derided, as it finally splashed into the water – only water, of course, could fully conquer the god of lightning by wetting his fireworks – reactions were not unmixed. The chronicler himself, favourable as he is to Russia's conversion, confesses that some of the Kievans wept at the sight, and this adds authority to his description of what followed. Vladimir sent heralds throughout the city ordering everyone to come on the morrow to the Dniepr to be baptized: male or female, old or young, rich or poor, working or begging, not one pagan would remain in the city to offend the Lord by his presence. John's 'baptism of repentance'[146] had been accomplished through the destruction of the idols; it was time for Kiev to accept the baptism of Jesus, and through him to receive the Spirit. As to the reactionaries whose sobs had mingled with the soldiers' insults and jibes, for their benefit Vladimir added the ominous words: 'If anyone does not come, let him consider himself my foe.' This was enough: no force was used to bring the entire population of Kiev to the bank of the Dniepr at the break of day, which is not as surprising as it may seem: the Viking prince was the *gode* (priest), the *Opferpriester* (in charge of sacrifices)[147] of his people; spiritually he stood head and shoulders above his subjects and they had few doubts that his decision in religious matters could only be in their common interest. This is why the populace enthusiastically exclaimed: 'If this were not good, the Prince and his boyars would not have accepted it.' What they knew about the Christian religion was next to nothing; still they were full of hope and ready to submit to the operation which was supposed to give them eternal life, as well as put them on a par with the civilized Greeks.

In the east, dawn peeped out, and 'a countless multitude'[148] assembled. A number of Vladimir's sons and daughters, legitimate or otherwise, joined the crowd, while the Great Prince himself, the Great Princess, the bishops and priests – Anna's chaplains and clerical reinforcements brought from Cherson, with Anastas prominent among them – remained in a group. Chanting and incense rose into the pure morning air, new sounds, new smells for the Slavs. Indicating their new flock to the all-seeing Eye of God, the priests prayed: 'Remove from them their former delusion and fill them with the faith, hope and love which are in Thee, that they may know that Thou art the only true God, with thine only-begotten Son, our Lord Jesus Christ and thy Holy Spirit . . .'

'Answer *amen*!' ordered Vladimir, and, for the first time, thousands of Russian tongues and throats formed the Hebrew word which means 'so be it'.

The time for the first exorcism had come, and one of the bishops addressed himself directly to the prince of this world:

The Lord puts you under ban, O Devil: He who came into the world, and made his abode among men, that He might overthrow your tyranny and deliver men; who also upon the Tree did triumph over the adverse powers, when the sun was darkened, and the earth did quake, and the graves were opened, and the bodies of the saints arose; who also by death annihilated death and overthrew him who exercised the dominion of death, that is you, the Devil. I charge you by God, who revealed the Tree of Life, and arrayed in ranks the Cherubim and the flaming sword which turns all ways to guard it: Be under ban. For I charge you by Him who walked upon the surface of the sea as it were dry land, and laid under his ban the tempests of the winds; whose glance dries up the deep, and whose interdict makes the mountains melt away. The same now, through us, puts you under ban. Fear, begone and depart from these creatures, and return not again, neither hide yourself in them, neither seek to meet them, nor to influence them, either by night or by day; either in the morning or at noonday; but depart hence to your own infernal abyss until the great Day of Judgement which is ordained. Fear God who sits upon the Cherubim and looks upon the deeps; before whom tremble Angels and Archangels, Thrones, Dominions, Principalities, Authorities, Powers, the many-eyed Cherubim and the six-winged Seraphim; before whom, likewise, heaven and earth do quake, the seas and all that they contain. Begone, and depart from these sealed, newly enlisted warriors of Christ our God. For I charge you by Him who rides upon the wings of the wind, and makes his Angels spirits, and his ministers a flaming fire: Begone, and depart from these creatures, with all your powers and your angels. For glorified is the Name of the Father, and of the Son, and of the Holy Spirit, now and ever and unto ages of ages.

And the people answered: 'Amen.'
Another bishop read the second exorcism.

God, holy, awesome and glorious, who is unsearchable and inscrutable in all his works and might, has foreordained for you the penalty of eternal punishment, O Devil: the same, through us, his unworthy servant, commands you, with all your hosts, to depart hence, from them who have been newly sealed in the Name of our Lord Jesus Christ, our true God. Wherefore I charge you, most crafty, impure, vile, loathsome and alien spirit, by the might of Jesus Christ, who has all power, both in heaven and on earth, who said unto the deaf and dumb demon, Come out of the man, and in nowise enter a second time into him: Depart! Acknowledge the vainness of your might, which has not power even over swine. Call to mind who, at your request, commanded you to enter into the herd of swine. Fear God, by whose decree the earth is established upon the waters; who has made the heavens, and has set the mountains with a line, and the valleys with a measure; and has fixed bounds to the sands of the sea, and a firm path upon the stormy waters; who touches the mountains and they smoke; who clothes himself with light as with a garment; who spreads out the heavens like a curtain; who covers his exceeding high places with the waters; who has made the earth so sure upon its foundations, that it shall never be moved; who gathers the water of the sea and pours it out upon the face of the whole earth: Begone, and depart from them who have made themselves ready for holy illumination. I charge you by the redeeming Passion of our Lord Jesus Christ, and by his precious Body and Blood, and by his awesome Coming-again; for He shall come, and shall not tarry, to judge the whole earth; and He shall chastise you and all your host with burning Gehenna, committing you to outer darkness, where the worm does not cease and the fire is not quenched. For of Christ our God is the dominion, with the Father and the Holy Spirit, now and ever and unto ages of ages.

As the people, happy to be taught, answered once more 'Amen', Vladimir, no doubt, remembered how the same ceremony had been performed over him. And it had worked! The devil had indeed departed from him, leaving him with a peace and a joy he had not dreamed were possible. Now a third priest, maybe Anastas himself, moved forward and read the third and final exorcism:

O Lord of Sabaoth, the God of Israel, who healest every malady and every infirmity: Look upon thy servants; probe them and search them and root out of them every operation of the Devil. Rebuke the unclean spirits and expel them, and purify the work of thy hands; and exerting thy trenchant might, speedily crush down Satan under their feet; and give them victory over the same, and over his unclean spirits; that having obtained mercy from Thee, they may be made worthy to partake of thy heavenly Mysteries; and may ascribe unto Thee glory, to the Father and to the Son and to the Holy Spirit, now and ever and unto ages of ages.

Three times a bishop asked of the people, 'Do you renounce Satan, and all his works, and all his angels, and all his service and all his pride?' Three times Vladimir, speaking not for himself but for his men, replied, 'We do renounce him', and they repeated it after him.

Then the bishop asked, likewise three times, 'Have you renounced Satan?' And Vladimir, as the godfather of his people, replied: 'We have renounced him.' 'Breathe and spit upon him!' ordered the bishop. Vladimir breathed and spat, and all the Kievans imitated him. 'Do you unite yourselves to Christ?' asked the bishop. 'We do unite ourselves to Christ.' 'Have you united yourselves to Christ?' 'We have united ourselves to Christ.' And finally: 'Do you believe in Him?' 'We believe in Him as King and God.'

After this oath of allegiance had been pronounced, the clergy turned toward the wide expanse of the quiet Dniepr and blessed its waters:

Great art Thou, O Lord, and marvellous are thy works, and there is no word which suffices to hymn thy wonders. For Thou, of thine own good will, hast brought into being all things which before were not, and by thy might Thou dost uphold creation, and by thy providence Thou dost order the world. When Thou hadst joined together the universe out of four elements, Thou didst crown the circle of the year with four seasons. Before Thee tremble all the Powers endowed with intelligence. The sun sings unto Thee. The moon glorifies Thee. The stars meet together before thy presence. The light obeys Thee. The deeps tremble before Thee. The water-springs are subject unto Thee . . . Thou didst hallow the streams of Jordan, sending down from heaven thy Holy Spirit, and didst crush the heads of the dragons who lurked there. Wherefore, O King who lovest mankind, come Thou now and sanctify this water, by the indwelling of thy Holy Spirit.

Three times the priests dipped the fingers of their right hands into the Dniepr and traced the sign of the cross over it. The whole river was now holy, and the people entered it, some up to their necks, others to their breasts, the younger remaining close to the bank, the older wading farther out. Looking toward the east, they immersed themselves three times, once in the Name of the Father, once in the Name of the Son, once in the Name of the Holy Spirit. Then they clambered back to shore, shivering a little in the autumn air, but feeling that a new Life had begun for them. The Dniepr flowed on, faintly rippled by the morning breeze.

Seized by a deep emotion, Vladimir lifted his eyes to heaven, and extending his arms over the people who had been his and whom he had just turned over to a greater Prince, prayed thus: 'O God, who hast created heaven, earth, sea and all that is in them! Look down upon these thy new men, and cause them to know Thee who art the true God, even as other Christian nations do. Continue in them a right and inalterable faith, and help me, o Lord, against the foe[149] who confronts me, so that hoping in Thee and in thy might, I may overcome his snares.' Slowly the people walked back to their homes, marvelling at the Spirit who had blown over them and rejoicing in a future which would have no end. Undoubtedly it was not to be as perfect and innocent as they then thought it would be; calamities would fall upon them and they themselves would sin abundantly and grievously. But the knowledge that sin is made to be forgiven would never leave their hearts. The voice of a Dostoievsky or of a Sergius Bulgakov still echoes, after a span of nearly one thousand years, the superhuman joy that prevailed in the city of Kiev on that brisk morning in the autumn of 989.[150] 'O what rapture, what jubilance there was on earth!' exclaims Jacob the Monk. 'Angels and archangels joined in the gaiety and the spirits of the saints made merry. Did not the Lord Himself say what joy reigns in heaven for one repented sinner? And numberless souls in all the Russian land had been brought to God by holy baptism. Such a deed deserves all kinds of praise, and it is filled with spiritual joy.' The joy was not all spiritual, either. Not to mention the banquet which no doubt celebrated the occasion, Vladimir had set all his slaves, men and women, free in honour of their baptism,[151] and the happiness of the new Christians, who were also new citizens, was probably not the least boisterous on that day. As to his wives and concubines, he liberally gave them in marriage to his companions,[152] which no doubt pleased the ladies, since now each would have a husband to herself.

2 The trumpet of the Apostles

So far, and with the exception of a few tears soon dried up, the evangelization of Russia had been a purely happy affair. Whereas Clodovicus of France had baptized his retinue after a defeat, Charlemagne had had to use force to christianize the Saxons, and St Stephen employ violence to make the Hungarians adopt the Western form of Christianity, Vladimir christened Kiev *verbis non verberibus*, by words not by blows.[153] Things did not go so smoothly in Novgorod and the northern provinces, where paganism was still very active, and it must be confessed, not without regret, that as so very often in history Christianity and intolerance appeared in Great Russia hand in hand. True, it is the unreliable Joachim who tells the story, but the details have a ring of truth about them, although the names may have been added later, as suggested by their relatively modern form.

It is here that Uncle Dobrynya, whom we had more or less forgotten, re-enters the stage. It is not known where he had spent the months of the Cherson campaign. It may be that Vladimir had called him back from Novgorod and entrusted the capital to him, or that, as soon as he heard the Great Prince had returned, he rushed south to pay his respects and, of course, get baptized in a jiffy. Religion, as far as Dobrynya was concerned, must have been a matter of military drill. 'Bring the Novgorodians to Jesus Christ? Yes, Sir, straight away, Sir.' A bishop and a good retinue was all he needed, and, having received both, he departed to execute his mission.

Did Vladimir know what he was doing when he sent Dobrynya on his evangelical expedition? There is little doubt that he did. It may even be surmised that he deliberately did not go to Novgorod himself, just as he managed to be away when Blud brought Yaropolk to the palace. There was no point at all in the Great Prince making himself unpopular with his faithful northern subjects; Dobrynya could attend to all the unpleasant aspects of the operation; Vladimir would appear himself when the time for reconciliation came. He did indeed travel to Novgorod eight years later, in 997, and had apparently no trouble recruiting soldiers there.

Pagans, as mentioned earlier, had no priests, but they had wizards whose influence could be strong. One of them, called Bogomil and nicknamed Solovey (Nightingale) for his eloquence, either because he was sincerely attached to pagan traditions or because he feared for the profits he derived from the practice of his art, excited the people in advance against submission to Christianity, so that when the baptizing party, which had cautiously landed on the market side, arrived at the famous Novgorod bridge, they found it partly disassembled, partly fenced up. An armed and resolute crowd stood behind the barricade; for the first time Dobrynya's authority was thwarted. He tried to parley – the Novgorodians would not listen. They had sworn not to let him enter and destroy their idols. Threats and blandishments were of no avail, and Dobrynya had to camp on the market side, where, after two days and much propaganda in markets and streets, Bishop Joachim,[154] a Chersonian, had succeeded in baptizing a few hundred citizens. This was not the kind of efficiency to which Dobrynya had accustomed his master.

To make matters worse, Ugonyay, the chief of the Novgorod militia, riding around the old city, encouraged his men to resist until death: 'It would be better for us to die than to allow our gods to be dishonoured.' It had begun like a riot, it was developing into an insurrection. The riffraff broke into Dobrynya's own house, wrecked it, looted his belongings, ferociously bludgeoned his wife and several of his kinsmen. There was no help for it but to counter-attack. Putyata, apparently Dobrynya's second-in-command, both a brave and an astute officer, took five hundred men, crossed the Volkhov under cover of night, circled the city, and entered it from the other side, passing for a defender instead of an assailant. Having arrested the sleeping Ugonyay and his aides, he sent word to Dobrynya by the same roundabout route that he had the situation well in hand. He had not. The Novgorodians had realized their mistake and five thousand of them set upon him. The battle raged. The houses of the Christians were plundered and the Church of the Transfiguration, probably Novgorod's only Christian place of worship, was torn apart. At dawn, with all the men he had left, Dobrynya rushed to the rescue and, resorting to desperate means, set the Podol on fire.

A few torches sufficed. The wooden houses blazed; it became imperative to extinguish the fire before the whole city burned. The Novgorodians abandoned the fight for their religion to save their belongings; the notables came to Dobrynya with their fur caps off and asked for peace.

The plundering stopped; the execution of the idols began: the wooden ones were burned down, the stone ones broken up and the remains thrown into the river. At the shocking sight, men and women began to cry. Weeping and sobbing, they begged for their gods as for human beings, but Dobrynya only laughed: 'You must be mad to pity such as cannot defend themselves. What use could they be to you?' Little did he know that he was paraphrasing what another God, the one he was so earnestly trying to serve at this very moment, had heard on the cross a thousand years before.[155] Perun, the glorious Perun who stood on the hill above the old city, toppled over with a resounding crash. Harnessed bulls pulled him over dung while soldiers bastinadoed him. 'Arise, our god!' cried men and women, running after him. But he did not arise. And while the God of love could consistently remain on the cross, it was bewildering that the god of brutal force, who had been supposed to make his followers invincible, should allow himself to be so insulted.

> Where is his might? Where is his sacred power?
> Was he no god?

asked the Novgorodians in awe . . . Perun was pushed off the cliff into the Volkhov, and doubts began to creep into the pagans' minds. Reconstructing the feelings of another people who went through the same experience, Aleksey Tolstoy concludes his poem *Rugevit* with these lines:

243

And when we woke from our first consternation,
We did not feel our former love for him,
And wandering off in sombre meditation,
We said: 'Swim on! You did not save our nation,
God made of oak, swim hence, we tell you, swim!'

The next day, a potter from Pidba, a village located some four kilometres from Novgorod on the left bank of the Volkhov, on his way to the great city where he hoped, notwithstanding the recent historical events, to sell some of his earthenware, found the idol stuck in a small cove. The good potter, with his arms akimbo, looked down at the great gormandizer floating at his feet, entangled in weeds and wearing the signs of heavy flagellation. It was a sorry sight, but it made the fellow laugh. 'Perun, you old hog,' he said. 'You have had your time eating and drinking. Now just swim off.' He took a long pole and shoved the thing back into the current.[156]

Meanwhile Dobrynya's heralds with the *posadnik* Vorobey (Sparrow) Stoyanov at their head – he had been educated at Vladimir's court and was, we are told,[157] a great orator – made speeches to the populace to persuade them to get baptized. Deprived of their pagan gods, most Novgorodians submitted willingly enough, knowing in their simple wisdom that a man cannot survive without one god or another. Those who resisted were persuaded by other means: the soldiers would grab them by the nape of the neck and duck them into the Volkhov, but not without method. Dobrynya had always been a great organizer and would not tolerate any confusion: men were baptized upstream from the bridge, women downstream. Some pagans tried to escape by pretending they were already baptized, but they counted without Dobrynya's administrative skills: after baptism, each citizen received a cross made of wood, or brass, or copper, to carry around his neck. Anyone who could not produce such a cross was dipped, and if it was the second time, well, no harm could come of it, could it? In a few hours there was not one pagan left in Novgorod – at least in theory – and Putyata was dispatched to Kiev to report 'Mission accomplished'. Centuries later Russians would still remember that 'Putyata had baptized Novgorod with the sword and Dobrynya had christened it with fire.'

During the next few years the evangelization of Russia kept Vladimir pretty busy. Obviously the destruction of idols and the baptism of pagans, whether enthusiastic or reluctant, could not be an end in itself. For Christianity to spread, it was necessary to have three elements: a ritual, churches and clerics.

The liturgical texts were of course Greek in origin, but only the Slavonic translations made by St Cyril (Constantine) were used, which shows that some Bulgarian influence must have been exercised at this point. This is verified by the presence of Bulgarian saints in the earliest Russian calendars and by numerous Bulgarian religious manuscripts discovered in Russia; it is also quite consonant with Vladimir's firm decision not to let Russia fall under an exaggerated Greek influence. Bulgars, on the contrary, were quite welcome: they had had the same problem, and at one point they had even sided with the Bishop of Rome to prove their independence from the Patriarch of Constantinople (in the 860s).

It was different with buildings. Willy-nilly some architects had to be imported from Greece, at least to erect the largest churches, and also craftsmen to decorate them properly with paintings and mosaics. But the Russians, who were supposed to be the best carpenters of their time, soon learned to emulate them, and, in a few years, churches sprouted all over the country without imported help, most of them wooden and as Vladimir had ordered, established in locations where idols had stood a short while before.[158] In Kiev the pagan pantheon was replaced by a church suitably dedicated to St Basil (it was later replaced by another, dedicated to St Peter). In Novgorod, not to be outdone, Dobrynya is said to have erected an oak Hagia Sophia with thirteen cupolas. In the North-east, Vladimir founded a new city, gave to it his own name, and built there a church dedicated to the Holy Theotokos (991).[159] True to his habit of alternating thrusts in different directions, the next year he founded another Vladimir, known as Vladimir-Volhynsk, on his western flank, with another Theotokos church, and later a third church also dedicated to the Virgin was erected in the north-eastern city of Rostov. To thank God for a narrow escape from the Pechenegs, yet another church was built in Vasiliev, in honour of the Transfiguration, for it was upon that day that Vladimir had been saved.

The architecture of all these buildings was of course conceived as an imitation of the Byzantine, but different materials and different climates produce different styles; soon the Greek structures had been adapted to Russian necessities, the classic stone cupola being replaced more and more by the onion dome made of wooden scales, and the various Russian *lady* (modes, orders) taking the place of Greek orders.

The largest church erected by Vladimir was once again dedicated to the Holy Virgin according to Jacob the Monk – some specify to the Dormition – as well as according to *The Chronicle*. It is probably by mistake that Thietmar refers to it as Hagia Sophia. It was built in 994–996, and burned down in 1017, but enough remains of it to give an idea of what it looked like.[160] Its surface was 1542.5 square metres; its length approximately 55

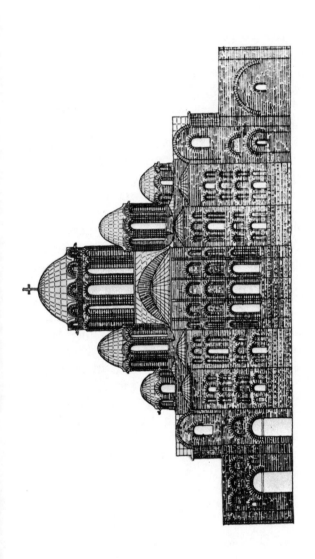

St Sophia, Kiev.
(Photo J. da Cunha-Plon. Courtesy of Mme Zalessky.)

metres, its width approximately 26 metres. It had one main cupola, four minor cupolas and probably twenty little ones. There were three naves separated by columns made of marble of Marmara; the walls were of stone, glass and Crimean jasper, partly covered with mosaics and frescoes; in the chancel the floor was a mosaic of multicoloured marbles; in the naves it was red slate from the Carpathians. The dedication of the church was celebrated on May 12 (996 ?),[161] which thus became the first Russian religious festival. If the church was indeed dedicated to the Dormition of the Holy Theotokos, the remarks made above[162] concerning the significance of this solemnity for the Orthodox apply again. A banquet, even more liberal than usual, and the distribution of much largess ensued. Vladimir was very proud of the building and begged the Theotokos to hear the supplications of whoever would pray in it. On this occasion he donated to this church one tenth of his property, to be spent on the living of priests, orphans, widows and poor people in general,[163] so that it came to be known as the Church of the Tithe. Anyone violating this promise, Vladimir declared, would be accursed. He embellished his favourite with icons, and placed in it all the sacred vessels and crosses he had brought back from Cherson, as well as the relics of St Clement. Significantly enough, he appointed Cherson priests, not Greeks from Greece, to officiate at the Tithe, and entrusted its administration to the notorious Anastas, who may or may not have become a bishop in the meantime.

Treasury and treason seem to go well together, and it is difficult, at this point, to refrain from New Testament associations. The following course of events seems to indicate that such thoughts are not completely groundless and that it was indeed difficult for Anastas to keep away from the good things of this world. Was Vladimir mistaken in him? Or did he believe that traitors are useful and that crooks make on the whole good administrators? Who knows?

Beside the relics of St Clement was laid Olga's body, which had remained intact after her death, as anyone could see who might peer through a window opened in her coffin. Here also were kept the standard weights and measures to which all others, in the markets of Kiev, must conform. This last point is extremely characteristic of a period when religion was deemed to be the key, the only key, to the whole world. Besides, in a land where a Dostoievsky would write, 'If there is no God, everything is permissible', it was especially fitting for the Holy Virgin to keep watch over the standards of honest trade.

The question of the recruitment of priests was apparently no great problem: Christianity was such a success in Russia that Chersonians and Bulgars were soon replaced by local products. Monasteries flourished already in Vladimir's lifetime, or at least very soon after his death; the schools he created dispensed an excellent religious education; the sophisticated eloquence of an Hilarion shows that the Russians were quite ready for intellectual progress, and that it was afforded to them. One can only marvel at the ease with which classical civilization was grafted on to the Russian stock, be it only on to one small part of it.

It is rather where clerical hierarchy was concerned that difficulties arose. Much has been written by competent scholars about this particular point, and little can be added here to the numerous and contradictory demonstrations, which, in the absence of coherent source material, tend to prove either that the Russian Church was autonomous, or that it was under direct Greek control, that its primates were metropolitans, or that they were archbishops, that it was administered by Tmutorakan, or by Cherson, or that it was an extension of the Bulgarian Church. It is not the present author's intention to enter the lists since, important as it is for Church history, the point does not, strictly speaking, belong to Vladimir's biography.[164] Still, one observation may be in order: the very fact that nothing certain is known about such a prominent question and that such contradictory evidence can be produced about it, may be interpreted as showing simply that, as long as Vladimir lived, no definite status was adopted for the Russian Church, and excellent reasons could be found for such a state of things. While the Patriarch of Constantinople tried to keep Russia under his thumb by considering it mission territory, Vladimir strove to make it if not already autocephalous, at least as independent as he could, and they both preferred not to spell out problems which they both hoped to solve by-and-by to their respective advantages. Vladimir's marriage to Princess Anna – the irretrievable gauge – allowed him to maintain *vis-à-vis* Constantinople a comfortably relaxed attitude, and it fell to the lot of his descendants, Yaroslav in particular, alternately to quibble with the Patriarchs and to submit to their authority in religious matters. In the meantime complete political autonomy had been secured,[165] while the vagueness of the Russian Church's constitution did not hurt her vitality in the least. The figure of Kuchug,[166] the Pecheneg prince converted to Christianity, who became a vassal and a favourite of Vladimir's, may be more legendary than historical, but it is symbolic of an indubitable fact: as opposed to France, Russia might be the Church's youngest daughter, but it was growing fast.

This growth was systematically organized. Vladimir

had surrounded himself with a council of bishops with whom he consulted frequently to find better ways of establishing Christianity – real Christianity – among the new converts.[167] A document which is undoubtedly apocryphal, since it begins with a grandiose anachronism,[168] but which still appears to contain authentic information, emphasizes the organized aspect of the reform. It is presented in the form of an edict signed by the 'Prince Basil, also called Vladimir, son of Svyatoslav, grandson of Igor and of the holy Princess Olga', and it makes the following points:

1 foundation of the tithe: the tenth squirrel skin of the judicial dues in the districts of the princedom, the produce of the tenth week from commercial imposts, and for every house and family the tenth part of the income from cattle and reaped corn, would go to the Church – there may be some confusion here with the establishment of the Church of the Tithe to which the Prince, and the Prince alone, had promised one tenth of his revenues

2 foundation of an ecclesiastical judicial power: the Church would have its own tribunals and no one but the Church would take cognizance of the following cases: divorce, adultery, fights between married persons, abduction, incest, magic, poisoning, witchcraft, incantations, accusations of fornication, poisoning and heresy, biting, striking of a father or of a mother by a son or by a daughter, or of a mother-in-law by a daughter-in-law, contests about legacies among siblings or descendants, robbing of churches, robbing of a dead man's clothes, mutilation of the cross or of the walls of a church, introduction of cattle or dogs or birds into a church without great need (one wonders what the great need could have been), other unbecoming actions in church, in the case of a fight between two men the sexual mutilation of one by

251

the other's wife (O devoted Russian better halves!), intercourse with four-legged creatures, heathen worship in barns, in woods and by streams, abortion. To simplify, it can be said that the Church held jurisdiction over family, sexual and religious matters. The intolerant mention of heathen worship 'in barns, in woods and by streams' is somewhat disturbing: did Vladimir by any chance organize a kind of Inquisition? No. There is no trace of such an institution in the whole history of the Russian Church (with the regrettable exception of the group of prelates who persecuted old-believers in the seventeenth century). Moreover one must remember that the Vikings' judicial traditions were extremely mild: if the worst came to the worst, it would have been a question of a fine and not of the stake

3 entrusting of markets to bishops: the bishops would be responsible for the supervision of measures, weights, scales and balances. This, as confirmed by what we already know about the Church of the Tithe, should not surprise us. But what is characteristic of Vladimir is that he found it necessary to specify that the bishops must 'neither increase nor diminish' the measures, and that 'on the universal day of judgement they shall answer for this as well as for the salvation of souls' – do we detect here an allusion to Anastas?

4 amalgamation of parts of the population with the Church: the Church would administer directly monasteries, hospitals, establishments for the care of guests and strangers, and also certain categories of subjects who, from then on, could be tried only by ecclesiastical courts of justice: these were, quite suitably, priests, deacons and their families, monks, nuns and all sorts of clerics; they were also stewards of church estates, women in charge of baking holy bread, cloistered pilgrims, and, more curi-

ously, physicians, miraculously healed people, slaves released by their masters if this was done for the good of their souls, strangers, the blind and the lame

5 finally, limitation of the powers of the Church: if any contest arose between one of these people and another man, the tribunal appointed to take cognizance of the case would be composed jointly of ecclesiastical and lay judges.

Metropolitan Hilarion describes the evangelization of Russia with his customary enthusiasm: the Prince 'ordered . . . everyone to become a Christian, the small and the great, the slaves and the free, the young and the old, the rich and the indigent, and there was no one who resisted his beneficial order; if some lacked love, they were baptized for fear of him who had ordered it, for his piety was combined with might, so that at the same time all our land rendered glory to Christ with the Father and the Holy Ghost.' The prelate has no illusions concerning the spiritual value of such an instantaneous and collective conversion; he realizes it is just a beginning, but he also knows that future developments would confirm it in depth.

Then the darkness of idolatry began to recede from us and the dawn of true devotion appeared, then the gloom of demonic service perished and the sun of the Gospel shone on our land, the temples were shattered and the churches grew, the idols crumbled and the icons came into sight, the devils fled, the cross illumined the cities, pastors took care of the spiritual sheep of Christ, bishops, priests and deacons offered their pure sacrifices, and all the clergy brought beauty to dress up holy churches.

And he concludes with the flamboyant peroration:

The trumpet of the Apostles and the thunder of the Gospel have resounded through all the towns; incense exhaled to God has sanctified the air; on mountains monasteries have risen; men and women, small and great, have filled holy churches rendering glory with these words: 'One is holy, one is Lord, Jesus Christ, to the glory of God the Father, amen.'[169] Christ has triumphed. Christ has conquered. Christ is King. Christ is glorified. Thou art great, O Lord, and admirable are thy works. Glory to Thee, our God.

3 War and peace

As a pagan prince, Vladimir used to behave kindly and mercifully;[170] once he had become a Christian, his generosity knew no bounds. Social security and welfare organizations would soon have gone bankrupt in his happy realm.

I cannot even enumerate all his charities: not only was he charitable toward people in his own house, but to all the city, and not only in Kiev but in all the Russian land and in the towns and villages, he would practise charity everywhere, clothing the naked, feeding the hungry and refreshing the thirsty, setting foreigners at ease by his charity, showing love and favour to clerics and providing for their needs, taking care of paupers and orphans and widows and the blind and the lame and the over-burdened and everyone.

So writes Jacob the Monk. Hilarion adds that Vladimir would free labourers and redeem debtors. Beggars would assemble in his courtyard every day, and he would receive them always and give them what they asked for, food, drink, or even marten skins and money. As to the sick and the weak who could not come and ask, the Great Prince organized a whole service for them: wagons would be loaded with bread, meat, fish, fruit, also casks of mead and of *kvas* (Vladimir would not dream of depriving a poor ne'er-do-well of a healthy drink), and driven around

Kiev. The driver – sometimes one of Vladimir's own sons, generally Boris – would call out, 'Where is there a poor man who cannot walk?' and be sure that everyone received what he needed.[171] On Sundays, Vladimir's famous banquets were especially plentiful, with three separate ones being prepared: one for the clergy, one for the poor, one for the Prince and his retinue. If the Prince was travelling, the banquets would still take place, and it is to be assumed that everyone would repeatedly drink the absent host's health at his expense.

It is difficult to please everybody (when you are not a gold coin, as the French say), and the *byliny* have preserved the memory of many a conflict between Vladimir and his closest companions, who obviously were as boisterous a bunch of drunkards and brawlers as ever served a Viking prince. Anyway the tradition of the Kiev court was anything but absolute monarchy, and although times were changing and Greek customs were gradually transforming the Konung into a Basileus, Vladimir was still in great need of his retinue. Besides, he was fond of the fellows: they knew how to swear a good oath, fight a good fight, drink a good tankard. So when, after especially hearty libations, they began to grumble at their lack of privileges, he tried to give them satisfaction as well as he could. The chronicler tells us that one day they showed disgust at having to use plain wooden spoons. Vladimir laughed and had silver ones cast for them. Silver versus retinue – it was, he reflected, a little like the egg and hen problem: which comes first? Still, experience had taught him that a good retinue could provide as much silver as was needed, but that silver could not always buy a good retinue. Therefore, although for religious matters he had now his council of bishops, for worldly matters he went on consulting his boyars, generals, *ognishchane* and city elders. In this permanent consultation with the thinking heads of his people may lie one of the secrets of his success. Their advice must have been sound most of the time and he must have put it to good use, for in spite of dangerous times and the spiritual revolution which was in progress, Vladimir met with very few failures and obtained considerable achievements in most fields.

First of all, he began to mint coins, which no other Kiev prince had ever done before him: rather crude gold and silver pieces they were, stamped with an engraved hammer and bearing a representation of Jesus Christ, the Great Prince in imperial attire, or the hereditary trident.[172] The minting of coins is one of the main attributes of sovereignty, and it is characteristic of Vladimir to have attempted it with the help of Russian craftsmen rather than to entrust the job to Greek artists, who would doubtless have created a product more satisfactory from the aesthetic point of view: the coins of a Russian prince had to be minted by Russians, who would eventually learn to make them smoother, more detailed and symmetrical. The proud inscriptions read 'HERE IS VLADIMIR ON HIS THRONE. AND THIS IS HIS GOLD.'

For a nation in full development, the founding of cities was of course essential. Izyaslavl, Vladimir, Vladimir-Volhynsk were supposed to pin the nation down to the land. Belgorod, a village, was extensively settled so as to become a town, presumably as a bulwark for Kiev against Pecheneg incursions.

Then there was education. Vladimir may not have been a great scholar himself, but he was determined to make Russia a civilized nation. So, like Charlemagne, he created schools, and sent there the children of the best families, to study 'book learning'. This was as drastic an innovation as any Peter the Great would impose on his

The trident, which seems to have been the emblem of
the Rurikids, on a coin minted under Vladimir.
Hermitage Museum, Leningrad.

people, and the poor mothers 'mourned their sons as if they were dead', which reminds one of the famous Mrs Prostakova in Fonvizin's *The Minor*: the lady objected to her son learning geography because it was a science for hansom cab drivers. Meek as he had become, Vladimir did not relent, and his son Yaroslav, for instance, learned among other things to speak five languages and to love books. He read them continually day and night, mentions the chronicler with approval and sententiously adds, 'Books are like rivers that water the whole earth; they are the springs of wisdom.'

Vladimir's foreign policy was firm and effective. He remained true to the Greek alliance and some of his men even fought for the Greeks against the Bulgars (although not against Sclerus who, having finally consented to take off the red boots, submitted to Basil and retired into blindness and old age). In return Constantinople kept providing Russia with religious goods, icons and vessels. We know that some, in particular, arrived in 1007 and were deposited in the Church of the Tithe.[173] Excellent relations were entertained with Stephen I of Hungary, Udalrich of Bohemia and, up to a point, with Boleslav the Brave of Poland. Missions were sent to such far-away countries as Jerusalem, Egypt and Babylon, or so at least one chronicler tells us.[174] The Volga Bulgars received permission to trade with Russian merchants, so long as they abstained from contacts with the rest of the population, just as Russian merchants could not go to Bulgar without a valid passport:[175] obviously Vladimir did not want what he considered pernicious Moslem influence to spread among his people.

Although Kiev always remained faithful to the Eastern brand of Christianity, close diplomatic ties were kept with the Bishop of Rome. Expressions of mutual 'love and honour'[176] were exchanged when ambassadors arrived from the Pope or were sent to him. Different authors indicate that the following missions came and went:

989	Rome to Cherson	From and to John xv
981	Rome to Kiev with Polish and Czech envoys	
994	Kiev to Rome	
1000	Rome to Kiev with Czech and Hungarian envoys	From and to Sylvester ii
1001	Kiev to Rome	

This was happening at a time when relations between the Eastern and Western Churches were more and more strained. Fifty years hence, St Theodosius would express only horror at the Western faith, although he did recommend that even Roman Catholics – Latins, as he calls them – should be helped if they were naked, hungry, cold or in any misery. But in matters of religion, segregation was the word. His instructions to Vladimir's grandson Izyaslav would be:

Not to join the Latin faith; not to adopt their customs; to avoid their communion; to avoid all their teachings; to despise their traditions. To watch over daughters, neither take nor give any in marriage; not to treat them as brothers, nor to greet them, nor to kiss them, nor to eat or drink from the same bowls with them, nor to accept drinks from them. On the other hand if they ask food or drink from us in God's name, give them some but in their bowls; if they have no bowls, give them some in our bowls, but then wash and pray, for they do not believe rightly and their habits are unclean: they eat with dogs and cats . . . They eat lions and wild horses and asses and strangled animals and carrion and bears and beavers and beavers' tails, and during Lent they eat meat after dipping it in water. During the first week of Lent on Tuesday their monks eat bacon, and they fast on Saturday and when the evening comes they eat milk and eggs. When they sin, they do not ask forgiveness from God, it is their priests who forgive them for a consideration. And their priests do not contract legitimate marriages . . . but they go to war and they serve wafers. They do not kiss icons or relics of saints, but they kiss the cross after drawing it on the ground, and when they get up they tread over it, and they lay their dead with the legs facing west and the arms underneath. They can marry two sisters and they are baptized with only one immersion (we take three); when we are baptized, we are anointed with myrrh and oil, but they pour salt into the mouth of the baptized; they do not give him the name of a saint but baptize him with any name the parents care to make up. And they say that the Holy Spirit proceeds from the Father and the Son; and they do many other things which are evil.

In the face of such rampant bigotry, Vladimir kept a cool head and went on exchanging love and honour with the Pope – maybe because he was not too interested in the technicalities of religion, maybe because he had decided that Russia would never become a satellite of Constantinople and had to give himself some leeway.

This worked out quite pleasantly as we know from the written report of one Bruno von Querfurt, otherwise known as Boniface, a German missionary monk who, dissatisfied with his work in Hungary, resolved to evangelize the Pechenegs and wandered into Vladimir's palace one fine day in 1007. Any foreigner was a guest in Kiev; if he was a cleric, so much the better. Vladimir received Bruno with open arms and kept him for a month. He would gladly have kept him longer; all the time he tried to persuade him not to waste his zeal on those savages. But Bruno held fast: far from frightening him, martyrdom appealed to him: he longed to suffer for Christ. Vladimir, always the realist, saw no great use in martyrdom for its own sake, but finally a helpful dream persuaded him to allow the missionary to have his wish. Still he would not let the holy man go without accompanying him to the border, with a party of armed men. The trip took two days – a matter of some seventy kilometres – we do not know along which road: probably the Zalozny one, to the east-south-east, or the Greek one, due south, since the Solony, which also went into Pecheneg land, crossed the Russian city of Rodnya a hundred and fifty kilometres from Kiev. At the border a thick hedge had been grown as a protection against the nomads. This was the last outpost of a more or less civilized Europe; on the other side of the hedge lay the wild East.

Vladimir dismounted and accompanied his guest through a gate. While the Russians remained standing there, Bruno and his party climbed the first hill of their territory. There, cross in hand, Bruno began to sing a hymn which opened with the words, 'Peter, lovest thou me? Feed my sheep.' When the singing was ended, Vladimir sent one of his companions to Bruno to try for the last time to persuade him to come back. The Great Prince had taken him into enemy land: it would be such a disgrace if Bruno lost his young life without cause or profit. And Vladimir had a presentiment (or feigned one): the next day, before the third hour, Bruno would die a horrible death. The missionary replied: 'May God open his Paradise to you as you have opened for me the road to the heathens.' He went on his way with his followers, and Vladimir returned to Kiev with a heavy heart.

But either the Great Prince was no good as a prophet or he had lied to Bruno; for not only did Bruno not die on the morrow, but he spent five months in the Pecheneg steppes, succeeded in baptizing some of them in the name of the Western Church, and even in arranging for a temporary peace between them and Vladimir, one of whose sons, it appears, was used as a hostage. True, Bruno faced many serious dangers, but he escaped all of them. Somewhat ironically, his wish for martyrdom was gratified only two years later, on February 14, 1009, when he was beheaded not by the Orientals on whom he had set his heart, but by pagan Prussians. Anyway Vladimir had not hesitated to receive the Western missionary as hospitably as he could and later to avail himself of his services: it is clear that theological differences between East and West were no concern of his.[177]

Vladimir's greatest problems arose in the administration of justice. The pagan tradition of the bloodwite[178] was profitable for the treasury, but had no moral significance, as was indeed normal in a society founded rather on practicality than on morality. This shocked the Greeks. Moreover, after Vladimir's baptism, the crime rate rose alarmingly, probably because he was giving more thought to his social work than to his police responsibilities. So the council of bishops wanted to know why the robbers and bandits whose number grew so fast were not punished more severely: in Christian Constantinople, where, at least in theory, one was beheaded for observing a servant drop a plate in the Basileus' presence, they would have been impaled or flayed alive at the very least. Vladimir made a grimace. War was war, but capital punishment did not agree with his outlook on life, and now he had been touched by the love of Christ, it seemed particularly repugnant to him. Besides, was it not written, 'Thou shalt not kill'? He still wanted to be on the right side of that picture representing the Last Judgement. The bishops smiled respectfully and pointed out to the ignorant Prince that he was appointed by God both for 'the practice of mercy toward the righteous' and for 'the chastisement of malefactors'; it was perfectly fitting for him to punish the guilty in order to protect the innocent; the only thing that was needed was a fair trial. Vladimir was willing to be guided by the Church in matters of morals, and humbly complied. Gallows grew here and there out of the Russian soil and began to bear their gruesome fruit. But not for long: financial expediency did not escape the holy fathers' attention, and since money was needed in the treasury, especially in connection with necessary wars, they expressed willingness to forgo their exalted principles and to let the nation benefit from the old amoral tradition. With a sigh of relief Vladimir returned to the gentler (and more profitable) custom of his forefathers.

The incident is interesting in more aspects than one. Russian mores were often ferocious, and some of Ivan the Terrible's or Peter the Great's initiatives in that field still make one shudder, but that is no reason to forget that Russia was also the first country to abolish capital punishment as such, although she repeatedly went back to it: Elisabeth, Peter's own daughter, put the executioners temporarily out of business in the middle of the eighteenth century, at a time when in 'douce France' molten lead was still being poured into select criminals' wounds before they were drawn and quartered. Little did that Princess know that she was following the example of her distant predecessor, the Great Prince of Kiev. Also the very process by which the final decision was reached, with due attention paid alternately to moral considerations and to practical necessities, illustrates the way the two foreign cultures on which Russian culture is based were progressively blending together. Finally the conflict shows again Vladimir's natural mercifulness. The not very reliable *Nikon Chronicle* gives one more example of it by describing how, in 1008, the robber Mogut, having been captured by ruse, obtained the Great Prince's pardon, was converted to Christianity and never again left the Metropolitan's residence: here we find the first illustration of that great theme of Russian folk literature: the Repentant Brigand.

During the first part of his reign, Vladimir had been quite a warlike Prince, but after the 988–989 Cherson campaign, sources differ widely as to the hostilities in which he participated. According to Joachim, the Sagas and later chronicles all quoted by Baumgarten, there was a campaign against the Poles in 992, with Misczyslaw of Poland beaten on the Vistula, one against the Croats in 993, one against the Danube Bulgars in 994, one against the Volga Bulgars in 997, the same year one against the Esthonians, one more against the Danube Bulgars in 1000, with the conquest of Pereyaslavets to which Svyatoslav had been so attached, and constant fighting against the Pechenegs. *The Chronicle*, which so far we have found reliable on the whole, mentions only the Croatian expedition (in 992 instead of 993) and many Pecheneg incidents, most of them in quite legendary terms, with anecdotes about Russian peasants so strong they could tear the skin off charging bulls and Pecheneg bumpkins so stupid they believed Russian land produced brewed porridge.

It is difficult to thrash out any truth from this imbroglio. There is no reason why *The Chronicle* would have kept silent about successful wars, and so our first tendency would be to assume all those it does not mention are imaginary. On the other hand it is not improbable that Vladimir lent a hand to his brothers-in-law against the Bulgars, and he may have had to push back the Esthonians to protect his earlier conquests. The same might apply to

265

the Poles (or Lyakhs). As to the Croats, it is generally thought that they were a remnant of a Slavic tribe which stayed in East Galicia after the rest had moved to what is now northern Yugoslavia: Vladimir would have attacked them to acquire some breathing space on his western flank, or to prevent them from allying themselves with the Poles. Whatever the truth of the matter, the Great Prince seems to have travelled extensively in connection with these hostilities, whether wars or rather skirmishes we shall probably never know: his presence in Novgorod is mentioned several times by various chronicles, in particular in 997 and 999. Consequently if campaigns were indeed undertaken against Esthonians and Volga (Silver) Bulgars, the base was probably Novgorod, not Kiev.[179]

One thing is clear, and that is that Vladimir's main concern was his south-eastern flank. The Pechenegs were becoming more and more aggressive, and it was impossible to crush them in one big offensive because they were nomads and resorted to guerrilla warfare: you could never find them when you were looking for them. In 992 a conflict with one of their princes was solved by means of a single combat won by a Russian somewhere around Pereyaslavl,[180] which they had attacked during Vladimir's campaign against the Croats. In 996 they attacked Vasiliev; the Great Prince himself, having fearlessly sallied forth to meet them with only a small detachment, was defeated and had to hide under a bridge in order to escape being captured or killed;[181] in 997 they came even closer, besieging and nearly taking Belgorod. In 1000, when Vladimir may have been on the Danube, it was, according to the *Nikon Chronicle*, the turn of the Polovtsy – a tribe related to the Pechenegs and well known[182] of all opera lovers – to attack. They besieged Kiev itself, which was saved, we are told, by the personal prowess of one

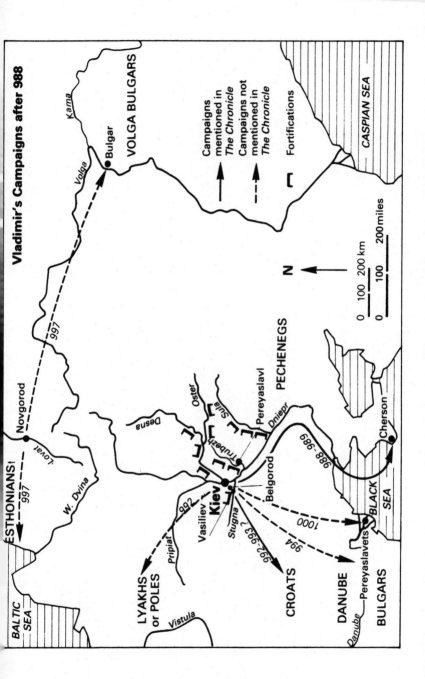

Alexander Popovich who killed the Polovets chieftain
Volodar and his brothers, for which he was generously
rewarded. In 1001 the same Popovich is said to have
counter-attacked and, with the help of Yan Usmoshvets
of bull-flaying reputation, to have captured the Pecheneg
prince Rodman and his three sons, which of course was
the occasion of an even more lavish banquet than usual,
with the distribution of even more largess. Nevertheless
in 1004 Belgorod was again besieged by the Pechenegs,
although without success. A truce was concluded in
1007,[183] but in 1015 hostilities had resumed, and
Vladimir's son Boris went looking for the Pechenegs east
of the Trubezh.

The details of this almost unceasing guerrilla warfare
may not be accurate, but the very fact that it was made
into a legend shows how serious, how essential it was.
From a certain standpoint anything that is *not* turned into
a legend is negligible. Vladimir may or may not have
fought the Bulgars, popular memory was not impressed
by such a conflict, neither was history marked by it. But
he did stand sentinel for Europe against Asia, history
knows it and poetry has recorded it in its own terms.

Bruno von Querfurt noticed a hedge and a gate. There
was more than a hedge: natural borders were put to good
use and forts erected on the Stugna, the Desna, the Oster,
the Trubezh and the Sula. They all looked toward the east
and the south-east whence so many enemies were going
to assail Russia in the years to come, and they were
doubled by a line of settled towns, for instance
Vasiliev,[184] which formed the backbone of the defence
and in whose interest it was to see that the Pechenegs stay
out of Russian territory. But it was the outposts in the 'Far
East' which caught the imagination of the bards: the
solitude of the few bogatyrs who manned them, the re-

sponsibilities laid 'on so few for so many', their vigilance and their exploits, had all the poetry of the American frontier and more, because the Middle Ages somehow lent themselves better to poetry than the nineteenth century, and battleaxes are even more appealing to the imagination than Colts and Winchesters:

> Not a rider will ride through,
> Not a foot soldier will march through,
> Not a beast will run through,
> Not a bird will fly through,
> And, if it does, not without losing a feather.[185]

On the whole, then, a mainly defensive attitude prevailed during Vladimir's later years, which is consonant with his mission as Basileus: a certain land had been entrusted to him; he would make it Christian and would take good care of it in all the ways he could, but he did not see why he should try to make it much larger or to plunder his neighbours' possessions or to threaten their lines of communication. He had reached his limits. He knew it. He would not go beyond them. But he would guard them with as much efficiency and gusto as he had used to set them where they were.

4 *Nunc dimittis*

In the early summer of 1015 Vladimir was ill and confined to his bed in his summer palace of Berestovo; he was approximately fifty-five years of age, which was pretty old for the period. He had reigned eleven years as a pagan and twenty-six years as a Christian, thirty-seven years in all, over a land which he had completely transformed. Spiritually, he had given it a religion which was to become so much a part of it that from then on it would be

known as Holy Russia; geographically, he had multiplied
its area at least by two: it extended now from the southern
shores of the Ladoga lake (without counting Novgorod's
Arctic colonies) to the cataracts of the Dniepr, and from
the northern slopes of the Carpathians to the Volga-Oka
junction, plus the mysterious enclave of Tmutorakan;[186]
he had also laid the foundations of an authentically
Russian civilization, fecundated by Greece, but independent of her.

Russia did not know – and it was her misfortune in the
years to come – the rigorous principle of absolute *droit
d'aînesse*, which, especially in the next centuries, was to
give so much stability to France, England, Spain, and
other Western European countries. No one knows what
Vladimir would have done if he had lived longer, but it
appears that during his lifetime he was perfectly content
to reign as Great Prince in Kiev, while distributing the
princedom piecemeal between his sons, who functioned
partly as vassals, partly as viceroys, governing in his
name and paying a tribute to him.

Sources give contradictory information as to the order
of birth of these sons, as well as to their mothers, and it is
very doubtful whether it will ever be possible to know
exactly who was whose. Did Vladimir himself know? Or
did he care? Or should we? The one salient fact is that,
given not only the natural dialectics of generations but
also a very clumsy system of inheritance, Vladimir, by
using his twelve legitimate sons as lieutenants and his
whole race as a cement for the nation, managed to con-
solidate all that was important to him: the predominance
of Kiev, the authority of the Great Prince, the independence of Russia and the implantation of Orthodoxy.

We have no way of knowing what kind of father
Vladimir was. We only know about those of his children

The three bogatyrs, by the nineteenth-century painter Vasnetsov, look eastwards, where the danger lies. From left to right: Dobrynya Nikitich, Ilya Muromets and Alyosha Popovich.
(*Photo J. da Cunha-Plon. Courtesy of Mme Zalessky.*)

who reigned (except one daughter, Predslava), but he must have had so many that he scarcely could have smothered them with excessive attention. The only indication we have is that none except two gave him trouble, as far as we know, and so we may be tempted to conclude that in his family – if such a caravanserai can still be called a family – he showed as much tact and authority as we have seen him display elsewhere.

Although he probably sent his twelve legitimate sons to their respective seats as they grew up and not all at once, as *The Chronicle* would have it, we can still imagine some festive occasion, St Basil's day perhaps, say in 1000, on which they all would have been reunited. Here he sits, in his customary armchair, and here they stand, surrounding him, their heads respectfully bowed and the blood of a youthful race playing merrily in their veins. Twelve young princes listening carefully, while history dawns on their land . . .

Here is Vysheslav, Prince of Novgorod, the eldest, twenty-three years of age, probably the future Great Prince, if he lives long enough. Here is Izyaslav the tender, the meek, the reader of Holy Scripture, the one who nearly saw his father kill his mother, and who has ruled independently in Izyaslavl ever since; he has a sickly look upon his face: next year his meekness will have its reward and his son Bryacheslav will inherit his seat. Here is Yaroslav, the lame, nicknamed Crooked-shanks, the scholar, the linguist, the Prince of far-away Rostov: the frontier . . . If Vysheslav dies and leaves the rich Novgorod seat vacant, since Izyaslav is settled for good in Izyaslavl, Yaroslav will not cry too long. Svyatopolk, Prince of Turov, comes next. He is not Vladimir's son at all, but a nephew, the posthumous child of Yaropolk; he has been adopted and he scowls at his so-called brothers, his subjects they should be, yes. And as to his so-called father, to whom he has to show love and respect, this is nothing but a usurper, Svyatopolk's real father's murderer, his mother's lover, a Claudius to his Hamlet. Let him beware. Beside Svyatopolk stand Vsevolod, Prince of Vladimir-Volhynsk, maybe Olaf's favourite, and Svyatoslav, Prince of Dereva. Then comes Mstislav, with his big body and his dark complexion, Mstislav the open-hearted, the chivalrous, bold in battle and merciful in victory, good old Mstislav who rolls his big eyes in all directions and is always ready to share everything with everyone, Mstislav the Prince of Tmutorakan who is always poking fun at Crooked-shanks. Next to Mstislav stands Boris, tall and handsome, with his broad shoulders and his narrow hips, looking more like an angel than a man, too young yet to have a government, but he will get Rostov if it is ever left vacant; then come the real boys, Gleb, who cannot move one step without Boris, but will have one day to settle down in Murom; Stanislav, the future Prince of Smolensk, Pozvizd – he will get Vladimir-Volhynsk after Vsevolod's demise – and the baby, Sudislav, who is still sucking his thumb and does not realize he will reign one day over Pskov.[187]

Vladimir looks at them, one after the other, wondering what happiness and unhappiness, what successes and what failures, what glories and what shames Fate has in store for them, and he tries to explain to them what a Christian prince should be.

Understand, my children, how merciful, how very merciful indeed is God, who loves mankind. We men are sinful and mortal, and if anyone does evil to us, we want to destroy him and are in a hurry to shed his blood, but our Lord, who rules over life and death, suffers us to commit sins higher than our head. Now He punishes us out of love, like a father his child,

without touching our lives, now He holds us close to Him.
Also our Lord has shown us how to conquer the foe, how to
wear him out and overcome him by three good pursuits: repentance, tears and almsgiving. So easy, my children, is the
commandment of God: by these three pursuits you will wear
out your sins and attain the Kingdom. But, I beg of you, do
not be lazy for God's sake, and do not forget these three. They
are not difficult! It is not through solitude, monasticism or
hunger such as some good men endure, but through these
small pursuits that one obtains the grace of God . . . Listen to
me, and if you do not accept everything, accept a half. When
God softens your heart, shed tears over your sins and say: 'As
Thou hadst pity on the adulteress and the thief and the pub-
lican, have also pity on us sinners.' Do that in church and
when you go to sleep. Without missing one night, bow to the
ground if you can, be it only three times if you are sick, but do
not forget it, do not be lazy: through those nightly pros-
trations and hymns a man conquers the devil, and whatever
sins he has committed in the daytime, he wears them out.
When you ride your horse and are not busy with anyone, if
you do not know any other prayers, just repeat, unceasingly
and in silence, 'Lord, have mercy': this is the most beautiful
prayer of all, and so much better than thinking idle thoughts.
Above all things, do not forget the poor, but as much as you
can, feed and assist the orphan, and defend the widow, and do
not allow the strong to destroy any man. Do not kill the just
or the unjust, neither have them killed; and if any deserve
death, at least do not destroy the soul of any Christian. When
you speak, either good or evil, do not swear by God nor cross
yourselves: that is unnecessary. If you kiss the cross to confirm
an oath made to your brothers or to anyone, test your heart to
be sure that you can keep what you have sworn, and, having
kissed, abide by your oath, so that by transgressing it you do
not perish. As to bishops, priests and priors, receive their
blessings with love, and do not shun them, but love them and
provide for them as much as you can, so that they might pray
to God for you. Above all things do not have any pride in your

hearts and minds, but let us exclaim: 'We are mortal: today we live and tomorrow it is the grave for us; all that Thou hast given us is not ours but Thine, entrusted to us for a few days.' Do not hoard in the earth: this for us is a great sin. Honour the old as your father and the young as your brother. In your homes do not be lazy, but see to everything; do not count on your steward or your servant, lest your guests laugh at your house or at your table. When you set out to war, do not be lazy, do not count on your generals; do not spend your time drinking, eating or sleeping; set your sentries yourself, and having set them, sleep among your soldiers, and get up early, and do not take off your armour without looking around, for it is through laziness that a man suddenly perishes. Guard against lying, drunkenness, vice, which destroy soul and body. Wherever you go in your land, let not your servants or any others do evil to the villages or to fields, lest you be cursed for it. Wherever you go, wherever you pitch camp, give the poor to drink and to eat; show great honour to any stranger, wherever he may come from, be he humble or noble or an ambassador, and if you have no gifts for him, ply him with drink, for these are they who, by travelling, make a man's reputation in all lands, as a good or as a mean person. Visit the sick; accompany the dead, for we are all mortal; pass no man without greeting him, give him a kind word. Love your wives but give them no power over you. The end of all things is to hold the fear of God above all else . . . What good things you know, do not forget them, and what you do not know, learn . . . First of all go to church: let not the sun catch you in bed! . . . Having praised God before dawn, then, when the sun rises and you see it, render glory to God with joy and say: 'Thou hast illumined my eyes, O Christ God, and Thou hast given me thy beautiful light. Give me some more years, O Lord, so that I may repent my sins, justify my life and thus praise God.'[188]

In 1015, when we resume the thread of our story, Vladimir was something of a patriarch, surrounded mainly by daughters, nine of them we are told,[189] since his

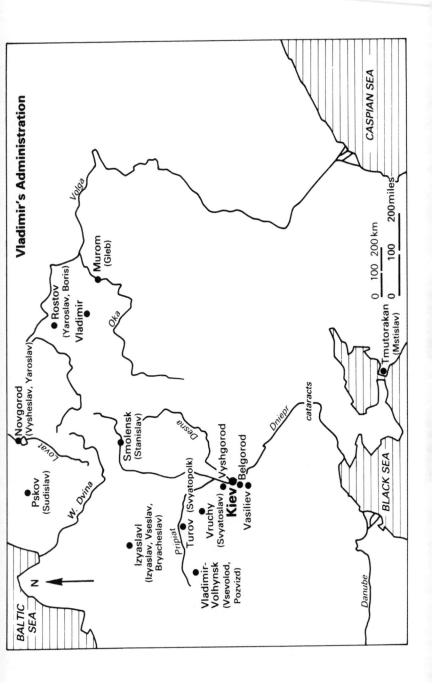

Vladimir's Administration

BALTIC SEA

CASPIAN SEA

BLACK SEA

N

Novgorod (Vysheslav, Yaroslav)

Pskov (Sudislav)

Rostov (Yaroslav, Boris)

Vladimir

Murom (Gleb)

Smolensk (Stanislav)

Izyaslavl (Izyaslav, Vseslav, Bryacheslav)

Turov (Svyatopolk)

Vladimir-Volhynsk (Vsevolod, Pozvizd)

Vruchy (Svyatoslav)

Vyshgorod

Kiev

Belgorod

Vasiliev

Tmutorakan (Mstislav)

Volga

Oka

Lovat

W. Dvina

Desna

Pripiat

Dniepr

cataracts

Danube

0   100   200 km

0   100   200 miles

Boris and Gleb, sons of Vladimir. Collection
of Konrad Onasch.
(*Photo J. da Cunha-Plon. Courtesy of Mme
Zalessky.*)

sons were away, each one in his seat. As will happen to
older men, people had begun to die around him. Around
1000, two former wives, Rogned and Malfrid, had
died.[190] In 1001, it was gentle Izyaslav's turn. It seemed
only yesterday that he had held out a sword to his father in
the middle of the night with the words, 'Did you think
you were alone here?' How nobly he had said that! And
now he was gone for ever. In 1003, Vseslav died: the boy
had been Izyaslav's son, and there was something particularly shocking about surviving one's own grandson. Still
there is no reason to believe that Vladimir was morbidly
sensitive to that death: a number of other grandsons
would soon console him for the loss of the first one. His
loins had provided Russia with all its future nobility. In
1011, Anna herself, the Basilissa, the Purple-born, died.
What her death meant to her husband we do not know,
but we do know that he buried her in the Church of the
Tithe, next to Grandmother Olga and beside the place he
would himself occupy one day.[191]

According to Baumgarten, who, for once, presents a
pretty good case, the Great Prince married again around
1013. This in itself is not unlikely since he was barely
fifty-three at the time, and his twenty-two-year-old
bride is supposed to have been a granddaughter of Emperor Otto the Great (to be precise, the third daughter of
Count Cuno von Oechlingen and Otto's daughter
Richlinte). The match was not an impossible one from
any standpoint, and it would have been quite in
Vladimir's style to seek a matrimonial alliance in the West
to balance his religious involvement with Constantinople. This Fräulein von Oechlingen would have
been the mother of Dobronega-Maria who married
Casimir of Poland, and that stepmother of Yaroslav's
mentioned by Thietmar as captured by Boleslav of

Poland in 1018. Baumgarten goes so far as to assert that it was Vladimir's remarriage which triggered Svyatopolk's and Yaroslav's subsequent revolts, which makes little sense, since neither of them could have been deeply attached to the memory of Anna, who had taken the place of both their respective mothers; as to fearing the competition of a 'legitimate' heir, this was out of the question in a country where legitimacy was still a very relative concept and sharing a father's possessions between brothers would still go on for centuries. It should be noted also that no trace of a second Christian marriage of Vladimir's has been preserved, and, given the number of early or late chronicles in which he plays an important part, that itself is a powerful argument against any such marriage having taken place. Historians have their pet temptations, and there is no doubt that Baumgarten, a Normanist and a Roman Catholic, was only too ready to find even flimsy ways to link his hero with the Roman West. The present author is no exception, but his temptations are different: he will not conceal that, for his part, he would prefer not to spoil Vladimir's later monogamous record, and to keep him faithful to his Greek vocation as well as to the memory of a woman who may have played a determining part in his life. The enigmatic remark in the Public Library manuscript, that 'Vladimir committed many acts of lechery and finally he was attracted by a wife and finally he found the grace of God', and the chronicler's observation that he loved Anna 'without measure because she was pleasing to God' seem to hint at some mysterious way in which Anna would have been for Vladimir *le plus court chemin de l'homme à Dieu* (woman is man's closest route to God, said Paul Claudel). This, it must be confessed, may be a sentimental interpretation, and the historian dares not insist that Anna was Vladimir's final vision of *das*

Ewigweibliche, which would probably preclude any hint of remarriage, although the novelist would be only too glad to adopt such an interpretation. To conclude the digression, Baumgarten's arguments are worth some attention, but they are not unassailable, far from it, and in the absence of any proof, the reader may enjoy the privilege of deciding for himself whether Vladimir's last two years were spent remembering his happy years with the sister of the Basileus or finding a second youth with the granddaughter of the Emperor.[192]

Shortly after Anna's death, Vladimir had had serious trouble with Svyatopolk. The lad had been raised on an equal footing with his cousins, but he could not forget whose son he was; maybe anxious to show his nephew that no difference was observed between him and them, Vladimir had made a mistake: he had sought and obtained for Svyatopolk the hand of Boleslav of Poland's daughter. In spite of their excellent diplomatic relations, Boleslav would naturally not resist trying to trip up his Russian counterpart, if only he could. Svyatopolk's nomination to the seat of Turov, not far from Poland's border, would make things easy for him. The young fiancée did not arrive alone; among her luggage she brought to Russia a Bishop Reinbern of Kolberg. For centuries to come Polish potentates would try to convert Russia to Roman Catholicism – just as Russians would try to convert Poland to Orthodoxy – and it seems scarcely likely that the Bishop would have travelled so far with the only purpose of taking a vacation in Turov. How easy it must have been for him to whisper in Svyatopolk's ear: 'If your father had not been foully murdered, you would have been his heir, reigning now over rich Novgorod instead of paltry Turov, or maybe even, if, God forbid, he had died early in life, you would already have been Great Prince, sitting on the throne of your fathers in Kiev. Now this could easily be arranged . . . Justice must be done . . . If ever you needed troops . . .' Svyatopolk was a murderous young man; scruples never bothered him much; anyway it was not difficult for him to rationalize the situation: he had an hereditary right to the throne and all effective means to obtain it would be virtuous enough for him. As to that beautiful Polish girl his wife, how easy it was for her to insinuate at every opportunity how much more beautiful she would be in the attire of a Great Princess, and to report regularly to her father on how the idea was progressing in her husband's mind. In case of doubt, the Bishop was there to bless whatever needed to be blessed. In 1013 – Svyatopolk was approximately twenty-four – the plan was ripe. As soon as Boleslav had finished his current German war, the necessary steps would be taken.

Fortunately Vladimir's intelligence service was as active as ever. One fine day, Svyatopolk, his wife and the Bishop were arrested and thrown into gaol, presumably into one of those convenient dungeons which had no doors. What followed is a matter of surmise. It seems that the princely couple was freed after a short imprisonment and that Svyatopolk was reassigned to Vyshgorod, where it would be easier to keep an eye on the rebel. As to Bishop Reinbern of Kolberg, it was very unfortunate, but he had died in his cell . . . There was nothing the Great Prince could do about it, even to please his royal friend and brother Boleslav the Brave.[193] Vladimir, it appears, had not lost any of his aptitude for finding simple solutions to complicated problems.

This had happened two years ago, and Svyatopolk had behaved properly since then, but now new problems had arisen with Yaroslav, that living paradox of a boy: an addicted bookworm, Crooked-shanks could fight when the need arose; an ambitious bungler, he knew how to compromise when there was no other way out; a slow learner, he might one day become greater than his father had been. After Vysheslav's death, Vladimir had promoted him to his own old seat, Novgorod, where he was doing quite well so far. In earlier years, Vladimir could have wished for no better heir than Yaroslav – hence the nomination to Novgorod – but times had changed, and other possibilities also seemed attractive.

With these thoughts, Vladimir's eyes turned to young Boris, Anna's son, the newly appointed Prince of Rostov, who, on learning about his father's illness, had rushed to his bedside. Strong in body, princely in manner, his kind and merry eyes shining in a round, still lightly bearded face, Boris was so appealingly pure and earnest! Yes, he lacked the ruthlessness, the cunning, and even the ambition which make the great sovereigns of this world, but what a prince he would be for any truly Christian land! If, at any time, Caesar and God could be reconciled, he would be the one to do it. He belonged entirely to the clean, new world of grace and goodness which Vladimir himself had entered twenty-six years ago, and which the necessities of the government of men had forced him to leave from time to time, although he had always come back to it. Should not the new, heavenly Kiev belong to a heavenly Basileus? Yaroslav was also a good Christian, fond of priests, churches and good books, but without anything of the angel about him. On the contrary, he had a tendency to dig in his heels rather viciously. As a matter of fact, it was precisely what he was doing now. While all Vladimir's viceroys punctually sent him the assigned taxes they levied from their appanages, Yaroslav had suddenly decided to withhold the 2000 grivnas (approximately one thousand pounds of gold) which was his yearly contribution. This, although not surprising in itself – young blood yearns for independence – was not to be tolerated. On the day when the news had been brought to the Great Prince, he had not flown into a rage, he had not moaned about filial ingratitude, he had given two orders, short and to the point: 'Repair roads. Build bridges.' He would take his retinue to Novgorod and give his son, for all his thirty-seven-odd years, the sound thrashing he deserved. Yaroslav could hire as many Vikings as he liked – intelligence reports indicated that he was doing some recruiting – his father could still teach him a trick or two. If only this illness would go away! It had come at a very awkward time, the more awkward as the Pechenegs were again stirring in the south-east. Well, Boris would take care of them. Boris was an angel – he was even reluctant to get married, so deeply was he attached to things spiritual – but, thank God, he did not mind striking a good blow to protect Holy Russia.

Such were probably Vladimir's thoughts as he lay on what was to be his deathbed. Worries he had, plenty of worries, what with Yaroslav and his unpaid taxes, Svyatopolk and his plotting wife, the Pechenegs always ready to seize a moment of weakness or inattention in order to wipe out the civilized nation that was gradually pushing them back into their steppes. But on the whole, everything, he reflected, was pretty well in hand. A loose assemblage of tribes had been converted into a nation, and this nation had been torn away from the stagnant, backward darkness of paganism and offered to the rays of the God of light. Churches and schools growing out of the ground, justice administered, the enemy contained, friends made among other nations . . . Much remained to be done, but to do it there was an army of sons, who had

Vladimir, on his sickbed, sends Boris to fight the Pechenegs. Fifteenth-century miniature. (Lichechov, 1907.)

their faults, of course – except, maybe, Boris – but who were all strong upholders of Russia, that original blend of Slav, Viking and Greek elements. True, among the twelve, there was the one black sheep, Svyatopolk, but one traitor among twelve faithful disciples sounds like the right proportion. There was a precedent and it had helped the dough to rise. If only God would grant a little more time to his Basileus to take Yaroslav down a peg or two and to settle the question of the succession to the throne . . . but if He didn't, that was his will, and Vladimir prayed every day that it might be done.

Vladimir had not been an early worker – but not one of the eleventh-hour kind either. He could use a little more time, but he had had a lot already. If a greater Prince than he deemed that it was enough, who was he to object? By accepting power from heaven, he had learned a certain measure of humility. When he sent his sons here or there, they went, and when he called them back, they came: would he be a rebellious son and quibble about rendering his accounts? This Russia that he called his was but an appanage granted for a time by the Lord of all. If the hour had come when it had to be surrendered, well, so be it. Lying in the dark, with just an oil lamp flickering in front of a reddish icon painted by the Russian apprentice of a Greek master, with Boris' white form growing dimmer and dimmer as if seen through a thickening mist, Vladimir prayed: 'My Lord God, I did not know Thee as God, but Thou hadst pity on me and didst illumine me through holy baptism, and then I knew Thee, God of all, holy Creator of all creation, Father of our Lord Jesus Christ! Glory be to Thee with thy Son and thy Holy Spirit. O God and Master! Do not remember my wickedness: I knew Thee not while I was a pagan, but now I know and I see Thee.' And, with a startling ingenuity, he added this bizarre but passionate cry of love: 'My Lord God! Have pity on me. But if Thou wantest to torment and torture me for my sins, then do it Thyself, O Lord, and deliver me not unto the devils.'[194]

Characteristically enough, Vladimir's last order was to send Boris away to face the Pechenegs. And then, on July 15, 1015, in the glorious solitude of the really great, 'he peacefully surrendered his soul to the Angels of the Lord'.[195]

CHAPTER SEVEN

Saint

1   Turmoil[196]

When great men die, the consternation is such that, for a time, it often appears that their work amounted to nil. The enemies whom they had crushed but not exterminated suddenly swarm over their dead bodies; their friends find themselves pushed into the background by revolution and reaction combined; the trinkets they loved suddenly seem outmoded and ridiculous. On the surface, their world changes overnight and it takes a few years for the winds of history to blow off the ephemeral films of fashion and changing taste. Then the edifice to which they had devoted their lives is discovered in all its solid, sturdy durability: it becomes evident that it will endure for centuries to come, and even, in a sense, become eternal. So it was with Alexander, with Caesar, with Louis XIV: empires split, civil wars raging, testaments broken by Parliament, could not prevent centralization and classicism from moulding the future destinies of France, the Roman Empire from taking the place of an outdated republic, hellenistic civilization from spreading throughout the Mediterranean and the Near East.

Shocking events followed Vladimir's death. He had hoped to recover and failed to designate an heir. There were three possible candidates: Yaroslav in Novgorod, who was busy arming himself against his father but could use for another purpose the Vikings he had been recruiting in addition to his own retinue; Boris, out east, facing the Pechenegs with eight thousand men; and Svyatopolk in Vyshgorod, at Kiev's doors. Vladimir's friends decided to conceal his death for a time, because they were aware of Svyatopolk's ambitions and wanted Boris to come back and assume power. So, while messengers galloped eastward, the Great Prince's apartments on the second floor of Berestovo summer palace were put under heavy guard, and health bulletins issued from them as usual. But Svyatopolk had his own men in the palace, and they apprised him of his hated uncle's death. He was quick to seize the oportunity, and ordered the body to be stolen. This was done at night, by taking apart the flooring of the apartment. With gruesome buffoonery, the body of the great man was then wrapped in a rug and lowered with ropes to the ground. In compliance with a Slavic tradition, it was placed on a sledge in spite of the warm season and dragged to Kiev, where it was laid in the Church of the Tithe, with all the appearance of mourning and respect.[197] Mighty and lowly flocked to the church to cry over a sovereign who had ruled for thirty-seven years with such firmness, such kindness, and such jolliness. Truly the Red Sun had set over Russia. The country would have a number of gifted and beloved rulers, but never again one so universally popular. The funeral was of course Christian, and all the pomp of the Russian Church was unfolded to bid farewell to its founder. Russian icons already adorned the walls of the church, and Russian tones and modes were beginning to replace the Greek ones. Clouds of incense rose toward the dome and sobbing mingled with singing when Vladimir was laid in a marble coffin next to his wife Anna and to his grandmother Olga, to sleep the well earned slumber of a second Constantine.

But while boyars and beggars alike cried over the dead

master – who would ever protect Russia's independence
with such energy? Who would ever again have mead
delivered in casks to the residences of the poor and sick?
– Svyatopolk was already at work. In the daytime he was
distributing largess to the Kievans and sending messengers to Boris to assure him that he desired to live at peace
with him; at night he rode to Vyshgorod where he had
acquired friends, or rather accomplices. Four of these
gentlemen, Putscha, Talts, Elorich and Lyashko, met
him secretly. He asked them: 'Are you devoted to me?'
'We shall give our lives for you,' they replied. 'Then say
nothing to any man, but go and kill Boris.' They
promised, saddled and were off.

Clearly Svyatopolk considered Boris as his main rival:
he could not feel secure in Kiev so long as he had not
disposed of Vladimir's favourite, who was also dear to
the common people, for he had often himself taken food
and drink to the sick and done many kind deeds in imitation of his beloved father, caring not only for the lame
and the poor, but loving everyone with the same serene,
evangelic love. Such men are dangerous and should not
be permitted to live.

In spite of all his tenderness and his scantily bearded,
round face, Boris, with his powerful stature and laugh-
ing eyes, looked every inch a prince, and he had
frightened the Pechenegs; without a confrontation, they
had melted away into their steppes. So that when the sad
messenger reached him, he was already heading for
home, hoping to see his father alive at least once more.
The news that Svyatopolk had occupied the throne was
brought to him a little later, but it failed to anger or
frighten him. Although his men expressed the desire to
fight for him, he shook his head: 'Let my older brother
be like a father to me,' he said. And having kissed his

eight thousand soldiers one by one, calling the younger ones brothers and the older ones fathers, he sent them off to their homes, so that they would have no part in the bloody events which he foresaw. Without haste but with a prayerful determination, disregarding all contrary advice, he proceeded with his trip back to Kiev.

On the 24th of July, he had reached the Alta river and had pitched camp for the night when Putscha, Talts, Elorich and Lyashko found him. It was dark. Boris was sitting in his tent and reading the Bible by candlelight. When he heard the horses' hoofs clattering outside, he called his chaplain and they began to sing matins. The chanting made the murderers pause: they could kill happily, but they could not bring themselves to interrupt a religious service. What a medieval trait! When Boris had finished singing, he kissed his followers, lay down on his fieldbed and called out to the men whose presence he felt outside and whose faces he had not yet seen: 'Come in, brothers, and accomplish the will of the one who sent you.' They must have been beside themselves with horror at what they were doing, for they butchered him so inefficiently that when they brought him to Svyato-polk in a canvas and unwrapped him, he was still breathing. The aspiring Great Prince had to send two Vikings to finish him off. The murderers felt fewer qualms about massacring Boris' followers, among them a Hungarian servant called George, who tried to protect his Prince with his own body, and whose head they cut off to get at an expensive torque Boris had given him.

The favourite was dead, but Svyatopolk did not feel as comforted as he should have. He was not afraid of Mstislav, who was too far away, of Pozvizd and Sudislav, too young, of Bryacheslav, just a child; he may have worked out some kind of deal with Stanislav, and as to Yaroslav,

видѣвъ же штрокъ єго верже и на нь тѣло єго,
крекыи; да неш станутъ єгѝ на моєго дра
гыи. да и дѣ же кработа тъ єв ла тъ воєѝю
ѹ в а дає. тоу и дѧ єшъ єленъ єбудꙋ. и жі
во тъ єконча ти бл ше же. єрод шоугринъ
й менє гєоргіи. бл ше єѝ во ложи сана нь
гривнꙋ злата х. и єкла въ єв ба рнеш пачемꙋ;
тоужеѝ тъ ого пробадоша; и поб . єи дъ єко
чиѹь шъ пра во сторо єѝ. нача ша глати

The assassination of Boris in his tent.
Fifteenth-century miniature. (Lichechov,
1907.)

he knew that Crooked-shanks would not be outwitted and that the day would come soon enough when he would have to be faced in the field. But there remained Svyatoslav and Gleb, of whom it was necessary to dispose. Murderers were sent after Svyatoslav; he fled; they overtook and assassinated him.[198] As to Gleb, in his far away Murom, it would be safer to lure him out of his fief before assailing him. So, since he could not yet know about the latest developments, couriers were sent to him with the message: 'Come in haste. Your father calls you. He is very ill.' Gleb, an obedient young man, hurried accordingly, laming his horse in the process.

Meanwhile, disapproval of Svyatopolk's usurpation was brewing. One of Vladimir's daughters, Predslava, had a secret line of communication to Yaroslav and kept him informed. He in turn did his best to save Gleb, and dispatched to him a messenger who caught up with him on September 5, in Smolensk, as the young Prince was boarding a boat which would take him down the Dniepr. 'Do not go to Kiev,' said the messenger. 'Your father is dead and your brother has been slain by order of Svyatopolk.' The boy had been extremely attached to his older brother; he used to spend days and nights listening to him reading the Bible, or lives of saints, or just talking about sacred things. Without Boris, Gleb felt lost in the world. Tearfully, he called upon him: 'If you have received encouragement from God, pray that I may endure the same passion, for it would be better for me to dwell with you than in this deceitful world!' At this very moment, Svyatopolk's assassins, led by a man called Goryaser, rode down to the shore. They seized the boat by the rope and drew their swords. But not one of them dared strike the first blow at the boy, Vladimir's son. Goryaser, at a loss, turned to the Prince's cook,

Torchin, and ordered him to do the deed, or else he would die a fearful death. The cook caught his master by the hair, threw him on his knees, and cut his throat.

Yaroslav himself was in deep trouble. In his desire to rule autonomously, he had, as mentioned previously, hired some Viking mercenaries as his father had done before him. But, at thirty-seven, he did not possess the authority of Vladimir at twenty, and he could not keep the men in hand: for lack of anything better to do, they began beating up the Novgorodians and raping their wives. The Novgorodians objected. There was a riot in the market-place, and the Vikings were exterminated to a man. Pale with anger at the affront, Yaroslav left the city, and, settling in a suburban castle, let it be known that he would not try to avenge the mercenaries: let only the leaders of the uprising come to him to discuss the situation. They came and he killed them. At that point Predslava's letter arrived, and Yaroslav learned that Vladimir was dead. One may be unwilling to pay one's taxes and still not wish for one's father's death; so Yaroslav wept for the one against whom he had rebelled. Besides, he knew that, if the worst came to the worst, he could always have submitted to his father and expected mercy from him, but now he found himself not only with an uprising on his hands, but also with a homicidal brother bent on ruling the whole country alone. It took tremendous daring and astonishing humility to do what he did in that predicament. He rode straight to Novgorod, assembled the people, and, wiping away his tears, laid the facts before them. We can only assume he had been extremely popular until the recent bloody misunderstanding, for the people forgave him the death of their kinsmen and swore to fight for him.

The next year was spent by both brothers mustering

The assassination of Gleb by his cook, acting under
threat of death. Fifteenth-century miniature.
(Lichechov, 1907.)

armies. In the autumn of 1016, Yaroslav came to Lubech and, craftily pushing Svyatopolk's army on to the thin ice of a lake, carried the day. Thereupon he ascended his father's throne, but not for long. Svyatopolk had fled to his father-in-law, the brave Boleslav, who, concluding a truce with the Germans, arrived with reinforcements. Budyi,[199] Yaroslav's tutor and one of his generals, scoffed at the fat Polish King: 'We'll pierce your fat belly with a lance!' But they didn't: it was Boleslav who, unexpectedly fording the Western Bug, overthrew the Russians. In 1018, Kiev, Vladimir's throne city, surrendered to the victors. The bishops and priests wearing their vestments met Svyatopolk at the gates as the lawful Prince; nine of Yaroslav's sisters, his stepmother, and, according to Thietmar, his own wife, were seized. As to Predslava, his informer, she was thrown into the fat Polish King's bed, with Svyatopolk smirking in the background. Vladimir's princedom had not survived him three years. Or so it seemed.

2 Balance

Yet, twenty years later, Yaroslav, Vladimir's continuator, was master of a Russia extending from the Black Sea to the Baltic and from Hungary to Asia, a powerful great-princedom which he ruled with vigour and moderation, earning the name of 'Wise'. The Poles were forced back, the Pechenegs vanquished. The relations with the Greek Patriarch were being progressively normalized. Christianity was triumphing without the use of force. Churches, monuments, monasteries, seemed to be growing out of the ground. Coins were minted. Religious books were translated, schools were opened, an authentically Russian culture was being born under the impulsion of a Prince who was himself a scholar and a linguist. A set of laws, magnificently known as The Russian Truth, was being promulgated. As to relations with foreign powers, they had never been so intimate; Yaroslav had enough children to count most of Europe's royalty among his in-laws: himself the husband of Ingigerd of Sweden, he gave his oldest daughter Elisabeth in marriage to King Harald of Norway, his youngest, Anastasia, to King Andrew of Hungary, and his middle one, Anna, to Henry I of France, who learned from her how to read and write. His sons also made brilliant marriages. Truly Kiev was becoming a northern Constantinople. And this was only the beginning of a dynasty which was to reign for five hundred years more – its last representative on the throne was Theodore I who died in 1598 – and to give to Russia most of its authentic aristocracy, many members of which can still rightfully boast that Vladimir's blood runs in their veins. When the Rurikids were finally replaced on the throne by the Romanovs, the pre-eminence of the founder of the Russian State was duly recognized: 'After Svyatoslav a brilliant star began to shine, a great sovereign, his son, the Great Prince Vladimir Svyatoslavich. He illumined the darkness of faithlessness and drove away the charms of idolatry, and he enlightened all Russia by holy baptism, so that he was called "equal to the apostles", and because he had enlarged his estates he was named "autocrat", and now he is worshipped and glorified by all.'

How was the situation overturned?

Partly through Svyatopolk's folly. Having once started to kill, he could not stop. As soon as the great-princedom had been delivered to him by Boleslav, he ordered his Russian supporters to massacre the victorious Poles, who thought they were among friends. This was duly executed, and it is quite possible that a similar fate would have been reserved for Boleslav himself had he not left Kiev in a hurry, taking with him many treasures and that notorious treasurer Anastas. What Anastas' intentions were this time is open to surmise. Maybe he simply could not bear the idea of leaving the treasury, now that he had become accustomed to administer the funds of the Tithe, maybe he was a convert to Western Christianity, maybe he hoped to convert Boleslav to the Eastern one.

Meanwhile Yaroslav had tried to flee to Scandinavia from Novgorod, as Vladimir had done before him, but his cousin Kosnyatin, Dobrynya's son, hacked his boats to pieces. When the Novgorodians had decided to be faithful to a prince, they could easily be *plus royalistes que le roi*.[200] 'We can still resist,' they said. 'If you have no money, take ours.' The city bled itself to gather the necessary funds for the campaign: the commoners gave 4 kunas each, the elders 10 grivnas, and the boyars 18 grivnas apiece. New Vikings were recruited; this time Yaroslav had learned his lesson and no problems of discipline arose. The army set out. Svyatopolk came out to meet it with a host of Pecheneg allies. As Fate – or Yaroslav – would have it, the encounter took place on the Alta, where Boris had been slain. 'The blood of my brother cries to Thee, O Lord !' exclaimed Yaroslav. Also: 'My brother, although you are absent in the body, yet help me with your prayers against this impudent murderer.' On a Friday, at sunrise, the two armies rushed at one another. The slaughter went on for the whole day. The sun was setting when the wounded Svyatopolk finally fled. His end, as described by the chronicler, is truly frightful. As he was fleeing, *a devil came upon him and his bones were softened*, so he could not ride. His retainers carried him in a litter. Although no one was in pursuit, from time to time he would cry out loud, 'Run faster! They are after us!' Part of the time he was in a faint, but when he recovered his senses, he would again hurry the carriers. So he fled through Poland and into Bohemia,[201] where he died of his wounds. 'And since his death,' gleefully concludes the chronicler, 'he abides in bonds and torture everlasting. His grave is in the wilderness even to this day, and an evil odour issues from it.'

But Svyatopolk's stupidity and his wickedness (which the chronicler attributes to the circumstances of his birth: a nun's child could only be a monster) were only the occasion, not the cause, of Yaroslav's triumph. In a manner of speaking, and even if Boris and Gleb did not actually pray for the success of his arms, his victory was theirs. Very soon the people were to demand that the two princes be canonized as martyrs, and although they had not died for their faith, only as Christians, the clergy complied. Just as the human body accepts some substances and rejects others, Russia craved to have saints of her own, and would not be ruled by a treacherous fratricide. A nation needs martyrs – Boris and Gleb came in very handy – it also needs villains: Svyatopolk, whom the people nicknamed the Accursed, was cut out for the part. Vladimir's work had been in such harmony with the requirements of his people – and Yaroslav's, then Vladimir Monomach's work was going to prolong it so satisfactorily in the right direction – that any rule but theirs seemed to be, and actually *was*, usurpation and tyranny. When Svyatopolk began distributing his largess, the people 'accepted it but their hearts were not with him, *because their hearts were with Boris*'. Boris also would have continued like Vladimir, and he would have

Four of Vladimir's granddaughters, the daughters of Yaroslav. Unlike icons, which always show their subjects in a state of transfiguration, this fresco gives some idea of the models' actual physical appearance. Eleventh-century fresco at St Sophia, Kiev. (*Photo J. da Cunha-Plon. Courtesy of Mme Zalessky.*)

been accepted by the living organism of Russia. But he lacked the willingness to use evil for the cause of good, which is indispensable for truly effective princes. So he made a truly effective martyr instead, and the people turned to Yaroslav, also Vladimir's son, also Vladimir's continuator, but who was ready to roll up his sleeves and do the dirty work that had to be done. Such is the logic of history, and it is probably as true to say that Svyatopolk *could not* have remained on the throne, as it is to maintain with Tolstoy that Napoleon *could not* have stayed in Russia, if he had been ten times a genius. Boris refused to resist Svyatopolk on the Alta river, but in the end, on the Alta river, it was Boris who won, and it could not have been otherwise because Vladimir's favourite son had become the soul of Russia.

This is remarkable in itself. One new generation had scarcely had time to reach maturity since the baptism of the land, and already its values had radically changed: violence, pride, courage, which so recently had held first place, were now relegated to second; non-violence, humility, submission, had suddenly become more admirable and more admired. The reluctance of the Kievans to accept Svyatopolk's largess is significant in this respect, but no more so than the unexpected choice made by the Novgorodians: they preferred a prince who had killed their brothers to one who had killed his. The very fact that the young men's Christian sacrifice was understood (and not despised) shows that something basic had changed in the Russian people. Their hearts were not with Svyatopolk because they were with Boris. It was as if the exorcisms on the shores of the Dniepr had actually worked.

Not entirely. Russia's history is definitely one of the bloody ones (what country's isn't?), and the excesses of an Ivan the Terrible or of a Peter the Great, which were child's play compared to the bloodbath of the Revolution, indicate that the devil did not obey the bishops' orders unreservedly and did keep a comfortable *pied-à-terre* in holy Russia. But that is only part of the picture. Other features beside cruelty and bloodthirstiness are inscribed at least as deeply in the Russian character: an unparalleled respect for innocence, the cult of chastity, the willingness to suffer and die for an ideal, not so much as a sacrifice as a vocation, these also are Russian traits, endlessly exemplified in history and literature, not forgetting a certain inimitable gentleness or rather sweetness: who has ever dreamed of a policeman with a sweet voice? Yet it was 'a sweet and sympathetic voice' which woke Dostoievsky up at five a.m. on April 23, 1849, when they came to arrest him! These, it will be observed, are typically Christian traits, which means that, but for Vladimir's reform, there would have been no Alyosha Karamazov, no Saint Seraphim, no Prince Myshkin, no Saint Sergius, no Plato Karataev, no 'Russian pilgrim', no Nicholas II – only Razin and Berya, Lenin and Pugachev. Dostoievsky thought that Russia would save the world by her sound, theocratic, orthodox inspiration. In this he was mistaken, but, on the other hand, who will deny that Russia has the vocation of martyrdom, and that the blood of martyrs achieves apparently impossible results? It could probably be said of the Russian people, even when they give proof of the utmost savagery, because their minds have been seduced and their instincts given a free rein, that at least 'their hearts were with Boris'.

Vladimir's Christian reform had met with a stunning – some would say a providential – success. The canonization of Boris and Gleb by popular acclamation

Saint Boris and Saint Gleb. Collection of
Konrad Onasch.
(*Photo J. da Cunha-Plon. Courtesy of Mme
Zalessky.*)

is but one sign of it. The number of churches built is another. Russia was baptized in 989. In 1017, there was a great fire in wood-built Kiev, and, according to the *Nikon Chronicle*, seven hundred churches were destroyed. Nevertheless Thietmar says that, in 1019, four hundred of them were in operation. Even if the figures are exaggerated, one is amazed, not so much at the number of buildings, as at the proportion of the population which was active in clerical or para-clerical professions. The North was much less easily converted. In 1071 there was a pagan meeting in Novgorod, and while the Prince and his retinue sided with the bishops, many common people still had, and expressed, more confidence in their traditional soothsayers. This had not prevented them from having a Dobrynina Street, in honour of the man who had attempted to baptize them with fire . . . At the end of the century, there were religious uprisings in Murom, and as to the obdurate Vyatichans, they preserved pagan burial customs as late as the thirteenth century. Nevertheless Christianity was progressing at a fast pace: in 1134 a quarter of Novgorod burned, including ten churches; in 1211, four thousand three hundred houses and fifteen churches went up in flames. Some tact was obviously being used by the clergy, since those pagan rites that could not be eradicated were christened: Midsummer's Night became St John's Feast, churches dedicated to St Elias, the Hebrew patron of thunder, were erected where Perun's sanctuaries had stood, and St Vlas, whose name sounds in Russian very much like Volos, appeared on icons surrounded by cattle, as would have been fitting for his heathen homonym. Soon there remained no unbaptized Russians: even the dead had to convert if they were important enough; in 1044, Yaroslav, with typical thoroughness, ordered the remains of Yaropolk and Oleg the Wizard to be exhumed, baptized and buried properly in the Church of the Tithe.

This prodigious growth of Christianity was accompanied by an efflorescence of religious literature, including great names like Metropolitan Hilarion or Cyril of Turov, a multiplication of chronicles and at least one great epic poem: the *Tale of Igor*. As to the plastic arts, no sooner had Russian painters begun to imitate Greek icons, than they equalled or surpassed their masters. The same is true of religious music: Russian chanting, with its richness and purity, constitutes one of the great spiritual treasures of humanity, still little known in the West.

One of the indirect but greatest benefits conferred by Christianity upon Russia was Russian. This is not the place to expand on the beauties of the language, but the fact that it first 'jelled' as a sacred tongue must be mentioned. The consequence is extreme solidity in vocabulary and forms. Texts written in the early eleventh century can still be read and understood by an educated reader with only occasional recourse to the dictionary. This, in spite of three hundred years of Tartar oppression, and at a time when practically all the population was illiterate! Had it not been for the unbending skeleton provided by what is now known as Church Slavonic and the religious inspiration to preserve it at all costs, it is more than likely that Russian would have disappeared as Celtic had in France, or would have blended completely with Mongol dialects as Saxon with French in England. The fact that, after three centuries of submission, the whale of the Russian fairy-tales did find the strength to shake off the Tartar fences and houses planted in her skin, and, leaving shore, to drown in the

314

offing the foreign parasites living off her back, shows the sturdiness of the structures national, spiritual and linguistic, rooted in Vladimir's reform. If one wonders why the reaction was not more immediate, why the Tartars were allowed to settle on the whale's back in the first place, one should reflect that Russians are not renowned for the speed of their reactions. When they are ready, however, they are ready with a vengeance. One of their most popular heroes, Ilya of Murom, remains paralysed, 'sitting like a sitter' for thirty years, but once he has drunk three steins of beer, give him a pole from here to the sky and a ring embedded in it, and he will grasp the ring and overturn the earth. For Russia, that magical and inebriating beer was Christianity. From Vladimir to Dostoievsky, and later to Berdiaev, to Sergius Bulgakov, to Aleksandr Solzhenitsyn and to Abram Tertz, Russia has stayed drunk on Christianity for one thousand years. That this addiction is, in large part, linguistic, is shown, among other things, by contemporary Soviet vocabulary, where the Thank God's, the Glory be to God's, the God may grant it's, the God be with you's abound – although, by official *ukaz*, the initial letter of the word 'God' must always be printed in lower case.

To go deeper into the study of the consequences of Vladimir's reform would be to write a history of Russia and her civilization.

3 Myth

Survival on earth is possible for man only in the form of myth. That the Red Sun became a Russian myth, as much as Arthur in England, Charlemagne in France, Barbarossa in Germany, is a patent fact.

This was not the work of intellectuals. Heraskov published a *Vladimir Regenerated* in 1785 and Elagin a *Vladimir the Great* in 1829; Zhukovsky intended to write a '*romantisches Heldengedicht*' about Vladimir, but never got down to it; Pushkin mentioned him in conventional terms in *Ruslan and Ludmila*, and Aleksey Tolstoy chose him to embody, in several poems, a Russian ideal as far removed from the plodding, well-meaning efforts of the Slavophiles as from the uprooted, snobbish nostalgias of the Westernizers. Add a few historical novels and short stories, and that is all the contribution of the literary intelligentsia to Vladimir's myth.

On the other hand, the popular bards of the Kievan cycle represented him consistently as a central figure, not a very active one, and sometimes even ridiculous – the same happened to Arthur, probably by a compensation reflex: too much grandeur without any comic relief would be resented – but fatherly, majestic and good-natured, holding gargantuan banquets, showing mercy and hospitality, always ready for a good song and a good drink, concerned with his subjects' family problems, a solar figure if ever there was one, radiating light and warmth. A complete survey of the matter would take us too far from our theme – as a matter of fact it would be an excellent subject for a doctoral dissertation – but a few generalities might prove useful here. In the *byliny*, Vladimir appears as tall, handsome and blond, with a thick beard; he is generally qualified as *laskovy*, which, in this case, would best be rendered as debonair. To serve him is to serve Christianity, since the only infidels around are supposed to be the Tartars, quite an anachronism of course, but a typical one: Vladimir rooted Christianity in Russia so deep and so fast that the people forgot he had done it at all; Russia was Christian and had

316

Saint Vladimir shown wearing the diadem of the
Basileus. On his left is the heraldic trident of the
Rurikids. Coin minted under Vladimir.
Hermitage Museum, Leningrad.

obviously always been so. His bogatyrs obey him faithfully but without servility. Their number is undetermined; the most popular are Dobrynya Nikitich, a gentleman; Ilya of Murom, a peasant, and the sly Alyosha Popovich, a priest's son. All together, they are as much of a Russian archetype as the besiegers of Troy were a Greek one.

Our physical representation of Vladimir is based mainly on the gold and silver coins minted during his lifetime, which show him to have had a long skull with a powerful jaw and chin, a long moustache, and an air of great nobility about him. A number of icons painted centuries after his death represent him as older than he ever could have been, and it is doubtful whether they contain any resemblance to his actual appearance, with the exception of the elongated face and the noble bearing, matched by piercing eyes looking from under heavy brows.

But it is neither in his appearance, nor even in the folklore surrounding his memory, that Vladimir's claims to mythical status lie, and by mythical we do not mean imaginary, but, on the contrary, truer than accidental truth. In a poem written to commemorate Edgar Allen Poe, Stéphane Mallarmé coined the expression '*en lui-même enfin l'éternité le change*': finally eternity transforms him into himself. It is in this spirit that we are using the term *myth*: it is only when he becomes a myth that a great man is finally divested of the superficial aspects of his personality and life, and that the quintessence of his person and influence are revealed. Therefore there is one last adventure of Vladimir's that we must examine, a posthumous adventure which the pagans would have called apotheosis, and which in the Christian Church is known as canonization.

What is a saint? Somebody whose name is in the calendar, after whom Catholic and especially Orthodox families call their children, and who is venerated – although not worshipped – in church? Yes, but how did he get into that calendar, or rather what does his presence there mean? It means that, the immortality of the individual being considered as revealed by God, and the only doubt being as to which of the two (or three) places each separate individual is sent to after his death, the Church has officially expressed her assurance that this given person has immediately upon his or her demise reached the right place, and consequently that prayers can be properly addressed to him or to her, to be, so to speak, relayed on to God by an act of benevolent intercession. This assurance can be based on a variety of considerations, although the performing of miracles is held to be essential in the Roman Catholic Church. A person who has led a blameless life is a likely candidate, but no more. One who has been martyred for Christ is nearly automatically on the list. If his or her body does not decay, this is a good although not a necessary indication that the person has already achieved his or her physical transmutation into the Kingdom. Contrary to popular belief, asceticism is not indispensable; it can be a means, it definitely is not an end. Sinlessness is not even deemed possible, but on the other hand repentance is indispensable. In most cases, when there is some reason to believe that a certain person should be inscribed among the saints, to render to that person the proper honours as well as to edify the people, the Church organizes a detailed investigation, not unlike a police one, checking the deceased's virtues and sins, looking into possible manifestations of the supernatural before or after death, and establishing a complete dossier on the probability of immediate admission among the Elect.

In the Roman Catholic tradition, very strict forms are used, with one of the hierarchs playing the part of the prosecutor before the holy tribunal, under the picturesque title of devil's advocate; the Orthodox are, as usual, somewhat more relaxed in their attitude, more open to individual cases, and, rightly or wrongly, tend to rely more heavily on a consensus of the Church rather than on the observation of rules. Traditionally, the saints receive different ranks, corresponding to the degree of seniority they are supposed to have attained in the hierarchy of holiness, a custom obviously somewhat open to ridicule. It may not be manifest to all, especially not to those raised in the Protestant spirit, that God will set much store by the artificial differences discerned by men between, let us say, martyrs and confessors, canonization and beatification, and the like. It is presumed that if God treated Joan of Arc as a saint, He did so even before her posthumous intercession cured some Frenchman's ulcer around the year 1900. On the other hand, there may be nothing wrong with an attempt on the part of the Church to express herself clearly and to use – in the good sense of the word – discrimination. Be that as it may, if a blameless life or ascetic habits had been *sine qua non* conditions for becoming a saint, Vladimir would not have made it. Indeed, he had trouble making it with the rules being what they are.

Whereas Boris and Gleb were easily enough accepted as saints by the Greeks who, at that time, were responsible for the heavenly registers (at least in the East), the Russians themselves for a long time had their doubts about Vladimir. Although the second part of his life was undoubtedly both virtuous and charitable, his conversion sincere, his repentance complete, his good deeds without number, his popularity unequalled, the merry banqueter – not to mention the former *fornicator immensus* – did not exactly meet the usual, although not obligatory, standards of innocence and austerity of most saints. He had been so alive, so earthy, there was something so physically radiant about the man! It was hard to imagine that he would surrender the sword to strum an ethereal harp, or give up his arduously earned crown of gold and pearls to don the flimsy diadem of the godly. If only he had been burned, tortured, devoured by wild beasts . . . But no, he had died in his bed at a ripe old age, after thoroughly enjoying all the good things of life. Some kind of a malaise definitely prevailed among his contemporaries concerning his advancement in heavenly matters. The chronicler writes:

It is indeed marvellous what benefits Vladimir conferred upon the Russian land by its conversion. But we, Christians though we are supposed to be, do not honour him as this benefaction deserves. For if he had not converted us, we should now be a prey to the devil's crafts, as were our perished ancestors. If we had shown zeal for him and had offered prayers to God on his behalf on the day of his death, God, seeing our zeal, would have glorified him.

It is not exactly clear what is meant here by glorification: probably some visible sign of Vladimir's accession to heaven, for instance the preservation of his body. Everyone remembers what scandal accompanies, in *The Brothers Karamazov*, the decaying of Father Zossima's remains. It may be presumed that a comparable emotion reigned around Vladimir's marble coffin. Jacob the Monk testifies to an embarrassment of this sort when he says:

The blessed Prince Vladimir resembled the holy kings David the Prophet, King Ezechias, the very blessed Josias and the great Constantine, they having chosen and preferred God's law above all else and having served God with all their hearts and having received the grace of God and inherited Paradise and obtained the Kingdom of Heaven and having gone to rest with all the saints who pleased God: so did the blessed Prince Vladimir, having served God with all his heart and soul. Let us not be surprised, beloved ones, if he performs no miracles after his death; many righteous saints performed no miracles, and still they are saints. St John Chrysostom speaks about it somewhere: how shall we know and recognize a holy man, by miracles or by deeds? And he replies: he shall be known by deeds, not by miracles. Even soothsayers have performed miracles by devilish inspiration; there were holy Apostles and there were false Apostles; there were holy prophets and there were false prophets, servants of the devil; by a miracle Satan himself can be transformed into an angel bright. But a saint should be known by his deeds, as the Apostle said: 'But the fruit of the Spirit is love, patience, faith, goodness, meekness and temperance, against such there is no law.[202]

So that was another problem: Vladimir was not performing any miracles. He was to perform one, however, if this can be said without any irreverence intended, a miracle quite in his character and style. With as much economy of means as efficiency in achievement: he was going to be recognized as one of the greatest saints that ever lived – his Russian title is *ravnoapostolnyi*, literal translation of the Greek *isapostolos*, which means equal to the Apostles – recognized by both the Eastern and the Western Churches, at a time when relations between them had been completely severed, recognized so fully that even an extremist like Pope Urban VIII could not demote him, and not one trace of the official procedure of canonization has ever been found by anyone. How this was managed has still not been clearly determined.

Hilarion had called him 'among rulers an Apostle',

and Jacob 'an Apostle among princes', as early as the first half of the eleventh century, but that was the private initiative of these two clerics. Around 1249, a nephew of King Daniel of Galicia received, in addition to the name Vladimir, the Christian name John, which shows, at that date and at least in Galicia, that Vladimir was not yet considered to be a calendar saint. The term *saint* is applied to him for the first time in 1254 (*Hypatian Chronicle*) and the continuation of the Laurentian mentions him as venerated as a saint in 1263. The first church dedicated to him was erected in 1313 by Archbishop David – curiously enough in Novgorod and not in Kiev, so that his first seat as a prince was also his first seat as a saint. Nothing else is known about the matter.

Suppositions, of course, have been put forward. It has been maintained that Vladimir was recognized as a saint so long after his death because an understandable Greek reluctance had to be dispelled: he had got so much out of them and given them so little in return. Maybe. They may also have resented whatever influence the Bulgarian Church exercised over the Russian one. But all this is imaginary: no sign of Greek opposition has ever been pointed out. Another supposition links Vladimir's canonization with the great victory over the Swedes which gave Prince Alexander of Vladimir (the city) his surname of Nevsky, for the battle had taken place on the Neva. The date, July 15, 1240, the anniversary of Vladimir's death, may have been chosen by Alexander as a good omen, and it is more than likely that the young prince did call upon his famous kinsman for help. The victory – in which Boris and Gleb are supposed to have mystically participated – would then have been received as the long expected miracle. Suitably enough, on his first icons, Vladimir appears not alone, but with the two sons who preceded him into statutory holiness.

The Russian proverb says: 'It takes a clap of thunder to make a man cross himself.' The many misfortunes which fell upon Russia when she was torn by feudal wars, invaded by Tartars, threatened by Teutons, probably did bring the memory of the blessed Prince who had made Russia one and strong, closer to the hearts of the people. At a time when religion and nation were inseparable, it was natural for them to appeal to the one who had given them both, and to appeal to him in religious terms, because they seemed the only eternal ones: 'O most glorious Vladimir, . . . thou hast been like Paul, the great Apostle, having left all idolatry as being the false wisdom of thine infancy, and come to the fullness of man's estate, thou hast been adorned with the purple of divine baptism. And now, standing in joy by Christ our Saviour, pray Him to save thy Russian land and its many people.' James V, 20, was interpreted in Vladimir's favour: 'He which converteth the sinner from the error of his way shall save a soul from death, and shall hide a multitude of sins.' What sins, anyway? Who remembered them? They had crumbled to dust. A great flow of gratitude mounted from the nation toward its teacher. 'How shall we thank thee, through whom we have known the Lord and rejected idolatry? . . . How shall we call thee, who didst love Christ? Truth's friend, Wisdom's vessel, nest of Mercifulness?' exclaimed Hilarion. And Jacob exulted: 'All Russian people have known God by you, divine Prince Vladimir!' There is no doubt that Vladimir's exalted rank helped. In the eleventh century no one had yet heard about class conflicts, and the common people were fond of a top-drawer saint. (In the pre-Tartar period, out of some hundred and eighty saints one third were rulers: maybe it was all a tremendous misunderstanding, but it must have been nice to live at a time when it was still deemed possible to serve Caesar and God through the same office.)

The Germans are said to believe that one day Friedrich Barbarossa will rise again and save Germany. The Russians entertain no such hopes. But if one of their sovereigns could fill the part, it would be Vladimir.

The French feel that their nation was saved once and somehow for all by Joan of Arc. All subsequent saviours – and God knows that the Church's eldest daughter needed saving more than once – were understood to be, in a manner of speaking, reincarnations of the not so humble girl from Domrémy; this was particularly obvious, for instance, in de Gaulle's case. The Russians entertain no such faith. But if Russia were ever to be saved, it would be by a man who had some of Vladimir's qualities and could win as much love as he.

Not that everyone approves of Vladimir. There was about him an uncanny propensity to eat his cake and still have it, which gets on some people's nerves. The man was just a little too successful for the taste of the stricter kind of judges. The younger son, the bastard, the sickly boy, accomplished more than many more famous characters. Napoleon's epopoeia is a tale of failure compared to his. Not only did Vladimir obtain on earth everything that his heart could desire, and having obtained it, kept it, but he also managed to reinvest all his outlay in heavenly granaries 'where neither moth nor rust doth corrupt'. Two birds with one stone again. The advocates of unhappiness as a system of salvation frown. The cynics doubt: was the man really so good? Did not Dame History use a little of her make-up on him? Is not the Church cheating a bit in favour of a man who was of great service to her?

No attempt will be made to answer these questions. The present author has little patience with the aggravating tendency which consists in systematically depreciating all the great figures of the past. It leads to an automatic depreciation of all human values, for the hero is the golden standard of the human bank, and if the gold is fool's gold, what will the paper be worth?

Vladimir's contemporaries were disturbed because, at a time when miracles were in fashion, he did not perform any. This may be a paradox, but we would tend to see in the very fact that no sanctimonious legends surround his name one more proof of his sterling greatness: such stature forbids petty tinkering with pseudo-holy visions. As to real miracles – if indeed there is a heavenly Jerusalem – what greater miracle could there be than to take a whole pagan flock and herd it in a few years into the fold? One believes in immortality and the intervention of saints in human affairs or one does not. If one doesn't, Vladimir's accomplishments in his lifetime will have to stand and be judged on their own value. If one does, one may wish to establish a connection between Vladimir the First's prayers on behalf of the Church he created and Vladimir the Last's lack of success in destroying it. In that sense it is possible to recognize here and there prophetic inflections in the peroration of Hilarion's *Discourse on Law and Grace*.

A good witness of thy piety, O blessed one, is the holy church of the holy Theotokos, which thou didst build on a rightful foundation, and where thy valorous body now reposes, awaiting the trumpet of the Archangel; an exceedingly good witness is thy son George [Yaroslav], whom God created to replace thee in thy sovereignty, who does not destroy thy law

The Golden Gate of the city of Vladimir,
probably like that of Kiev, but of a later date.
The church built over the gate itself is the one
mentioned by Metropolitan Hilarion on
p. 333.
(*Photo Novosti Press Agency, Moscow.*)

but confirms it, does not diminish what was designed by thy piety but extends it, does not distort but accomplishes, who finishes what thou hadst left unfinished, even as for David did Solomon, . . . who has delivered thy people and thy city to the all-glorious Holy Theotokos: for her he has created a church above the Golden Gates in honour of the first festival of the Lord, the holy Annunciation, so that the Archangel will greet the city as he greets the Virgin; to her he will say: 'Rejoice, thou filled with joy, the Lord is with thee', and to the city: 'Rejoice, faithful town, the Lord is indeed with thee.'

Arise therefore, O honourable head, arise from the grave, shake off thy sleep, for thou art not dead but sleepest until the day when all will live again. Arise. Thou art not dead. It is not meet that thou shouldst die, who didst believe in Christ, the life of the whole world. Shake off thy sleep, lift thine eyes and behold what honour the Lord has granted thee in heaven, and how he has left thee unforgotten on earth thanks to thy son. Arise, behold thy child George, behold thy blood, behold thy beloved one, whom God has brought forth from thy loins; behold him embellishing the throne of thy land, rejoice, be glad. Also behold thy pious daughter Irina,[203] behold thy grandchildren and great-grandchildren, see how they live, how they are guarded by the Lord, what piety they preserve in fulfilment of thy teachings, how they frequent the holy churches, how they glorify Christ, how they venerate his name. Behold thy city radiant with magnificence, behold the churches blossoming, behold Christendom growing, behold the city gleaming with the icons of saints, fragrant with incense, resounding with praise and holy songs. Having beheld all this, rejoice and be glad and praise the beneficent God who constructed it. Look not with thy body but with thy spirit. For thy joy[204] and gladness the Lord will show thee these things. The radiance of thy belief was not burnt out by the heat of faithlessness, but, with the help of God's rain, multiplied into abundance of fruit. Rejoice, apostle among rulers! It is not dead bodies that thou didst resurrect, but our souls were dead, killed by the disease of idolatry, and thou didst bring them back to life; through thee we became as gods and knew the living Christ; we had been convulsed by demonic deceit, and through thee we were set right and entered the path of life; by demonic deceit we had been blinded in the eyes of our hearts; we were blind with not seeing, and through thee we discovered the triple sunlight of the Godhead; we were mute, and through thee we began to speak, and now, great or small, we glorify the consubstantial Trinity. Rejoice, our teacher, our master in piety. Clad in righteousness, girt with strength, shod with truth, crowned with sense and mercy as with a torque and golden ornaments, shine on!

Yes, shine on, truly *great* Prince, canonized by that strangest of all miracles, which, after one thousand years, you are still eliciting from us: our gratitude.

Shine on.

Notes

Foreword

1 For list of secondary sources, see bibliography.
2 Mykola Andrusiak in 'Kings of Kiev and Galicia'.
3 M. N. Tikhomirov in *The Origins of Christianity in Russia*.
4 Scarcely one line of this work is not based on historical evidence or the opinion of learned scholars. In order not to overwhelm the text with notes, the following documenting system is used throughout: if the evidence does not deal with Vladimir personally or if it is borrowed from *The Chronicle*, notes are not generally appended. All other information is noted and documented.

Chapter One   Boy

5 Pushkin, *Poltava*.
6 Remember Borodin's *Polovtsian Dances*.
7 Some write Patzinaks.
8 Otherwise known as Black Ugrians, or Hungarians.
9 Avenarius, *Ilya Muromets and the Tsar Kalin*.
10 *Ibidem*.
11 The question of Vladimir's birth date is a tricky one. The chronicler has not preserved it for us, and we can only try to deduce it from other known facts. According to *The Chronicle*, Svyatoslav is supposed to have been born in 944 (in 920 according to the fanciful Tatishchev), but in 946 he was already throwing spears at people. Although we are told the spears barely cleared his horse's head, it

seems reasonable to assume that he was at least 4, and so, if the 946 date is the right one, the youthful spear-thrower must have been born in 942. Of course Igor's death and the campaign against the Drevlyans could also have been misdated, and then Svyatoslav's birth date could be correct. *The Chronicle* shows that he began to rule independently, taking the reins from his mother's hands, in 964; it might also have been in 962, since this is the year when Adalbert, the Western bishop invited by Princess Olga, had to leave Kiev in great haste. The Rurikids had no formal coming-of-age procedure, and it follows that Svyatoslav began to rule at a maximum age of 22 if he was born in 920, and at a minimum of 18 if he was born in 944. (If he had been born in 920, he would have been 42 or 44 at the time, which is absurd.) Eighteen to 22 appears to be a sensible range, and so we may accept 942–944 as his approximate birth date. Vladimir is presumed to have been his third son, which is not certain and anyway does not mean much in a civilization where polygamy was taken for granted. Besides, Vladimir was probably born out of wedlock. Since it would not be reasonable to suppose that he was born before his father was 16, 958–960 is the earliest date at which he may have seen the light. Starting from the other end, some sources indicate that Yaroslav, Vladimir's son, died in 1054 at 76, which gives 978 as his birthdate. Vladimir must also have been at least 16 at the time, so he was born in 962 at the latest. But since *The Chronicle* gives Yaroslav in third position among Vladimir's sons, he was probably a little older, which leads us back to the 958–960 date. Other sources state that Yaroslav died at 66, which could move up Vladimir's birth to 972, but since in 968 he was already around and in 978 we find him busy raping princesses, this does not strike us as a very convincing hypothesis. Consequently it will be assumed here that Vladimir was born in 960 with a possible margin of minus two years.

12 The scene is described in *The Chronicle*; Vladimir stand-

ing at the window is a figment of the author's imagination.

13 In *War and Peace* Tolstoy attempts to prove that individuals can have no effect on history, which belongs to the masses.

14 At all times, historians have allowed themselves to invent dialogues, and even to add here and there a little touch of picturesque, provided the ideas expressed and the images brought forth were in keeping with the situation and personalities involved. We promise to use economy when availing ourselves of this traditional licence.

15 Such was Leo the Deacon's opinion.

16 Igor of Kiev (?–945), not to be confused with the Prince Igor of Borodin's opera, Igor of Novgorod–Seversk and Chernigov (1151–1202).

17 Was Olga a Viking or a Slav? And, to anticipate a little, was Malusha, daughter of Malk of Lubech, sister of Dobrynya, and mother of Vladimir, a Slav or a Viking? Historians entertain in this field such strong interests and prejudices that it is impossible to express one's opinion without hurting at least someone's feelings. Svyatoslav's portrait hints at a partly Slavic origin, although his male ancestry is, as far as we know, all Viking. Yaroslav's body has been dug up by the Soviets, and they claim that his measurements clearly indicate a Slav. Who his mother was is doubtful, and whoever she may have been, it is not known whether she was a Slav or a Viking. Olga had a Viking name (even spelled Helga by Constantine the Purple-born); Malusha had a Slavic name. To please some historians, it is possible to surmise that Olga was in reality a Slav and Malusha a Viking (Malusha would then be the diminutive of Malfried), but the general picture is really much simpler if we accept that Rurik's unknown wife was probably a Slav, Olga a Viking – she was born of the clan of Gostomysl (a Slavic name rather than a Viking one) according to Joachim, but Joachim is the least reli-

able of all the Russian chroniclers (he might even be an imaginary figure) – Malusha a Slav, and Yaroslav's mother, whoever she was (there is no lack of candidates), again a Slav.

18 That is according to Joachim, who also accuses Svyatoslav of destroying a chapel dedicated to St Nicholas and erected over Askold's tomb, and of torturing to death his only brother Gleb. But since no other trace of the very existence of such a brother can be found, that piece of information should not be taken too seriously.

19 *Nikon Chronicle*.

20 At least there is no reason to think that he ever had.

21 More precisely, 'to the most holy Mother of God'. Was that the name of a specific church? But there is no indication that any church except St Elias existed in Kiev at the time. The *Arkhanghelsk Chronicle* is one of the later ones and not extremely dependable.

22 Slavs and Greeks called them Varangians and sometimes Russes, as did the Arabs. Historians have not yet solved the question of their origin (Sweden? Denmark?) but, since all but the most extreme agree that they were Vikings, Vikings we shall call them, for simplicity's sake. This may be as good a place as any to mention that the word Russia itself is of widely and wildly contested etymology. Hundreds of pages have been published concerning it and the most fantastic origins have been defended tooth and nail. We are not going to join the mêlée, whatever the temptation, nor shall we use the historically correct but unusual term 'Rus' either for the people or for the land. For practical purposes the following axiom should suffice: Northerners coming from Scandinavia, having settled in the ninth century in a region extending from the Gulf of Finland to Kiev, mainly in Novgorod and Kiev itself, and having mingled with the local population, mainly the Polyan tribe, are to be called Russians, and the region is to be called Russia.

23 Tmutorakan is mystery land. Lermontov describes its

eerie atmosphere in his short story *Taman*; Catherine the Great's rival to the throne, a princess who may have been a daughter of Elisabeth I, chose Tmutorakan as her fictitious fief; and whatever historians do not understand in the development of Kiev – like the 860 attack on Constantinople, or the so-called first conversion of Russia, or the relative independence of the Russian Church in the first years after the 'second' (Vladimir's) conversion – they tend to explain by that magic name: Tmutorakan. When that peninsula became a Viking colony we do not know; in fact we cannot be sure it ever was one. What was its relationship to Kiev in the early Rurikids' time? Or even, was there such a relationship? Before indulging in ingenious hypotheses we have to confess ignorance, and, as far as we are concerned, we do not feel the need to go any further. In *The Chronicle*, the name appears for the first time when Vladimir's son Mstislav becomes prince of Tmutorakan.

24 Cf. Jean-Jacques Rousseau's political visions.

25 *The Chronicle* presents Rurik, the founder of the dynasty, as Vladimir's great-grandfather. One more 'great', however, would help with some dates, especially if Rurik and Rorik of Jutland (born around 800) are the same man, for, in that case, if Svyatoslav was born around 940 of, at best, a 60-year-old father, Igor was born around 880 of an 80-year-old one! True, if Rurik was born say in 810, Igor in 875, and Svyatoslav no later than 940, the genealogy proposed by *The Chronicle* would violate only probability, not nature. Still, one cannot help toying with the idea that Oleg might have been Rurik's (maybe illegitimate) son and Igor's (maybe secret) father. It does sound a little like Alexandre Dumas, but consider this. Oleg's words to the people of Kiev on presenting Igor, 'This is Rurik's son' (which we render by 'In his veins runs Rurik's blood'), would still be true, inasmuch as 'son' can mean 'descendant'. The curious fact that Oleg reigned until his death without surrendering the throne to the

boy for whom he had obtained it, would be justified. As to the touching scene of Rurik on his deathbed entrusting Igor to Oleg, could not Oleg have invented it for the benefit of the Kiev populace? Two sixty-five-year-old fathers in a row seem scarcely more likely.

26 Pushkin's hero.

27 Some write Oskold.

28 Amiable Patriarch Photius means the Russians.

29 The monetary system of the time is a specialist matter that cannot easily be explained here.

30 Pushkin, *Song of Oleg the Wizard*. This nickname of Wizard has always puzzled historians, the Russian word *veshchiy* having magical connotations. If Oleg conjured up a descendant for Rurik, his wisdom must truly have seemed to border on witchcraft.

31 Cf. p. 337, n. 17.

32 Unless some kind of *more danico* marriage had been performed between the prince and the housekeeper, which does not seem likely if we accept the version according to which Malusha was exiled. Viking indifference to legitimacy of birth throws some supplementary doubt over our Igor theory (p. 339, n. 25). On the other hand, it will be noted that among *Russian* Vikings few bastards ever reigned, and Vladimir did not advertise the fact that he was one.

33 Here arises the question of language. As already seen, the Vikings were not attached to Norse, and one can be certain that Vladimir had not the slightest knowledge of runes. As to Slavonic, it had two alphabets, the Glagolitsa and the Cyrillic, one of the two, probably the second, having been invented by St Cyril in the ninth century for the evangelization of Bulgaria. Specialists disagree as to which alphabet of the two would have been used in Kiev in Vladimir's time. Since the Cyrillic was the only one to survive, and since the only extant Russian literary monument of the tenth century (an inscription on a jar found near Smolensk, dated 900–950) is written

in Cyrillic characters, as well as the inscriptions on Vladimir's coins, it is reasonable to assume that Vladimir himself read and wrote the beautiful lettering still in use in the Russian Church today, with a few differences due to the passage of time and the change in styles.

34 Cf. Vladimir Monomach's memoirs.

35 Cf. p. 335, n. 11.

36 It is not absolutely certain that Novgorod lived at that time under Svyatoslav's rule, but indications according to which Olga had regularly collected tribute from it, as well as the present mission, hint at a relationship which might have loosened with the years but still was close enough.

37 Such is Joachim's tradition. Only one thing is certain: after Vladimir's victory over Yaropolk, the pagan party flourished.

Chapter Two   Teens

38 According to some, it was Dobrynya himself who erected a gigantic statue of Perun in Novgorod, to imitate what Vladimir had done in Kiev (Cf. p. 103); this, of course, happened much later, but there is every reason to believe that, at the time of Vladimir's arrival in Novgorod, there was already a statue of Perun there, even if it was not as impressive as Dobrynya's future one.

39 One grivna would buy a *strug* carrying 30 tons of goods.

40 In Novgorod, *posadnik* generally means city mayor; in other cities a *posadnik* is a prince's man, serving as governor.

41 Avenarius, *The Youth of Vasily Buslaev*. Rogatitsa was a street in Novgorod.

42 This aspect of Vladimir's life has been, for some reason or for no reason at all, underrated by most historians, which led to some misunderstandings concerning Vladimir's later conversion. The only direct authority we have con-

cerning actual sacrifices performed by Vladimir with his own hand is an Icelandic saga, not a chronicle. But any Viking prince's role as high priest in charge of sacrifices is an historical fact. Vladimir's personal devotion to pagan gods is not subject to doubt, and the prayer quoted here is an authentic one, preserved for us by Ibn Rusteh. Other details of the cult have been gleaned mainly in Ibn Fadlan. For modern commentators, consult bibliography.

43 *The Chronicle* has no record of such a marriage; the sagas mention a wife, Adlague or Alloguia, 'a very wise woman'; the unreliable Joachim names Olava, 'a Viking princess', and, later, among other wives, one called Adèle. We tend to think that Alloguia is none other than Olga: Norse bards were sometimes vague about chronology. As for Adlague, Adèle and Olava, it is impossible to determine if they existed or not. The only important point here is to know if Vladimir had already been married before he met Rogned in 978. Our reasoning goes as follows. *The Chronicle* lists Vladimir's sons in what may be presumed is the order in which they were born. First comes Vysheslav (mother: a Czech, according to *The Chronicle* and the *Nikon Chronicle*; Olava, according to Joachim). Then Izyaslav (mother: Rogned). Then Yaroslav (mother: Rogned, according to *The Chronicle*; Gorislava – another name for Rogned – according to Joachim and the *Nikon Chronicle*, but that is contradicted by the continuation of *The Chronicle*, which mentions an historical feud between Yaroslav's and Rogvolod's descendants, based on the fact that Izyaslav, Rogned's son and consequently Rogvolod's grandson, received the city of Polotsk as an independent appanage. The opposition thus established between Yaroslav's and Rogvolod's lineages indicates that Yaroslav was not Rogvolod's grandson and therefore that Rogned was not his mother). Now Yaroslav was born in approximately 978. Since the rape of Rogned also took place in 978, Izyaslav, if he was indeed older than Yaroslav, must have

been born a very few months before him. Vysheslav, the oldest, was born earlier, at a guess in 977, of some other union, or he may have been Yaroslav's mother's first son, Yaroslav being the second. In 978 Vladimir was approximately 18, he did not lead an especially chaste life, and sons must have come plentifully to him, whoever their mothers were. To summarize, Vladimir had had a wife before he met Rogned, and there is no reason not to give her the name retained by Joachim: Olava. Was she a Czech or a Viking? More probably a Czech, since, according to Soviet research, Yaroslav's skeleton presents Slavic characteristics.

44 Although it is difficult to determine how much – or how little – faith should be put in Icelandic sagas, there is no reason to reject their testimony altogether, inasmuch as it does not contradict what knowledge has reached us through more conventional channels. Since the story of Olaf Tryggvison throws some interesting light on Vladimir in his role of Prince of Novgorod, it is worth telling in some detail. Somewhat arbitrary choices will have to be made concerning which version of the sagas to use for which incident. For instance, Olaf's birthdate varies from 958 to 969 depending on the sources. According to one of them his relation to Vladimir suggests that he was younger than the Russian Prince; still, in 978 at the latest, and probably rather earlier, he broke Klerkon's head in Novgorod. Therefore we shall assume he was born around 963.

Chapter Three   Man

45 Descriptions of contemporary costumes to be found in Vernadsky.
46 Rogvolod, says *The Chronicle*, had come from overseas. His name does sound like the Norse Rognvaldr, and his

daughter's, like Ragnheidr. Some historians, however, think they were Slavs.

47 Continuation of the Laurentian manuscript.

48 *The Chronicle* mentions two sons.

49 Descriptions of contemporary costumes to be found in Vernadsky.

50 Ibn Fadlan.

51 *Ibidem*.

52 The continuation of the Laurentian manuscript, generally better acquainted, or so it seems, with the Polotsk side of the story, does not mention the two sons.

53 Thietmar. Vladimir's extraordinary appetites are also consistently mentioned in Russian chronicles. According to some historians, this aspect of his character may have been exaggerated for Christian purposes, in order to make the effects of conversion more striking. Thietmar is not suspected of such motives. (*Chronic. lib.* VII c. 52).

54 Joachim.

55 Tatishchev. Cf. also p. 341, n. 37.

56 Between Dorogozhich and Kapich, according to *The Chronicle*. Dorogozhich would be 'the flat elevation extending between the present north-west section of Kiev known as Lukyanovka and the locality of St Cyril's monastery'; Kapich, 'the site of the modern village of Belichi about ten kilometres west of Kiev on the highway to Belgorodka' (Cross). According to Joachim, Vladimir wanted to run away from Polotsk to Novgorod, but Dobrynya, knowing Yaropolk's unpopularity – Joachim also says Yaropolk was very popular – persuaded his nephew to bribe the Kievan generals and then to offer battle. Yaropolk would then have been defeated in the vicinity of Smolensk. If this battle on the Drucha did really take place, it was probably nothing more than a skirmish, which scared Yaropolk into shutting himself inside Kiev.

57 According to Baumgarten, it is the news of his death which brought Vladimir back from Scandinavia. This seems extremely doubtful.

58 Such coincidences, as Solzhenitsyn remarks, are not uncommon in history. Every Frenchman will gleefully tell
you that Joan of Arc's main judge was called Cauchon
(*cochon* = swine).

59 *Nikon Chronicle.*

60 There seems to be some confusion with Vladimirko Gal-
itskiy in the twelfth century.

61 The *Nikon Chronicle.*

62 It is tempting, as Cross puts it, to mix up this expedition,
whose date is uncertain, with Vladimir's dispatch of 6000
Vikings to Constantinople in 988, which will be
discussed later. The temptation resides mostly in the fact
that the first expedition is mentioned only in Russian
sources, and the second only in Greek and Arabic ones.
Nevertheless I think it should be resisted, in view of all
the details contained in *The Chronicle*: the marten skins,
the one-month delay, the granting of land, the letter to
the Emperor, none of which would be applicable to the
second expedition, organized at the Greeks' request.
Therefore I assume the first expedition really took place
in the circumstances described and at the date indicated
(978).

63 *The Chronicle* seems to be in error when it refers to one
god called Simargl instead of Sim and Rogl.

Chapter Four   Prince

64 Vernadsky is well informed about Kiev, Tikhomirov
about crafts. Vladimir's iconography and his *joie de vivre*
suggest that he was well dressed.

65 Avenarius, *Ilya Muromets quarrels with Prince Vladimir,
Ilya Muromets and the Tsar Kalin.*

66 The social structure of Kievan Russia was complicated
and is still not clearly understood. The fact that most of
the research is done by Soviet historians, who willy-nilly

have to come up with Marxist findings, does not help to clarify matters.

67 Cf. p. 20.
68 Avenarius, *Volga Vseslavevich.*
69 *Ibidem, Mikula Selyaninovich.*
70 Cf. pp. 56, 60, 341, n. 40.
71 Cf. pp. 29–30.
72 Cf. p. 10.
73 On the Pishchan, a tributary of the Sozh.
74 Chroniclers and historians have felt differently about this for centuries. Without going into ludicrous details – like reading *Serbian* instead of *Serebryanny* (Silver) – we can list the following arguments: 1 – The Danube Bulgars (the Bulgars of Bulgaria) were at that time fighting the Greeks, and the Greek sources could hardly avoid mentioning sudden help received from an unexpected quarter. 2 – *The Chronicle* describes Dobrynya's surprise at seeing the Bulgar prisoners wearing boots, but Danube Bulgars were a familiar sight in Kiev, and everybody knew what footwear they used. Besides, Bulgaria was already an organized nation and it would seem that an expedition in that direction would have been described in more detail. In particular, how could the chronicler have resisted mentioning that Vladimir the pagan was fighting a Christian Tsar? 3 – *The Chronicle* specifies that Vladimir set out by boat. This would have been rather obvious if his intention had been to sail down the Dniepr and up the Danube. On the contrary, the fact was worth mentioning if the objective was Bulgar, which was more readily reached by land. 4 – It is logical to assume that, after opening the Western trade routes, Vladimir decided to take care of the Eastern ones. The Danube Bulgars did not stand in his way, since he had a water route to Constantinople; the Volga Bulgars may have appeared to him as greedy middlemen on the silver road. 5 – If the Volga Bulgars are assumed to be in question, it still remains to ascertain from what direction Vladimir attacked them.

The Oka system appears to be the obvious choice, but here two factors may have their importance: a) *The Chronicle* mentions that Vladimir used the Torks as allies: they accompanied his boats on horseback. Now the Torks were cousins and neighbours of the Pechenegs, and they lived in the Don region. It was clearly easier to lead them against the Volga Bulgars than against the Danube Bulgars, especially if one was going to attack the Volga Bulgars by the Volga and not the Oka; b) *The Chronicle* ignores, but Jacob mentions, a dateless campaign against the Khazars, whom, according to him, Vladimir would have submitted and forced to pay tribute. This in itself is startling news. In Oleg's time, the Polyans were paying tributes to the Khazars, and now the state of affairs was reversed and *The Chronicle* has not one word to say about it? We are used to more boastfulness on its part. It seems more reasonable to suppose that the victory over the Khazars – if not a figment of Jacob's imagination, which it probably is not, imagination never having been Jacob's strong point – was just one incident in another campaign, and the tribute a one-time ransom. But the Khazars were completely out of Vladimir's way, unless he wanted to attack precisely the Volga Bulgars and precisely by the Volga, in which case he absolutely had to go through Khazar land. 6 – Psychologically it is quite likely that Vladimir wanted to repeat his father's fantastic 965 campaign, even on a slightly more modest scale. Such an idea – maybe a somewhat sentimental one – would have taken him on the very same itinerary the mention of Torks (*Chronicle*) and Khazars (Jacob) suggests. The trip Dniepr-Orel-portage-Donets-Don-portage-Volga could easily – though not obviously – be done by boat, as *The Chronicle* takes care to mention. The trip back was probably done by the shorter northern route. All this, of course, is a matter of surmise, and the author will not be unduly disappointed if it is ever proved that Vladimir travelled to Bulgar by the Oka, although of course the maps will have to be changed. He will be quite surprised, however, if he learns that the Danube Bulgars were the ones the chronicler had in mind. – Baumgarten's ingenious hypothesis, according to which Vladimir fought the Volga Bulgars but befriended the Danube Bulgars in their wars against the Greeks, has no foundation in Russian, Bulgarian or Greek sources. True, Arab historians mention that the Russians had been enemies of the Greeks until 988, but they do not specify how this hostility was expressed. Leo the Deacon does say that he was nearly killed in 986 by a Russian serving in the Bulgarian army, but there is nothing to show that this was a regular soldier in a Russian unit, rather than an isolated mercenary. In short, in the absence of any indication of a Bulgaro-Russian alliance, it seems more sensible to assume that, for the time being, Vladimir was not looking south. As to Baumgarten's argument that Tork cavalry could not have been brought to Bulgar because the area was too wooded, it might be worth considering, but the thickest woods began to the north of the Volga-Kama confluence, and if cavalry could operate on the Don, it presumably could do the same on the Volga, since the terrain conditions were approximately the same (cf. A. Linberg, *Classical Atlas of General Geography*).

75 Ibn Rusteh.

76 Cf. pp. 63–4.

77 St Vladimir's '*Prologue*' life.

78 Now a section of Kiev, on the bluffs overlooking the Dniepr. Excavations.

79 Vladimir is stressed on the second syllable.

80 A legendary bogatyr of noble birth, Dobrynya Nikitich, not to be confused with Vladimir's uncle.

81 Avenarius, *Volgà Vseslavevich*.

82 On the Irpen, 25 kilometres south-west of Kiev.

83 Cf. p. 93, p. 344, n. 53.

84 Continuation of the Laurentian. Second wife by our count; first according to *The Chronicle* (Cf. p. 342, n. 43).

85 Description borrowed from Ibn Fadlan; confirmed – minus the cremation, which was probably reserved for the upper classes – by numerous graves excavated in the region of Kiev and containing tenderly embracing skeletons, a man's and a woman's.

Chapter Five   *The Light on the Road*

86 St Paul.

87 Cf. p. 25.

88 Cf. p. 41.

89 Mainly from the so-called Normanist school, whose purpose it is to prove that Russia was in fact evangelized by Roman Christians and not by Greek ones.

90 There is some disagreement among historians as to whether this church was a cathedral. The term *sborney* used by the chronicler lends itself to various interpretations.

91 Priselkov.

92 Dvornik.

93 Cf. pp. 102–3.

94 Some historians have completely denied the episode of the quest for three main reasons: a) that it is not mentioned in other sources, except the *Prologue Life* which post-dates *The Chronicle* by several centuries, b) that it contains anachronisms, c) that it is 'quite unlikely'. It is difficult to agree with such views since a) Jacob and Hilarion wrote eulogies, not histories, and rightly found it more tactful to insist on the 'true' faith which Vladimir finally adopted rather than to describe the 'false' ones he had considered and, for somewhat frivolous reasons, rejected; besides, Hilarion does say that Vladimir 'began to search for the only God'; b) anachronisms are to be found in all chronicles written after the event; people in the Middle Ages did not have the same sense of evolution that we have; besides, those anachronisms appear only in

the German incident: cf. n. 97; c) there is nothing unlikely in a man seeing through his own threadbare religion and addressing himself to representatives of other religions; as a matter of fact the Prince of the Khazars had done just that more than a century earlier, and, in spite of the great Constantine's (Cyril's) efforts to incline him toward Christianity, had selected Judaism (851); moreover Arabic sources confirm Vladimir's interest in Islam (cf. Marvazi), and Bandouri confirms his investigation in Constantinople, although he describes it in fantastic terms.

95 'If Cleopatra's nose had been shorter, it would have changed the face of the world.' Pascal, *Pensées*.

96 Cf. pp. 22, 25.

97 Corrupt as it is, the text says: 'They replied: "Fasting according to one's strength, but whatever one eats or drinks is all to the glory of God, as our teacher Paul has said." Vladimir told the Germans: "Go back, because our fathers did not accept this."' Paul is not Olaf's Paul but the Apostle, and the reference is probably to I Cor. X, 31. But who are 'our fathers'? The pagans? Is Vladimir rejecting – as his father would have done – the very idea of fasting? Or is the mention of fathers a later interpolation and does it illustrate in the chronicler's view one of the innumerable disputes between the Western and Eastern Churches as to when and how to fast? None of this sounds very satisfactory. Other explanations would be a) that Vladimir disapproved of shilly-shallying and, if this anachronism may be forgiven, of jesuitism: he wanted a yea or nay discipline, not a doctrine which would allow him to eat his cake without breaking fast; b) that Vladimir, for the time being, rejected any kind of asceticism; c) that he was, as suggested previously, manoeuvring his people and preparing them to accept the Christian faith from the Greeks; d) that a copyist's absent-mindedness has turned the whole text into gibberish.

98 The answer seems to indicate that the men were Jewish missionaries, not Khazar converts. Or else, the Khazars considered that by adopting the Jewish religion they had joined the race of the Elect. But Vladimir knew who the Khazars were. At different times tributes had been paid to them or received from them by the Kievans.

99 This incident is contested by some on the pretext that Boris of Bulgaria was also converted by an icon (not a canvas) representing the Last Judgement, which seems inconclusive: there is no reason why the same frightening image should not have made the same impression on two rulers of Slavic lands, nearly contemporaries at that; on the contrary, it could be argued that the Greeks had good reason to use a second time a trick which had worked once; finally, as is clear from what follows, Vladimir was not *converted* by the picture, just strongly impressed by it.

100 It rings like Louis xiv's famous '*Je verrai*'.

101 Such was until fairly recently the usual interpretation of the Bible, by both the Eastern and the Western Churches. It may seem intolerant to us, but it explains in depth some of the excesses of, say, the Inquisition: heretics would be burned in this world so that they would not burn in the next. Strange as the paradox must appear, it is nevertheless a fact that the religious wars, for instance, were, at least in part, a work of charity.

102 Bandouri's number, on the whole not unlikely.

103 Unless of course Vladimir had already been secretly baptized, as some historians maintain, and was organizing the whole show for the benefit of the people, in which case the envoys would have been recent and secret converts to the Greek faith. This does not seem to be a likely hypothesis, as mentioned previously (cf. p. 166).

104 Cf. pp. 21–2.

105 *The Orthodox Church*, September 1978.

106 It would appear that the Church of St Elias was closed by that time and that, although there undoubtedly were

Christians in Kiev, they could not or would not celebrate impressive public services. This is not in contradiction with traditional pagan tolerance in matters of religion. Even now, non-baptized persons are not supposed to attend the most solemn part of the Russian liturgy: 'Catechumens, leave!' sings the deacon. Although this is a Greek legacy, the Greeks were obviously more liberal, and allowed the Russians to see everything there was to see.

107 It is interesting to note what consideration surrounded women – not as women, which would be the Western chivalrous tradition, but as human beings – in early Russian history.

108 Another discrepancy concerns time and place. *The Chronicle* maintains that the search took place in 986–987, and that Vladimir was baptized in Cherson in 988. Others, it states, place the baptism in Kiev, Vasiliev or other places, but 'they do not know the truth'. The monk Jacob does not mention Cherson and gives no exact date, but declares that Vladimir was baptized in the tenth year after Yaropolk's death, which would be 987. 'Nestor' says Vladimir died in the twenty-eighth year after his baptism, which then would have taken place in 986. Much has been written about this problem, but it is doubtful whether chroniclers and orators in the eleventh century were as demanding as we are concerning exact dates. The systems of reference they favoured – either year so and so 'since the creation of the world' (or even more vaguely 'since Adam') or 'the umpteenth year before or after such an event' – did not encourage extreme precision. The fact that the year began in March and not in January does not help, at least from a modern standpoint. *The Chronicle* itself (Laurentian version) is unsure about the date of Vladimir's accession to the throne – it indicates, mistakenly, 980, but its own references to other events give 978, which is the right date – and historians might well be arguing about mistakes due

to a happy-go-lucky attitude toward chronology, not differences of opinion. What, frankly, is more important, is the conception according to which Vladimir was baptized more or less secretly, let us say in Vasiliev in 986 or 987, and baptized his land a few years later, in 988 or 989. Such a hypothesis is fancied by those who reject the whole Cherson episode. It is unclear why Vladimir would have waited such a long time to give to his people what he felt was absolute truth. On the other hand, his decision to go to a Christian land to be baptized and, so to speak, to bring truth back home, is in character. This would have satisfied his love of formalities (he could not even kill a wife without telling her to get dressed in her wedding gown) and would have given him much more authority as an evangelist. Obviously it was easier to return solemnly baptized from 'the country where God dwells' and then start religious reforms, rather than get up one morning and order everybody to jump in the Dniepr. Vladimir would have realized that. As to Jacob's and Nestor's dates, even if they are accurate, they can be explained simply enough: they refer not to Vladimir's actual baptism but to the first signs of his interest in Christianity.

109 What follows is the subject of endless disputes among competent scholars. Rather than try to settle each separate argument, it has been deemed more expedient to present, in the body of the text, only the author's interpretation of events, to stand or be rejected on its own merits. The problem is threefold.

a) *Silence of different sources on different events.* Four closely related events took place between 986 and 989: Vladimir's baptism; his marriage to Princess Anna, sister to the co-emperors Basil II and Constantine VIII; the siege of Cherson, a Greek city, by the Russians; the provision of Russian Viking reinforcements used by Basil against the rebel Phocas. Since everyone agrees that Vladimir's baptism took place before his marriage, and since the date of his baptism has already been discussed (cf. p. 352, n. 108), it will simplify matters a little if, for the present purpose, the marriage alone is taken into consideration, which leaves us with three facts: the marriage, the siege, and the provision of reinforcements.

Three groups of sources report on these facts: Russian (*The Chronicle*, Jacob the Monk, the different *Lives*), Greek (Cedrenus, Zonaras, Psellus, Leo) and Eastern (Arabic: Yahya, El-Macin, Abu-Shyjac, Ibn-al-Athyr; Armenian: Açoghiq). Their reports present the following singularities. The Russians omit to mention the substantial reinforcements sent to Constantinople; the Greeks mention the fall of Cherson in contexts unrelated to either marriage or reinforcements; the Easterners omit it altogether. Why?

One can presume that the fall of Cherson escaped the Easterners' notice and that the Greeks did not like to associate the humiliation of a misalliance with the humiliation of a defeat. But why did the Russians omit an incident which ought to have flattered their pride, since it was they who saved the Empire? No satisfactory explanation was ever given. It may be suggested that Vladimir's contingent of six thousand was composed of Scandinavian Vikings recruited through his mediation and called Russians by the Greeks because they came from Russia. This seems the more probable, as the same men, instead of returning to Russia, were seen eleven years later still in the service of the Basileus (Açoghiq). Such a hypothesis would also explain how Vladimir could afford to help the Basileus with one hand and to take a city from him with the other.

b) *Sequence of events.* The Russian sources do not mention the reinforcements provided and fail to explain why Vladimir suddenly attacked Cherson; the Greeks also fail to explain the motives for the siege; both Greeks and Arabs make the connection marriage-reinforcements, suggesting a deal between Vladimir and Basil: the one arranging for reinforcements, the other giving his sister's hand. Since enthusiasm for the marriage was obviously lacking on the Greek side, it is generally considered that the taking of Cherson had no other objective but to prod the reluctant Basileus into fulfilling his promise and that the prodding was suitably left out of history books. So far so good, and the order of events unanimously proposed by the Arabs fits the picture: the marriage comes first, then the reinforcements are produced. The full sequence would then be the following: 1 – mutual agreement to the deal; 2 – dilly-dallying on the part of the Greeks; 3 – Vladimir takes Cherson; 4 – marriage occurs; 5 – reinforcements are sent.

The problem with this logical sequence is that the reinforcements were already active at the battle of Abydos (April 13, 989) and at the preceding battle of Chrysopolis which took place at an undetermined date between the summer of 988 and February 989, whereas Cherson was taken *after* April 7, 989, since on that day (exact date from Yahya) was seen an aurora borealis which (according to Leo the Deacon) foretold, among other calamities, the fall of Cherson. Consequently, since the reinforcements were in action *before* Cherson was taken, the sequence of events must be modified as follows: 1 – agreement; 2 – reinforcements sent; 3 – Greek dilly-dallying; 4 – Cherson taken; 5 – marriage occurs. The only other solution would be to disregard the aurora and to assume that Cherson was taken in 988, as apparently indicated by *The Chronicle*, rather than in 989 as results from Jacob and Leo's observations.

Of course it is possible that Leo the Deacon made a mistake in his mystical interpretation of natural phenomena and that Cherson had already been taken when the heavenly sign appeared, apologizing for being late; still, it is not very satisfactory to make up such a poor explanation in order to discard one of the very few certain dates we have. On the whole, and since there is no way of keeping both the chronology and the sequence, it seems more reasonable to suppose that when the Arabs state that Vladimir was Basil's brother-in-law they apply the term a little loosely to a *future* brother-in-law, a promised brother-in-law. The Greeks do the same, but they might be doing it on purpose, so as to hide the inelegant – and ineffective – way in which Basil tried to go back on his promise: if Vladimir was already Basil's brother-in-law when he beat his enemies for him, well, of course there had been a misalliance, but a useful, therefore an excusable one. It is not unlikely that such could have been their reasoning. Therefore we would conclude that, as Leo and his aurora borealis have it, Cherson was taken in the spring of 989, before the marriage, but after the reinforcements had been provided. As to the date of 988 to be found in *The Chronicle*, the rectified sequence (advocated here) would be barely in contradiction with it: the year starting in March and Cherson being taken in April or May, the mistake would be only of one or two months. Moreover, what *The Chronicle* literally says is that Vladimir *set out* against Cherson in 988 (which is confirmed) and not that he took it that year. As to Jacob, he also alludes to a southern campaign in 988, and so, as far as dates are concerned, we are on relatively safe ground. It is true that *The Chronicle*, detailed as it is, does not establish any connection between the siege of Cherson and the marriage, but that is easily explained: the Russians did not care to stress how reluctant the Greeks had been.

c) *Number of delegations exchanged.* It is difficult, when writing about a period about which little is known, not to fall into the temptation of over-simplifying events by connecting sparse pieces of evidence and making one picture of them. It is also difficult, when one works on a character who has been for centuries the exclusive property of hagiographers, not to over-react against their limited point of view. Therefore it has been maintained either that Vladimir's search for a new religion had only one purpose – to provide diplomatic cover for Greek and Russian envoys negotiating the Deal (reinforcements in exchange for marriage) – or at least that the mission of the envoys was a double one: the Philosopher spoke openly of Orthodoxy and covertly of 'mercs'; the committee gaped at Hagia Sophia and haggled about Anna. Maybe. On the other hand, religious motives are not unknown in history, even in relatively pure forms, and to deny them entirely is but another variation of naïveté. The court of Constantinople had no lack of ambassadors and Kiev also could muster a few. In consequence, and with all possible reservations, the two matters will be treated separately here.

110 Bandouri, who may have had access to lost Greek sources, states that the service the Russians attended was either on the day of St John Chrysostom or that of the Dormition of the Theotokos. St John Chrysostom is honoured on January 27 and 30, on September 14 and on November 13. Only September 14 could be confused with August 15 (Dormition), and August seems the more likely month of the two, because of travel conditions. Still, Bandouri is completely unreliable, and it is only his expressing doubt concerning the date which suggests that for once he was using information rather than sheer imagination.

The details concerning audiences in Constantinople are authentic and, as well as other details of Byzantine life, borrowed from Bertha Diener. Of course, it is not known which particular audience room and ceremony were used in the case of the Russians.

111 Constantine VII Porphyrogenetus, *De Ceremoniis*.

112 It is generally believed that the Viking bodyguard was already in operation at the time. It may have originated with the contingent Vladimir sent to Constantinople in the autumn of 978 (cf. p. 102).

113 Cf. p. 102.

114 The tradition of colonizing through converting is not an invention of the eighteenth or fifteenth centuries, far from it. The Basileus felt that he was the supreme Christian ruler and that all other Christian rulers should recognize his authority, especially if they had been evangelized by missionaries of his nation. This seemed so obvious that in the fourteenth century the Sultan of Egypt, giving the Basileus his full title, still called him, among other things, *Rex Rhossorum*, king of the Russians.

115 Once again, Bandouri's date presents no guarantee whatsoever.

116 Molière's Tartufe 'makes arrangements'. The Russian style is different. Aleksey Tolstoy has described it in a short poem of which the following imitation may give an idea:

> If you love, love without measure,
> If you give, then give a treasure,
> If you swear, swear a good oath,
> If you burn one end, burn both.
>
> If you quarrel, quarrel bolder,
> If you strike, strike from the shoulder,
> If you spare, spare *hic et nunc*,
> If you banquet . . . Let's get drunk!

117 *Timeo Danaos et dona ferentes* (Virgil, *Aeneid*).

118 Some have wondered at the following lines in the *Prologue Life*: 'And he said in himself: Here is what I shall do; I shall go into their land, and I shall take a city of theirs, and I shall find a teacher.' Was it so difficult to find a teacher? Were not the Greeks only too happy to send missionaries? They were, and that is precisely the point: Vladimir had to manoeuvre so as to gain heaven without losing land.

119 The Constantinople dream was realized partly by Vladimir himself, in particular through his marriage to Anna, partly by his son Yaroslav, in particular through the building of the Kiev Hagia Sophia, the Kiev Golden

Gates, etc., partly by his descendant Tsar (the word comes from Caesar) Ivan the Terrible, who adopted Byzantium's two-headed eagle and created the myth of the third Rome – it could not be Kiev any more, so it was Moscow. The imperial vocation of Russia's sovereigns can be traced further down to Peter the Great, who chose to be called Emperor, and even to the present-day Soviet federal-monarchical structure, where one man rules over a conglomerate of theoretically autonomous nations.

120 Since, in all likelihood, the six thousand were not Russian regulars, there is nothing surprising in the fact that neither Jacob nor *The Chronicle* take any particular notice of them.

121 *Life*.

122 A ship is a masculine concept in Russian.

123 Avenarius: *Solovey Budimirovitch*. The last line is the author's contribution. The real line is: Young Solovey, son of Budimir.

124 Cf. Davidson.

125 Tolstoy, *War and Peace*, book VI, chapter 1.

126 There is no evidence to support El-Macin's unlikely opinion that Vladimir himself sailed with his men.

127 Psellus. The date of the battle of Chrysopolis is unknown. Various computations set it at between June 988 and February 989.

128 Berthier-Delagarde insists that Vladimir could not take such a risk while his own men were 'like hostages' among the Greeks. But they were probably not 'his own men', just mercenaries; besides, six thousand armed Vikings make rather uncomfortable hostages to handle; finally, at this very moment they were saving Basil's Empire for him.

129 This section will follow very closely Berthier-Delagarde, where military insights into the siege of Cherson are unparalleled. As to his debatable psychology and complete disregard for the aurora borealis, one has no obligation to agree with them. His article is based partly

on *The Chronicle*, partly on other chronicles, partly on different *Lives*. It is very carefully documented and the reader may refer to it for precise indication of sources.

130 Jacob.

131 Zernov's expression.

132 *Nikon Chronicle*. The legend according to which Vladimir kills the prince and princess (*sic*) of Cherson and gives their daughter in marriage to Zhdbern (Rumyantsevsky Torzhestvennik – seventeenth century) is an apocryphal variation on the Rogned theme.

133 Psellus.

134 This and other details in this section are borrowed from a number of different chronicles and *Lives* of Vladimir. Some may be the fruit of the authors' imaginations; only those that seemed in character have been used. These chronicles and *Lives* are difficult to obtain in the original, but Shakhmatov has blended them together in one continuous story, with every detail carefully documented. Therefore they will not be noted here. The reader is referred to Shakhmatov for precise information on the sources.

135 Byzantine costumes and customs from Diener.

136 'Lord Jesus Christ have pity on me a sinner.' Repeated thousands of times, it is one of the main instruments of Eastern Christian mysticism.

137 Confirmed by Thietmar.

138 Vladimir's baptism took place, according to different sources, in the church of St Basil, of St Sophia or of St Jacob. If we adopt the rule of the *lectio difficilior*, St Jacob's is the most likely, since St Sophia's has already played its part in Constantinople and St Basil's was erected by Vladimir. According to the *Life*, his companions were baptized in the church of the Theotokos.

139 The Pereyaslavl Chronicle in Shakhmatov.

140 Either Pope St Clement I or some other St Clement. Phoebus is Cross's interpretation, a likely one, of the Russian 'Fiv'. This character is otherwise unknown.

141 Tolstoy, *War and Peace*, book VI, chapter 1. Impossible to resist that quotation, but truth forces us to confess that it may not be appropriate as far as the season is concerned: this was early autumn or late summer, and the oak may still have had its full foliage.

142 Gal. I, 20.

Chapter Six   Basileus

143 Unless otherwise indicated, sources for this chapter are: the Laurentian version of *The Chronicle*, other versions of it, and Vladimir's *Life*. The text of the baptism ceremony consists of excerpts borrowed from the edition put forth by the Orthodox Church in America (New York, 1972) under the direction of Fr Paul Lazor.

144 Cf. p. 157.

145 Sources for the description of Vladimir's attire are a) his portraits on the coins he later minted: they show him dressed as a Byzantine Basileus, b) general information on the costume of the Byzantine Emperors, c) the famous charter sent by Patriarch Joasaph II to Ivan the Terrible in 1561 to confirm him as Tsar by divine right. The passage that interests us reads as follows:

> Our modesty has been informed and has been given verification, not only by word of mouth of many credible men, but also indeed by documented proof provided by chronographers, that the present Basileus of Moscow, Novgorod, Astrakhan, Kazan, Noga and all great Russia, the lord Ivan, is truly descended from the genus and blood of royalty, namely from that renowned Basilissa and Mistress the Lady Anna, sister of the Emperor the Lord Basil. The said Basil and the most pious Basileus Constantine, together with the then Patriarch and his holy synod of bishops, having sent forth the then Metropolitan of Ephesus and the Prefect of Antioch, crowned as Basileus the most pious Great Prince Vladimir, and presented him with the royal crown for his head and the diadem of pearls and all the other regal symbols and robes.

It is not absolutely clear what is meant by the crown *and* the diadem (probably the crown proper *and* the pendants), but that is a minor point. What is more disturbing is that a) it is now known that the charter was delivered by the Patriarch to obtain a bribe from the Tsar and that only two of the thirty-seven signatures supposed to authenticate the document are not forged: the Patriarch's and that of the Metropolitan of Euripe, who played messenger boy and took the charter to Moscow – the thirty-five others are counterfeit – b) the short text quoted here contains at least one obvious lie: Ivan the Terrible was not a descendant of Princess Anna, since his lineage was traced back to Yaroslav, who was twenty at the time when his father married that Princess. It is clear that the Patriarch believed there was only one royal blood on earth, the Greek one, and that, to please the Tsar, he resorted to genealogical legerdemain. Consequently everything the noble Patriarch has to say should be treated with some circumspection, and it is not necessary to impute to Svyatopolk the loss of a crown (Andrusiak) which may never have existed. Still, given the coins and the general situation, it seems likely that Vladimir was arrayed as a Basileus when he set foot again on Russian soil.

146 Acts XIX, 4.

147 Klint-Jensen, Mansikka.

148 Tens of thousands were present there. The exact location of the baptism is uncertain. It may have been on the Pochayna, the already mentioned tributary of the Dniepr; it may have been on the Dniepr itself at a place called Kreshchatik. There is no known foundation for the tradition (Gizel's *Synopsis*, a seventeenth-century compilation published in 1823) according to which Vladimir's sons were baptized separately in Kreshchatik's spring (at the junction of the present Ulitsa Revolutsii and the riverside road north from the Chain Bridge).

149 The chronicler seems to have the devil in mind. The

hagiographer is more down to earth: his text is 'help me against my enemies, so that I may conquer them'.

150 *The Chronicle* seems to indicate all this happened in 988.

151 This is what Jacob appears to mean.

152 Joachim.

153 Lactantius.

154 Not to be confused with the chronicler.

155 Luke XXIII, 35–37.

156 *Chronicle of Novgorod*.

157 Back to Joachim, not the bishop but the chronicler.

158 *The Chronicle*.

159 This and the following information quoted by Muraviev and confirmed by the existence of the two cities of Vladimir and Vladimir-Volhynsk.

160 Tikhomirov.

161 *Prologue*.

162 Cf. p. 189.

163 Jacob the Monk.

164 The interested reader is referred to excellent studies by Priselkov, Vernadsky, and especially Obolensky, Zernov and Honigman.

165 Modern parallels can be found for this situation. For instance, whereas the Russian Patriarchate has granted autocephaly to the Orthodox American Church, the Greek Church does not yet recognize it.

166 *Nikon Chronicle*.

167 Hilarion.

168 Vladimir is made to say: 'I . . . have received the saving rite of Baptism from . . . Photius, the Patriarch of Constantinople.' Photius died *circa* 895.

169 From the Liturgy of St John Chrysostom.

170 Cf. p. 158.

171 *The Chronicle, Life*, Hilarion.

172 The sign which we have chosen to call the Trident, and which the Republic of Ukraine adopted as its coat of arms in 1918, is considered as mysterious, and different historians have given it the most varied interpretations. It

was seen as a trident, but also as the top of a Byzantine sceptre, a Scythian sceptre, a crown, a triple candlestick, the Labarum, a banner, the dove of the Holy Spirit, the Greek *akakia* (purse containing soil), an anchor, the tip of a battleaxe, a bow and arrow, a helmet, a poleaxe, a crow, a portal, a monogram (Runic, Ukrainian or Byzantine), a geometrical ornament of Byzantine, Eastern, Slav or Viking origin. Studied in detail in *Vladimirskiy Sbornik*.

173 Joachim.

174 *Nikon Chronicle*.

175 *Ibidem*.

176 *Ibidem*.

177 Wilhelm von Giesebrecht.

178 Cf. p. 127.

179 Frankly, we tend to consider these campaigns most unlikely. What would Vladimir have wanted with the Silver Bulgars, besides commercial relations which he already had? How could he have fought the Volga Bulgars and the Esthonians the same year? *The Chronicle*'s version – he went to Novgorod to recruit troops in order to fight the Pechenegs – sounds more probable. The Sagas also mention a war between Vladimir, who was helping his friend Olaf, and Prince Eric of Norway. No such war is mentioned in any chronicle.

180 *The Chronicle* says that it was Vladimir who founded Pereyaslavl to celebrate his victories. This is scarcely likely since the town is already mentioned in the Russian-Greek treaties of 911 and 945. Vladimir probably settled it with colonists from the North, as he did with Belgorod.

181 The Church of the Transfiguration was erected in gratitude for this escape. Cf. p. 246.

182 Cf. p. 335, n. 6.

183 Cf. pp. 262–3.

184 Tikhomirov.

185 Refrain to be found in several *byliny*.

186 Cf. p. 338, n. 23.

187 The question of Vladimir's progeny is a complicated one,
as could only have been expected. Under the year 980,
The Chronicle states that by Rogned he had four sons:
Izyaslav, Mstislav, Yaroslav and Vsevolod, and two
daughters; that 'the Greek woman bore him Svyatopolk;
by one Czech he had a son, Vysheslav; by another,
Svyatoslav and Mstislav; and by a Bulgarian, Boris and
Gleb.' Under the year 988, the same *Chronicle*,
mentioning that Vysheslav was the eldest, lists twelve
sons, presumably in order of birth, but without stating
so: Vysheslav, Izyaslav, Yaroslav, Svyatopolk,
Vsevolod, Svyatoslav, Mstislav, Boris, Gleb, Stanislav,
Pozvizd and Sudislav. Later *The Chronicle* mentions by
name a daughter, Predslava. Other sources mention various numbers of other daughters, including one called
Premislava, and another named Dobronega-Maria. The
biographies of some of the sons (Yaroslav, Mstislav) are
well known; others, on the contrary, remain perfectly
mysterious, and one should beware of the guesswork of
some historians concerning possible identifications, marriages, etc. What follows is a brief summary of information borrowed from *The Chronicle* and other sources and
applying only to the twelve brothers.

1 – Vysheslav, born around 977, if he was older than
Yaroslav, and if Yaroslav was born in 978, as is generally
believed. Son of a nameless Czech woman according to
The Chronicle, and of Olava, according to Joachim.
Prince of Novgorod. Died 1010 (Joachim).

2 – Izyaslav, born around 978, son of Rogned. Treated
differently from his brothers: Izyaslavl was built for him
and he reigned there in his mother's right rather than as
his father's *posadnik*. Died 1001, and his son Bryacheslav
reigned in his stead. His son Vseslav died 1003. The *Nikon
Chronicle* describes him as meek, tearful, patient, tender
and a great lover of the Scripture.

3 – Yaroslav 'the Wise', baptized as 'George', born in
978, son of Rogned according to most sources, but of

another woman according to the continuation of *The Chronicle* (Laurentian) (cf. p. 342, n. 43). Prince of Rostov, then of Novgorod, then of Kiev, and Great Prince. At what date was he appointed to Novgorod? Probably in 1010, at Vysheslav's death, but some sources indicate that in 1015 he had been in Novgorod 28 or 18 years, which is not likely. Great Prince in 1019. Married to Ingigerd of Sweden. Died 1054.

4 – Svyatopolk 'the Accursed', son of Predslava according to Joachim, but of the Greek nun according to *The Chronicle*, the *Nikon Chronicle* and the *Passion and Encomium of Boris and Gleb*. Born around 979. Posthumous son of Yaropolk, adopted by Vladimir. Prince of Turov. Married to the daughter of Boleslav the Brave of Poland. Died 1019.

5 – Vsevolod, son of Rogned. Prince of Vladimir-Volhynsk. Married Astrid of Denmark, sister of Kanut the Great. According to Icelandic Sagas assassinated 1015, at instigation of his mother-in-law, Sigride 'Storrada', Olaf's implacable enemy (Baumgarten), or died in Scandinavia 995 (Presnyakov).

6 – Svyatoslav, canonized by the Church, son of a Czech woman according to *The Chronicle*, of Malfrid according to Joachim. Prince of the Drevlians with seat in Ovruch. Murdered 1015 by order of Svyatopolk.

7 – Mstislav, son of Rogned according to *The Chronicle*, of Adèle according to Joachim. Prince of Tmutorakan. Fought against Yaroslav, triumphed over him but allowed him to reign in Kiev, unmolested. Had one son Eustace who died before his father. The name Eustace presents a certain interest, because it was the Christian name of Plakida, to whom *The Life of Boris and Gleb* compares Vladimir himself (cf. p. 159). Mstislav died 1036 and his appanage returned to Kiev. Physical description appears in several chronicles, quoted here from Karamzin.

8 – Boris, son of the Bulgar woman according to *The

Chronicle, the *Nikon Chronicle* and the *Passion and Encomium of Boris and Gleb*, but of Anna according to Joachim, the Pliginsky and the Public Library manuscripts quoted by Shakhmatov. It seems extremely likely that Vladimir intended to leave his throne to the first-born son of his only Christian marriage: hence Boris is entrusted with his father's retinue and sent against the Pechenegs. The Christian name of Boris is 'Roman', maybe in honour of Tsar Roman of Bulgaria (Priselkov). Prince of Rostov. Physical description in *Hypatian Chronicle*.

9 – Gleb, baptized as 'David', maybe in honour of Prince David of Macedonia, murdered by order of Svyatopolk in 1015. Canonized. If Boris was Anna's son, it is logical to assume that Gleb was also. Why Christian boys should receive both Christian and pagan names is not quite clear, but the habit was preserved for some time, which is just as well for the variety of the Russian calendar, since pagan names became Christian when their bearers became saints. Gleb was Prince of Murom.

10 – Stanislav, Prince of Smolensk. According to Joachim, he was Adèle's son. In that case he would be older than Boris, since Vladimir, once baptized, gave up polygamy, and the order in which the twelve sons are presented in *The Chronicle* would lose all significance. Of course Stanislav may also have been Anna's son, although no source indicates that.

11 – Pozvizd, Prince of Vladimir-Volhynsk after Vsevolod's demise.

12 – Sudislav, Prince of Pskov, died 1063 (Baumgarten).

188 Borrowed from Vladimir Monomach's (our Vladimir's grandson's) testament, which appears to be written in our Vladimir's spirit.

189 Thietmar.

190 According to the Normanist school, Malfrid was Vladimir's mother Malusha. According to Joachim, she

was Svyatoslav's (Vladimir's son's) mother. *The Chronicle* announces her death as if it was perfectly clear to everyone who she was.

191 According to Cedrenus, Anna survived her husband. This is not what *The Chronicle* indicates. If she did, however, that would explain which stepmother Thietmar is referring to when he says that Boleslav the Brave captured Yaroslav's stepmother and nine sisters (cf. p. 302).

192 N. de Baumgarten, 'Le Dernier Mariage de Saint Vladimir', *Orientalia Christiana*, vol. 28 (1930).

193 Thietmar. Liaskorovski. Baumgarten.

194 Jacob.

195 *Ibidem*.

Chapter Seven   Saint

196 Based on *The Chronicle*, other chronicles, Thietmar, the *Life of Boris and Gleb*, the *Passion and Encomium of Boris and Gleb*.

197 This is our interpretation of a rather cryptic passage of *The Chronicle*. Others think that it was Vladimir's friends themselves who stole his body, but how could they have hoped that Svyatopolk would not notice it in the middle of the Church of the Tithe? The *Passion and Encomium of Boris and Gleb* indicates on the contrary that it was Svyatopolk who wanted to conceal Vladimir's death, but maintains that it was he who had the body taken to the Church, which is absurd.

198 In Hungary, says *The Chronicle*. Baumgarten interprets: on the Hungarian hill, in Kiev, which seems quite possible.

199 Or, according to the *Tver Chronicle*, Blud. It does not seem extremely likely that Vladimir would have chosen his brother's murderer as a tutor for his son (cf. pp. 95 *et seq.*).

200 'More royalist than the king'.
201 The original text lends itself to two interpretations. Either Svyatopolk died in Bohemia or 'heaven knows where'.
202 Approximate quotation from Gal. V, 25.
203 Better, daughter-in-law: Ingigerd of Sweden, baptized as 'Irina'.
204 Olga's theme: joy.

Select Bibliography

ANDRUSIAK, MYKOLA. 'Kings of Kiev and Galicia', *Slavonic and East European Review*, vol. 33, 1954–55.

AVENARIUS, V. P. *Kniga Bylin*. Saint Petersburg, 1880.

BAUMGARTEN, NICOLAS DE. (Généalogies et mariages occidentaux des Rurikides russes du Xe au XIIIe siècle', *Orientalia Christiana*, IX, 35, 1927.

——'Le Dernier Mariage de Saint Vladimir', *ibidem,* XVIII, 61, 1930.

——'Olaf Tryggvisson, roi de Norvège, et ses relations avec Saint Vladimir', *ibidem*, XXIV, 73, 1931.

——'Saint Vladimir et la conversion de la Russie', *ibidem*, XXVII, 1, 1932.

BERTHIER-DELAGARDE, A. 'Kak Vladimir osajdal Korsun', *Izvestia otdelenia russkago iazyka i slovesnosti imperatorskoi Akademii nauk*, vol. 14, Saint Petersburg, 1909.

CROSS, S. H., and SHERBOWITZ-WETZOR, O. P. *The Russian Primary Chronicle*, Medieval Academy of America, Cambridge, Massachusetts, 1953.

DAVIDSON, HILDA RODERICK ELLIS. *The Viking Road to Byzantium*. G. Allen and Unwin, London, 1976.

DIENER, BERTHA. *Byzanz, von Kaisern, Engeln und Eunuchen.* E.P.T.A.L. Leipzig-Vienna, 1937.

DOERGLER, F. 'Corpus der griechischen Urkunden des Mittelalters und der neuen Zeit'. Reihe A. Regesten, Abt I. *Regesten der Kaiserurkunden des oströmischen Reiches*, Teil I. *Regesten 565–1026*. Munich-Berlin, 1924.

DVORNIK, FRANCIS. *The Slavs in European History and Civilization*. Rutgers University Press, New Brunswick, 1962.

——*Byzantine Missions among the Slavs*. Rutgers University Press, New Brunswick, 1970.

GIESEBRECHT, WILHELM VON. *Geschichte der deutschen Kaiserzeit.* Leipzig, 1885.

GOLUBINSKY, E. *Istoria Russkoi Tserkvi.* Universitetskaia Tipografia, Moscow, 1904. New edition by Slavistic Printings and Reprintings, Mouton, The Hague-Paris, 1969.

GREKOV, V. P. *Kievskaia Rus'.* Moscow-Leningrad, 1939.

KARAMZIN, N. M. *Istoria gosudarstva rossiiskago.* Saint Petersburg, 1892.

KLINT-JENSEN, OLE. *The World of the Vikings.* Robert B. Luce, Washington-New York.

KLUCHEVSKY, V. *Kurs russkoi istorii.* Moscow, 1904.

KOSTOMAROV, N. I. 'Sobranie sochinenii', *Istoricheskiia monografii i izsledovania*, vol. 5, tomes XII, XIII and XIV. Saint Petersburg, 1905.

LAPPENBERG, J. M. *Monumenta Germaniae Historica.*

MANSIKKA, V. J. 'Die Religion der Ostslaven'. *FF Communications* Nio 43 Suomalainen Tiedeakatemia, Helsinki, 1922.

MINORSKY, V. *Sharaf-al Zaman Tahir Marvazi on China, the Turks and India*, Royal Asiatic Society, 1942.

MURAVIEV, A. N. *A History of the Church of Russia.* Saint Petersburg, 1938. New edition by AMS Press, New York.

OBOLENSKY, DMITRI. 'Byzantium, Kiev and Moscow: a study in ecclesiastical relations', Dumbarton Oak Papers no. 11. Harvard University Press, Cambridge, Massachusetts, 1957.

PRESNYAKOV, A. E. *Kniajnie pravo v drevnei Russi.* Saint Petersburg, 1909.

PRISELKOV, M. D. *Ocherki po tserkovno-politicheskoi istorii kievskoi Russi X–XII vekov.* Saint Petersburg, 1913.

RYDZEVSKAIA, E. A. 'Legenda o kniaze Vladimire v sage ob Olafe Trigvassone', *Trudy Otdelenia drevne-russkoi literatury*, vol. 2, 1935.

SEREBRIANSKY, N. S. *Drevne-russkia kniajeskia jitia.* Moscow, Sinodal'naia tipografia, 1915.

SHAKHMATOV, A. A. *Povest' vremennyh let. Izdanie imperatorskoi arheograficheskoi komissii.* Petrograd, 1916. New edition by Mouton, The Hague-Paris 1969.

——*Korsunskaia Legenda o kreshchenii Vladimira*. Lamanski Collection, Saint Petersburg, 1906.

SNORRE STURLESON, J. *Heimskringla Saga*. Peringskjöld, Stockholm, 1697.

SREZNEVSKY, I.I. *Drevnie pamiatniki russkago pis'ma i iazyka*, Saint Petersburg, 1863–82.

STOKES, A. D. 'The Statutes of the Russian Church 988–1037', *Slavonic Review*, vol. 37, no. 89, June 1959.

TATISHCHEV, V. N. *Istoria Rossii*. Saint Petersburg, 1768.

TAUBE, MICHEL DE. *Rome et la Russie avant l'invasion des Tartars* (IXe–XIIIe siècles). Paris, 1947.

TIKHOMIROV, M. *The Origins of Christianity in Russia*, 1959; *The Towns of Ancient Rus*, Foreign Language Publishing House, Moscow, 1959.

VASSILEVSKY, V. G. 'Variago-russkaia i variago-angliiskaia drujina v Konstantinopole', *Jurnal Ministerstva narodnago prosveshchenia*. Saint Petersburg, 1824, vol. 11, 1875, vols 2, 3.

VERNADSKY, G. 'The Status of the Russian Church during the first half-century following Vladimir's conversion', *Slavonic Year Book 1941*.

Vladimirskiy Sbornik. Belgrade, 1938.

ZERNOV, N. 'Vladimir and the origin of the Russian Church', *Slavonic and East European Review*, vol. 28, no. 70, November 1949; vol. 28, no. 71, April 1950.

373

Index

Numbers in italics refer to illustrations

375

Index

Index